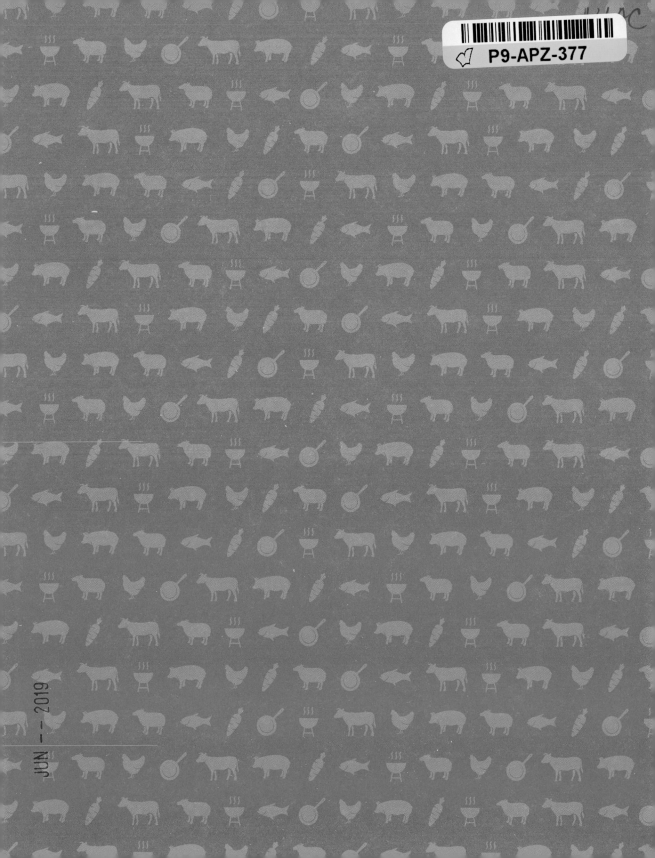

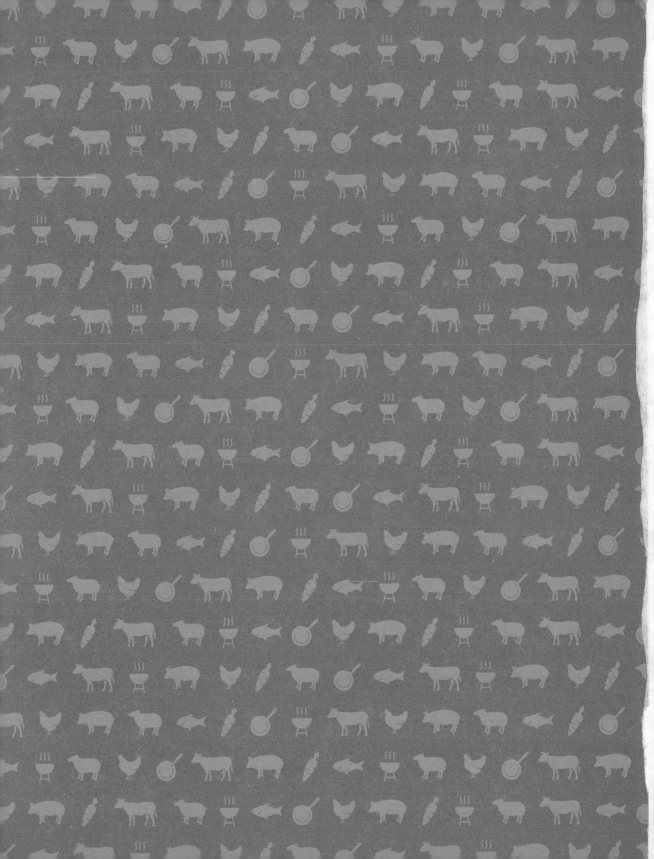

AMERICA'S
TEST KITCHEN

ALSO BY AMERICA'S TEST KITCHEN

The New Essentials Cookbook

Cook's Illustrated Revolutionary Recipes

Vegetables Illustrated

Tasting Italy: A Culinary Journey

Spiced

How to Braise Everything

How to Roast Everything

Dinner Illustrated

The Complete Diabetes Cookbook

The Complete Slow Cooker

The Complete Make-Ahead Cookbook

The Complete Mediterranean Cookbook

The Complete Vegetarian Cookbook

The Complete Cooking for Two Cookbook

Cooking at Home with Bridget and Julia

Just Add Sauce

Nutritious Delicious

What Good Cooks Know

Cook's Science

The Science of Good Cooking

The Perfect Cake

The Perfect Cookie

Bread Illustrated

Master of the Grill

Kitchen Smarts

Kitchen Hacks

100 Recipes: The Absolute Best Ways to Make the True Essentials

The New Family Cookbook

The America's Test Kitchen Cooking School Cookbook

The Cook's Illustrated Baking Book

The Cook's Illustrated Meat Book

The Cook's Illustrated Cookbook

The America's Test Kitchen Family Baking Book

The Best of America's Test Kitchen (2007–2019 Editions)

The Complete America's Test Kitchen TV Show Cookbook 2001–2019

Air Fryer Perfection

Cook It in Your Dutch Oven

Sous Vide for Everybody

Multicooker Perfection

Food Processor Perfection

Pressure Cooker Perfection

Vegan for Everybody

Naturally Sweet

Foolproof Preserving

Paleo Perfected

The How Can It Be Gluten-Free Cookbook

The How Can It Be Gluten-Free Cookbook: Volume 2

The Best Mexican Recipes

Slow Cooker Revolution Volume 2: The Easy-Prep Edition

Slow Cooker Revolution

The Six-Ingredient Solution

The America's Test Kitchen D.I.Y. Cookbook

THE COOK'S ILLUSTRATED ALL-TIME BEST SERIES

All-Time Best Brunch

All-Time Best Dinners for Two

All-Time Best Sunday Suppers

All-Time Best Holiday Entertaining

All-Time Best Appetizers

All-Time Best Soups

COOK'S COUNTRY TITLES

One-Pan Wonders

Cook It in Cast Iron

Cook's Country Eats Local

The Complete Cook's Country TV Show Cookbook

FOR A FULL LISTING OF ALL OUR BOOKS

CooksIllustrated.com

AmericasTestKitchen.com

PRAISE FOR AMERICA'S TEST KITCHEN TITLES

"A terrifically accessible and useful guide to grilling in all its forms that sets a new bar for its competitors on the bookshelf. . . . The book is packed with practical advice, simple tips, and approachable recipes."

PUBLISHERS WEEKLY (STARRED REVIEW) ON *MASTER OF THE GRILL*

"This encyclopedia of meat cookery would feel completely overwhelming if it weren't so meticulously organized and artfully designed. This is Cook's Illustrated at its finest."

THE KITCHN ON *THE COOK'S ILLUSTRATED MEAT BOOK*

"It's all about technique and timing, and the ATK crew delivers their usual clear instructions to ensure success. . . . The thoughtful balance of practicality and imagination will inspire readers of all tastes and skill levels."

PUBLISHERS WEEKLY (STARRED REVIEW) ON *HOW TO ROAST EVERYTHING*

"*The Perfect Cookie* . . . is, in a word, perfect. This is an important and substantial cookbook. . . . If you love cookies, but have been a tad shy to bake on your own, all your fears will be dissipated. This is one book you can use for years with magnificently happy results."

THE HUFFINGTON POST ON *THE PERFECT COOKIE*

Selected as one of the 10 Best New Cookbooks of 2017

THE LA TIMES ON *THE PERFECT COOKIE*

Selected as the Cookbook Award Winner of 2017 in the Baking category

INTERNATIONAL ASSOCIATION OF CULINARY PROFESSIONALS (IACP) ON *BREAD ILLUSTRATED*

"This book upgrades slow cooking for discriminating, 21st-century palates—that is indeed revolutionary."

THE DALLAS MORNING NEWS ON *SLOW COOKER REVOLUTION*

"If there's room in the budget for one multicooker/Instant Pot cookbook, make it this one."

BOOKLIST ON *MULTICOOKER PERFECTION*

"This book is a comprehensive, no-nonsense guide . . . a well-thought-out, clearly explained primer for every aspect of home baking."

THE WALL STREET JOURNAL ON *THE COOK'S ILLUSTRATED BAKING BOOK*

"Some books impress by the sheer audacity of their ambition. Backed up by the magazine's famed mission to test every recipe relentlessly until it is the best it can be, this nearly 900-page volume lands with an authoritative wallop."

CHICAGO TRIBUNE ON *THE COOK'S ILLUSTRATED COOKBOOK*

"The 21st-century *Fannie Farmer Cookbook* or *The Joy of Cooking*. If you had to have one cookbook and that's all you could have, this one would do it."

CBS SAN FRANCISCO ON *THE NEW FAMILY COOKBOOK*

"The go-to gift book for newlyweds, small families, or empty nesters."

ORLANDO SENTINEL ON *THE COMPLETE COOKING FOR TWO COOKBOOK*

"A one-volume kitchen seminar, addressing in one smart chapter after another the sometimes surprising whys behind a cook's best practices. . . . You get the myth, the theory, the science, and the proof, all rigorously interrogated as only America's Test Kitchen can do."

NPR ON *THE SCIENCE OF GOOD COOKING*

"This impressive installment from America's Test Kitchen equips readers with dozens of repertoire-worthy recipes. . . . This is a must-have for beginner cooks and more experienced ones who wish to sharpen their skills."

PUBLISHERS WEEKLY (STARRED REVIEW) ON *THE NEW ESSENTIALS COOKBOOK*

THE ULTIMATE
BURGER

PLUS DIY CONDIMENTS, SIDES, AND BOOZY MILKSHAKES

America's Test Kitchen

Library of Congress Cataloging-in-Publication Data

Names: America's Test Kitchen (Firm), author.
Title: The ultimate burger : plus DIY condiments, sides, and boozy milkshakes
    / America's Test Kitchen.
Description: Boston, MA : America's Test Kitchen, [2019] | Includes index.
Identifiers: LCCN 2019000933 | ISBN 9781945256844 (harcover)
Subjects: LCSH: Hamburgers. | Milkshakes. | Cooking, American. | LCGFT: Cookbooks.
Classification: LCC TX749.5.B43 .U47 2019 | DDC 641.6/62--dc23
LC record available at https://lccn.loc.gov/2019000933

AMERICA'S TEST KITCHEN
21 Drydock Avenue, Boston, MA 02210
Manufactured in the United States of America
10 9 8 7 6 5 4 3 2 1

Distributed by Penguin Random House
Publisher Services
Tel: 800.733.3000

Pictured on front cover: Loaded Nacho Burger (page 132)
Pictured on back cover (clockwise from top left): Banh Mi Burger (page 98), Spiced Cauliflower Burgers with Yogurt Sauce (page 174), Ultimate Chocolate Milkshakes (page 210), Thai-Style Turkey Sliders (page 82), Easier French Fries (page 179)

Editorial Director, Books **ELIZABETH CARDUFF**

Executive Food Editor **DAN ZUCCARELLO**

Deputy Food Editor **ANNE WOLF**

Senior Editors **NICOLE KONSTANTINAKOS AND SARA MAYER**

Associate Editors **JOSEPH GITTER, LAWMAN JOHNSON, AND RUSSELL SELANDER**

Senior Managing Editor **DEBRA HUDAK**

Assistant Editor **KELLY GAUTHIER**

Art Director, Books **LINDSEY TIMKO CHANDLER**

Deputy Art Directors **ALLISON BOALES, COURTNEY LENTZ, AND JANET TAYLOR**

Associate Art Director **KATIE BARRANGER**

Photography Director **JULIE BOZZO COTE**

Photography Producer **MEREDITH MULCAHY**

Senior Staff Photographer **DANIEL J. VAN ACKERE**

Staff Photographers **STEVE KLISE AND KEVIN WHITE**

Additional Photography **KELLER + KELLER AND CARL TREMBLAY**

Food Styling **TARA BUSA, CATRINE KELTY, CHANTAL LAMBETH, KENDRA MCKNIGHT, MARIE PIRAINO, MARY JANE SAWYER, ELLE SIMONE SCOTT, KENDRA SMITH, SALLY STAUB, AND SEAN WIDMAN**

Photoshoot Kitchen Team

   Photo Team Manager **TIMOTHY MCQUINN**

   Lead Test Cook **JESSICA RUDOLPH**

   Assistant Test Cooks **SARAH EWALD, JACQUELINE GOCHENOUER, AND ERIC HAESSLER**

Senior Publishing Operations Manager **TAYLOR ARGENZIO**

Production Manager **CHRISTINE SPANGER**

Imaging Manager **LAUREN ROBBINS**

Production and Imaging Specialists **DENNIS NOBLE, JESSICA VOAS, AND AMANDA YONG**

Copy Editor **ELIZABETH WRAY EMERY**

Proofreader **PAT JALBERT-LEVINE**

Indexer **ELIZABETH PARSON**

Chief Creative Officer **JACK BISHOP**

Executive Editorial Directors **JULIA COLLIN DAVISON AND BRIDGET LANCASTER**

CONTENTS

WELCOME TO AMERICA'S TEST KITCHEN

This book has been tested, written, and edited by the folks at America's Test Kitchen. Located in Boston's Seaport District in the historic Innovation and Design Building, it features 15,000 square feet of kitchen space, including multiple photography and video studios. It is the home of *Cook's Illustrated* magazine and *Cook's Country* magazine and is the workday destination for more than 60 test cooks, editors, and cookware specialists. Our mission is to test recipes over and over again until we understand how and why they work and until we arrive at the best version.

We start the process of testing a recipe with a complete lack of preconceptions, which means that we accept no claim, no technique, and no recipe at face value. We simply assemble as many variations as possible, test a half-dozen of the most promising, and taste the results blind. We then construct our own recipe and continue to test it, varying ingredients, techniques, and cooking times until we reach a consensus. As we like to say in the test kitchen, "We make the mistakes so you don't have to." The result, we hope, is the best version of a particular recipe, but we realize that only you can be the final judge of our success (or failure). We use the same rigorous approach when we test equipment and taste ingredients.

All of this would not be possible without a belief that good cooking, much like good music, is based on a foundation of objective technique. Some people like spicy foods and others don't, but there is a right way to sauté, there is a best way to cook a pot roast, and there are measurable scientific principles involved in producing perfectly beaten, stable egg whites. Our ultimate goal is to investigate the fundamental principles of cooking to give you the techniques, tools, and ingredients you need to become a better cook. It is as simple as that.

To see what goes on behind the scenes at America's Test Kitchen, check out our social media channels for kitchen snapshots, exclusive content, video tips, and much more. You can watch us work (in our actual test kitchen) by tuning in to *America's Test Kitchen* or *Cook's Country* on public television or on our websites. Listen in to test kitchen experts on public radio (SplendidTable.org) to hear insights that illuminate the truth about real home cooking. Want to hone your cooking skills or finally learn how to bake—with an America's Test Kitchen test cook? Enroll in one of our online cooking classes. However you choose to visit us, we welcome you into our kitchen, where you can stand by our side as we test our way to the best recipes in America.

facebook.com/AmericasTestKitchen

twitter.com/TestKitchen

youtube.com/AmericasTestKitchen

instagram.com/TestKitchen

pinterest.com/TestKitchen

AmericasTestKitchen.com
CooksIllustrated.com
CooksCountry.com
OnlineCookingSchool.com

BURGER BASICS

IN THIS CHAPTER

INTRODUCTION

What is the "ultimate" burger? We spent months in the test kitchen developing recipes in an attempt to answer that question. We came to the conclusion that the ultimate burger features a combination of flavors and textures that harmoniously come together in every bite.

We began our burger experimentation with the most fundamental component: the patty. Starting with beef, we tested and retested our way through every primal cut and discovered that ground sirloin steak tips or grass-fed chuck-eye roast made the most flavorful, beefiest burgers. And for our Grind-Your-Own Ultimate Beef Burger Blend we tested dozens of combinations until we found the perfect one: skirt steak, boneless short ribs, and steak tips. Along the way, we sussed out the secret to the ultimate turkey burger (grind collagen-rich turkey thighs and combine them with meaty mushrooms, a little gelatin, and a pinch of baking soda), and we developed a veggie burger that satisfies even the staunchest of carnivores. We then put our grind-your-own burger blends to work in exciting craft burgers with dozens of unique flavors and toppings.

Not inclined to grind your own meat? While we prefer our homemade burger blends, you can substitute store-bought ground meat in all of the recipes in this book. We share our shopping tips for buying ground beef and other meats, and our shaping and cooking techniques ensure that burgers made from store-bought meat are tender and flavorful.

While our burger recipes feature the combinations we loved best, you can use the components in The Perfect Patty chapter to try out new ideas. Create your own ultimate burger from scratch by mixing and matching endless combinations of burger blends, sauces, condiments, toppings, and buns.

This book has burger recipes for everyone, reaching beyond beef to include turkey, chicken, bison, lamb, pork, seafood, vegetarian, and vegan patties. With multiple burger options and a full chapter of side dishes and drinks to complete the meal—including fries, slaws, salads, and a few adults-only milkshakes—it's simple to cook delicious and foolproof ultimate burgers anytime.

Whether you want a beef burger or a cauliflower burger, are cooking on the stovetop or the grill, or want to try your hand at making homemade buns and condiments, the following pages are filled with recipes and ideas that will help you make *The Ultimate Burger*.

FIND WHAT YOU'RE LOOKING FOR

These icons let you know at a glance what each burger patty is made of and whether it is cooked in a skillet or on a grill.

 cook in a skillet

 cook on a grill

 beef or bison

 turkey or chicken

 pork

 lamb

 seafood

 vegetarian or vegan

ANATOMY OF AN ULTIMATE BURGER

No one element makes a burger ultimate; it's the result of a combination of flavors and textures coming together. We've given you recipes for specialty burgers so that you don't have to think about the various elements, but you'll also find multiple basic burgers to use as a blank canvas for creativity and experimentation.

BUN
Potato, kaiser, brioche, pretzel, donut: There's a wide variety of burger bun options. The structure of a good bun should support a juicy, well-stacked burger without falling apart. For the ultimate burger experience, we like to bake soft homemade buns (pages 218–233); we think the flavor and freshness are well worth the effort.

SAUCE
Sauces add another layer of flavor to burgers; they also contribute richness and moisture. Try one of our burger sauces or flavored mayos (pages 29–31).

TOPPINGS
The function of the vast array of topping possibilities is to add additional flavor and textural interest. We stack burgers with shoestring onions, candied bacon, slaws, and even nachos. They all taste incredible.

CHEESE
For classic flavor we like to melt American or Swiss cheese on top of a burger, but we also like to sprinkle on blue cheese or feta for bold tang; spread goat cheese or mascarpone over the bun for extra richness; and stuff Brie or pimento cheese inside a burger for a gooey surprise.

PATTY
Whether you're grinding your own meat, buying it preground, or going for a vegetarian, vegan, or seafood option, a flavor-packed patty is paramount; so be sure to follow our shaping and cooking tips for a perfect burger every time. When making a burger with beef or turkey, we strongly prefer grinding our own meat (see page 6), but our shopping suggestions (see pages 4–5) will help you create the best burger no matter what.

BUYING GROUND BEEF

The Dos and Don'ts of Store-Bought Ground Beef

Most burger recipes simply call for "ground beef," but, as any supermarket shopper knows, the choices are much more varied. The U.S. Department of Agriculture defines "ground beef" as ground fresh and/or frozen beef from primal cuts and trimmings containing no more than 30 percent fat. But that doesn't really help anyone understand the difference between ground round, ground chuck, and ground sirloin. And what about fat content, which can be as low as 7 percent? These dos and don'ts will have you buying ground beef like a professional butcher.

DO BUY GROUND CHUCK If you're set on purchasing preground meat, ground chuck is the best choice. This cut of meat will cook up into a juicier and more flavorful burger than ground sirloin or ground round.

DO BUY 85 PERCENT LEAN Unless a recipe specifically calls for fattier or leaner beef, 85 percent is our favorite choice for a burger with just the right amount of richness.

DO HAVE THE BUTCHER GRIND FOR YOU Not all markets offer freshly ground meat, but grocers who do grind beef in-house usually start with whole primal cuts. If you're lucky enough to find a butcher who will grind meat to order, you can ask for any cut, ground as coarse or fine as you like.

DON'T BUY GENERICALLY LABELED "GROUND BEEF" Any cut or combination of cuts can be labeled "ground beef," so consistency is a problem, and because ground beef may have as much as 30 percent fat, greasiness can also be an issue.

DON'T BUY BEEF THAT LOOKS BROWN A brown color in store-bought ground beef is a sign that the meat is not freshly ground and won't be as tender and flavorful as fresher, redder ground meat.

DON'T BUY MEAT WITH JUICES AT THE BOTTOM Don't be fooled by the liquid at the bottom of the package. It's not a sign that the meat is juicy; it's a sign that the meat may have been previously frozen and thawed.

GRASS-FED VERSUS GRAIN-FED BEEF

Most U.S. beef is raised on grain, but grass-fed beef is becoming an increasingly popular option. Grain-fed beef is generally considered to be richer and fattier with a milder flavor, while grass-fed beef is leaner, chewier, and more complex with a funky, gamy flavor.

We cooked many grass-fed and grain-fed burgers side by side in the test kitchen while developing recipes. In our taste tests, we noted a difference in flavor but we found no difference in the moisture content or the texture of the two meats. We also found that they cooked the same, so you can use them interchangeably.

GO BEYOND BEEF

Other Burger Patties

Beef may be the most common choice for a burger patty, but it's certainly not the only one. Try out new flavor combinations by changing the patty in your burger. These options will give you endless burger possibilities.

TURKEY When purchasing preground turkey, we recommend 93 percent lean ground turkey, which contains light and dark meat, instead of 99 percent lean ground turkey breast, which produces dry, chalky burgers. For the juiciest results, we recommend grinding your own turkey blend (page 26).

BISON Most bison meat is grass-fed and 90 percent lean; its gamy, iron-y flavor makes for a delicious burger. Bison meat is slightly leaner than standard 85 percent lean beef, but it makes a great alternative.

PORK Ground pork can take on intense flavorings as a burger (pages 97–105). Depending on how lean your ground pork is, it may retain some of its pink color after it cooks, making it difficult to judge doneness. Take the temperature of the burger (see page 9) to make sure it's fully cooked.

LAMB Lamb can be either grass-fed or grain-fed; grass-fed is more intense and less sweet than grain-fed. This flavor-packed meat can be bought preground at the supermarket so be sure to try it as a deliciously earthy, convenient burger option.

FISH For a rich and meaty fish burger the pronounced flavor of wild salmon can't be beat, but farm-raised salmon is available year-round. Grinding it in the food processor is super easy. We also like the distinctive flavor of tuna; to achieve the best texture we hand-chop tuna steak.

SHRIMP Chopped shrimp makes a surprisingly flavorful burger. But beware that supermarket raw shrimp is not always fresh; when shopping, look for frozen shrimp that's labeled "individually quick-frozen," or

IQF. We prefer untreated shrimp—those without added sodium or preservatives like sodium tripolyphosphate (STPP).

VEGGIE The quality of store-bought veggie burgers varies greatly so we focused on developing several nonmeat burgers. Our test cooks outdid themselves creating recipes for the best versions of burgers made from the usual beans and lentils as well as inventive burgers made from quinoa, millet, tempeh, and cauliflower.

FREEZING BURGERS

When meat is frozen, water vapor escapes from its surface, migrates through an air space in the package, and condenses on the inner surface of the package. The result is a piece of meat covered with ice crystals that can tear through the muscle tissue—what's commonly known as freezer burn. Freezer burn indicates a loss of moisture in the food and should be avoided. The food is still safe to eat, but the quality has suffered. To prevent freezer burn, stack patties, separated by parchment paper, wrap in plastic wrap, and place in a zipper-lock freezer bag.

BE YOUR OWN BUTCHER

Choosing the Right Cut

While preground meat can create a good burger in a pinch, meat ground at home has better texture and flavor than supermarket ground beef. Here in the test kitchen, we did a tremendous amount of testing to arrive at the perfect cut or cuts for each of our burger blends.

CHUCK Cut from the shoulder, ground chuck ranges from 15 to 20 percent fat and was favored by our tasters for its rich flavor and tender, moist texture. This is the best choice for burgers if you're using preground meat. In our Grind-Your-Own Ultimate Beef Burger Blend (page 24) we recommend using a portion of short ribs, a cut taken from the chuck area of the cow, to add rich juiciness and a mild, nutty flavor.

SIRLOIN Tasters found ground sirloin a bit dry in burgers, but loved its prominent beefy flavor. Cut from the midsection of the animal near the hip, ground sirloin usually ranges in fat content from 7 to 10 percent. In our Grind-Your-Own Sirloin Burger Blend (page 20) and Grind-Your-Own Ultimate Beef Burger Blend (page 24) we recommend using steak tips, a cut taken from the sirloin area of the cow, for their solidly beefy flavor.

PLATE On its own, plate meat is usually too tough and fatty to make a burger, but in combination with other cuts this meat can round out the flavor and richness of a patty blend. In our Grind-Your-Own Ultimate Beef Burger Blend (page 24) we recommend using a portion of skirt steak, a cut taken from the plate area of the cow, for its deep, beefy flavor and hint of earthiness.

GRINDING BEEF AT HOME

Grinding your own meat doesn't have to be intimidating and doesn't require any special equipment. In fact, we've found that a food processor is as good a tool as at-home meat grinders, producing a coarse grind that's perfect for burgers. The food processor doesn't grind the meat as finely as a commercial meat grinder, but stray pieces of gristle are obvious once the meat has been spread over a baking sheet and can easily be removed.

1. Arrange ½-inch pieces of meat in single layer on rimmed baking sheet. Freeze until firm and starting to harden around edges but still pliable, 15 to 25 minutes.

2. Working in batches, pulse meat in food processor, stopping to redistribute meat as needed for an even grind.

3. Spread ground meat over sheet, discarding any long strands of gristle and large chunks of fat.

GET READY TO COOK

The more you handle ground beef, the denser and more rubbery it becomes when cooked. Our favorite technique is to start with a loosely packed ball of meat and then gently pat it down into a disk. Some of our recipes call for freezing patties briefly before grilling; this helps to ensure that the patties hold together without overworking the meat. Patties typically bulge as they cook, and can end up looking more like golf balls than burgers. We found that creating a slight divot in the patty helps burgers stay flat as they cook.

1. Divide meat into 4 lightly packed balls.

2. Gently flatten into patties of desired thickness.

3. Using your fingertips, press center of each patty down until about ½ inch thick, creating slight divot.

4. Season formed burgers on the outside only. (We do not incorporate salt into the meat mixtures because it toughens the meat.)

Get Out the Right Skillet

Although we love the char and flavor grilling contributes to a burger, there are times when cooking indoors is the better technique or is simply more convenient. For most burgers, we prefer to use a traditional 12-inch skillet, which comfortably fits 4 patties. But for burgers that are extremely sticky or fragile, we sometimes recommend a nonstick 12-inch skillet to make flipping the burgers just a little easier. For our recommended skillets, see page 10.

SEAR THEN BAKE GRIND-YOUR-OWN BURGERS

The key to cooking tender grind-your-own burgers with a crisp, well-browned exterior and a juicy interior indoors is a two-step process: First, sear the burgers on the stovetop to create a nice brown crust, and then move them to a relatively low, 300-degree oven to bring the interior of the burgers to medium-rare or medium without leaving the exteriors leathery or burnt.

To Toast or Not to Toast?

Whether or not to toast burger buns is a source of great debate, so we let you decide. We think that toasting the buns adds extra flavor as well as a nice bit of texture. To toast buns indoors: Broil split buns 6 inches from the broiler element until lightly toasted. On the grill: While the burgers rest, grill split buns until lightly toasted, 30 to 60 seconds.

TIPS FOR GRILLING SUCCESS

Choose Your Grill

Fire up the grill! When cooking outside, we prefer to use a charcoal grill rather than a gas one. We love the great crust and smoky flavor charcoal grilling gives our burgers, and we've found that it's easier to control the heat of a charcoal fire. But if you're grilling with gas, don't fret: All of our grilled recipes also include instructions for cooking your burgers on a gas grill.

CHARCOAL GRILL
The **Weber Original Kettle Premium Charcoal Grill** is our favorite for its great construction and design.

GAS GRILL The **Weber Spirit II E-310 Gas Grill** is our favorite because its burners allow for varying heat levels and the most cooking control.

Regardless of whether you're cooking on a charcoal or gas grill, a stuck patty is a recipe for disaster. To ensure your burgers release with ease, heat your grill before cleaning the cooking grate with a sturdy grill brush. Any residual debris will come off a hot grate much more easily than a cool one. For further insurance against sticking, grab a wad of paper towels with a pair of long-handled tongs and dip it in a bowl of vegetable oil, then run it over the cleaned grill grate.

GRILL SETUPS

Arranging your coals is an easy way to modify the heat in your charcoal grill and gives you better control over the cooking. We recommend vent and charcoal setups with each of our grilled recipes to ensure the best possible result, but these two simple setups will help you grill any burger like a master.

SINGLE-LEVEL FIRE This simple arrangement is suited to foods that you want to brown but that can also overcook quickly, such as burgers. To set up the fire, distribute ash-covered coals in an even layer across the bottom of the grill.

CONCENTRATED FIRE Corralling the coals in a disposable pan concentrates the heat to create an intense fire ideal for quick-cooking foods that we want to give a substantial char, such as burgers. To set up the fire, poke holes in the bottom of a large disposable aluminum pan, place the pan in the center of the grill, and pour the ash-covered coals into the pan.

IS IT DONE YET?

Temp It

The finger test, the touch test, the color check—there are many methods for checking a burger's doneness, but the foolproof way to ensure a perfectly cooked center is to check your patty's temperature. To temp a burger, leave the patty in the pan or on the grill and slide the thermometer into the burger at the top edge, pushing it toward the center. Be sure to avoid touching the thermometer to the surface of your pan or grill grate. Then, use the doneness chart below to ensure your burgers are cooked to your preferred doneness.

Give It a Rest

Who hasn't eaten a burger on a bun so saturated with meat juices that it was practically falling apart? There's an easy way to mitigate that problem: Let your meat burgers rest to allow the juices to redistribute throughout the patty. For perfect burgers (and buns), let the burgers rest on a platter for at least 5 minutes before transferring them to buns. Be sure to leave the burgers uncovered while they rest. If tented with foil, the steam trapped inside will turn the burger's nice crust soggy.

DONENESS CHART FOR BURGERS

BEEF, BISON, AND LAMB BURGERS	
Medium-rare	120–125
Medium	130–135
Medium-well	140–145
Well done	150–155
POULTRY BURGERS	160

PORK BURGERS	150
SEAFOOD BURGERS	
Salmon (medium-rare)	125
Wild Salmon (medium-rare)	120
Tuna (medium-rare)	125
Shrimp	140–145

THE BEST EQUIPMENT FOR BURGER MAKING

TRADITIONAL SKILLET

With its ample cooking surface; steady, even heat for excellent browning; and low, flaring sides for good evaporation, the **All-Clad d3 Stainless Steel 12" Fry Pan with Lid** offers everything you need in a 12-inch skillet.

NONSTICK SKILLET

The **OXO Good Grips Non-Stick 12-inch Open Frypan** came slick and stayed that way. It cooks and releases food perfectly, thanks to its darker finish and excellent nonstick coating.

RIMMED BAKING SHEET

Everything prepared in the sturdy, warp-resistant **Nordic Ware Baker's Half Sheet** cooks appropriately and evenly. Best of all, our new favorite is a few bucks cheaper than our old winner.

ALL-AROUND SPATULA

Flipping delicate burgers requires a spatula with a perfectly proportioned head that is moderately thin and flexible. The **Wüsthof Gourmet 12" Fish Spatula** excelled at getting under food, and users found its handle easy to hold.

GRILL SPATULA

Testers loved the **Weber Original Stainless Steel Spatula**'s slim handle, remarking on the agility, sense of control, and confidence that it inspired. Particularly when the grill is really packed, this is your spatula.

TONGS

A good pair of tongs feels like a natural extension of your hands, and with a silicone-padded handle and scalloped, uncoated pincers the **OXO Good Grips 12-Inch Tongs** feel very precise.

CHEF'S KNIFE

The **Victorinox Swiss Army Fibrox Pro 8" Chef's Knife**'s super-sharp blade is silent and smooth, and it retained its edge after weeks of testing. Its textured grip feels secure for precise, effortless cuts.

FOOD PROCESSOR

For perfect home-ground meat and fish, a food processor with a powerful, quiet motor; responsive pulsing action; and sharp blades is a must. The **Cuisinart Custom 14 Food Processor** aced every test and is easy to clean.

DIGITAL SCALE

Perfect portioning requires a kitchen scale. The **OXO Good Grips 11 lb Food Scale with Pull Out Display** has sturdy construction, responsive buttons, precise decimal measurements, and a removable platform.

THERMOMETER

Don't guess at burger doneness; the **Thermoworks Thermapen Mk4** is dead accurate, fast, and so streamlined and simple that it's a breeze to use. The automatic backlight and large digits are legible in any lighting.

KITCHEN TIMER

A reliable kitchen timer ensures the perfect cook, and we thought the **OXO Good Grips Triple Timer** was simple and intuitive. It displays all three of its timers at once, so you can check everything at a glance.

KITCHEN RULER

To measure the perfect burger width and thickness, we love the **Empire 18-inch Stainless Steel Ruler** because it's easy to read, use, and clean. The inches are divided into 32nds on one side and 16ths on the other.

THE BEST STORE-BOUGHT BURGER FIXINGS

HAMBURGER BUNS
A great burger deserves an equally tasty bun, with a subtle sweetness that complements but doesn't upstage the patty. We thought **Martin's Sandwich Potato Rolls** were the fluffiest and moistest around.

KETCHUP
Our tasters wanted ketchup that tasted as they remembered it from childhood. Juggernaut Heinz topped the pack, but the saltier and tangier **Heinz Organic Tomato Ketchup** outranked the classic version.

YELLOW MUSTARD
Yellow mustard is a barbecue mainstay, and our tasters liked the smooth texture and balance of sweetness and acidity in **Heinz Yellow Mustard** best.

BROWN MUSTARD
Unlike the yellow stuff, we reach for brown mustard when we want to feel the burn. Our panel liked **Gulden's Spicy Brown Mustard** for its smooth texture and bright and classic, yet complex, taste.

MAYONNAISE
Our winner, **Blue Plate Real Mayonnaise**, had the shortest ingredient list and was the only brand that used egg yolks alone (no whites) for a richer, deeper flavor that's almost as good as homemade.

BARBECUE SAUCE
Our tasters wanted their barbecue sauce to be tomato-forward yet complex and balanced. They found all that and more in **Bull's-Eye Original BBQ Sauce**, with its subtle smoke and spice notes.

BREAD AND BUTTER PICKLES
Don't skip the pickles—their snappy crunch adds crucial dimension to a burger. **Bubbies Bread & Butter Chips** are made with real sugar rather than high-fructose corn syrup, and our tasters could tell the difference.

SWEET PICKLE RELISH
Having trouble achieving maximum pickle coverage? Relish to the rescue! While other brands were mushy and full of out-of-place flavors, **Cascadian Farm Sweet Relish** was piquant, sweet, and fresh.

BACON
Step aside over-easy eggs; burgers are bacon's new best friend. **Oscar Mayer Naturally Hardwood Smoked Bacon** had thin slices with a good balance of chew and crispness, thanks to equal amounts of fat and protein.

AMERICAN CHEESE
The best American cheese is mild, but not bland, and melts like a dream. We found **Boar's Head American Cheese** to be familiar-yet-sophisticated with a complex sharpness and nutty, rich flavor.

CHEDDAR CHEESE
Sometimes, a slice of warm bubbling cheddar on a burger is the way to go. **Cabot Vermont Sharp Cheddar** took top honors among our crew for its almost smoky caramel notes and buttery, creamy texture when melted.

SWISS CHEESE
A pockmarked wedge of Swiss may be instantly recognizable, but it's rarely celebrated for its flavor. **Boar's Head Gold Label Switzerland Swiss Cheese** had premium meltability and a great mineral taste.

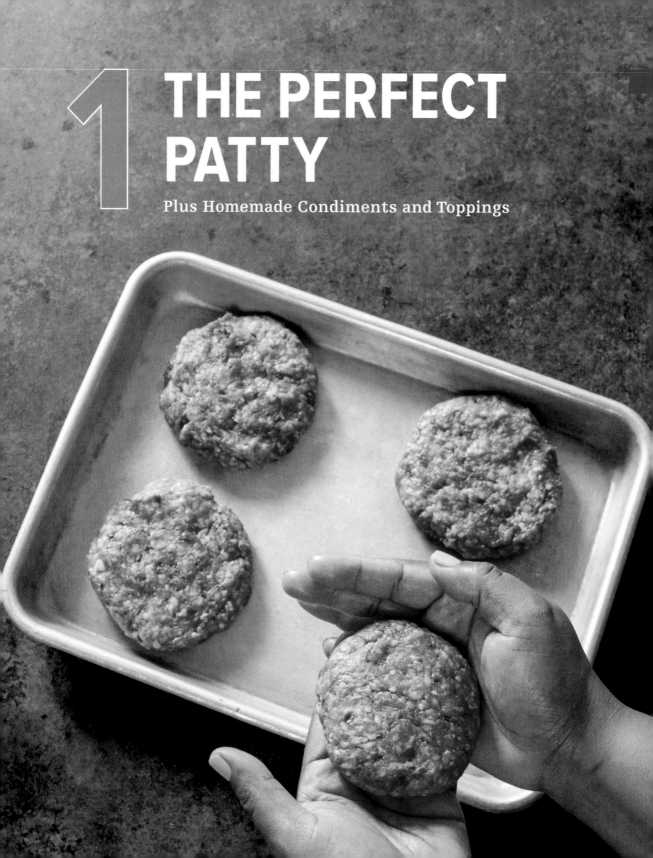

1 THE PERFECT PATTY

Plus Homemade Condiments and Toppings

IN THIS CHAPTER

CLASSIC BEEF BURGERS

SERVES 4 |

Why This Recipe Works   Sometimes simple is best, and for quick weeknight burgers or a backyard barbecue for a crowd, store-bought ground beef is certainly convenient. But with so many options available in supermarkets, we knew we would need to find the right cut of beef with the ideal amount of fat to produce tender, juicy burgers. Generically labeled "ground beef" can be a combination of different cuts with little beefy flavor that yields fatty, greasy, or mushy burgers. Hoping for better luck with singular cuts of meat, we tested ground sirloin, round, and chuck. Ground sirloin left us with dry burgers and ground round was flavorless and gristly, but 85 percent lean ground chuck gave us burgers with rich flavor and a tender, moist texture. Our first few batches of burgers puffed up like tennis balls, but we quickly figured out that slightly indenting, or dimpling, the center of each burger helped the burgers cook to a perfectly even thickness. You can serve these burgers simply with classic condiments, lettuce, and sliced ripe tomatoes. But if you're looking to branch out beyond the basics, try one of our homemade toppings on pages 28–39.

1½ pounds 85 percent lean ground beef

½ teaspoon table salt

¼ teaspoon pepper

1 teaspoon vegetable oil, if using skillet

4 slices cheese (4 ounces) (optional)

4 hamburger buns, toasted if desired

1 Divide ground beef into 4 equal portions, then gently shape each portion into ¾-inch-thick patty. Using your fingertips, press center of each patty down until about ½ inch thick, creating slight divot.

2A **For a skillet**   Season patties with salt and pepper. Heat oil in 12-inch skillet over medium heat until just smoking. Transfer patties to skillet, divot side up, and cook until well browned on first side, 2 to 4 minutes. Flip patties, top with cheese, if using, and continue to cook until browned on second side and meat registers 120 to 125 degrees (for medium-rare) or 130 to 135 degrees (for medium), 3 to 5 minutes. Transfer burgers to platter and let rest for 5 minutes. Serve burgers on buns.

2B **For a charcoal grill**   Open bottom vent completely. Light large chimney starter filled with charcoal briquettes (6 quarts). When top coals are partially covered with ash, pour evenly over grill. Set cooking grate in place, cover, and open lid vent completely. Heat grill until hot, about 5 minute s. Clean and oil cooking grate. Season patties with salt and pepper. Place patties on grill, divot side up, and cook until well browned on first side, 2 to 4 minutes. Flip patties, top with cheese, if using, and continue to cook until browned on second side and meat registers 120 to 125 degrees (for medium-rare) or 130 to 135 degrees (for medium), 3 to 5 minutes. Transfer burgers to platter and let rest for 5 minutes. Serve burgers on buns.

2C For a gas grill

Turn all burners to high, cover, and heat grill until hot, about 15 minutes. Leave all burners on high. Clean and oil cooking grate. Season patties with salt and pepper. Place patties on grill, divot side up, and cook until well browned on first side, 2 to 4 minutes. Flip patties, top with cheese, if using, and continue to cook until browned on second side and meat registers 120 to 125 degrees (for medium-rare) or 130 to 135 degrees (for medium), 3 to 5 minutes. Transfer burgers to platter and let rest for 5 minutes. Serve burgers on buns.

CLASSIC TURKEY BURGERS

SERVES 4 |

Why This Recipe Works A lean, flavorful turkey burger is a delicious alternative to the classic beef burger, and we wanted to create a simple and satisfying patty using store-bought ground turkey. To start, we took a close look at the ground turkey sold in supermarkets and found a few kinds: ground white meat, ground dark meat, and 93 percent lean ground turkey. Our tasters preferred the flavor of 93 percent lean ground turkey. Melted butter provided welcome richness and ensured moist, juicy burgers. A little bit of Worcestershire and Dijon mustard added plenty of flavor and a pleasant tang to the mild meat. Be sure to use 93 percent lean ground turkey, not 99 percent fat-free ground turkey breast, or the burgers will be tough. You can serve these burgers simply with classic condiments, lettuce, and sliced ripe tomatoes. But if you're looking to branch out beyond the basics, try one of our homemade toppings on pages 28–39.

1½ pounds ground turkey

2 tablespoons unsalted butter, melted and cooled

2 teaspoons Worcestershire sauce

2 teaspoons Dijon mustard

½ teaspoon table salt

¼ teaspoon pepper

2 teaspoons vegetable oil, if using skillet

4 slices cheese (4 ounces) (optional)

4 hamburger buns, toasted if desired

1 Break ground turkey into small pieces in large bowl. Add melted butter, Worcestershire, and mustard and gently knead with hands until well combined. Divide turkey mixture into 4 equal portions, then gently shape each portion into ¾-inch-thick patty. Using your fingertips, press center of each patty down until about ½ inch thick, creating slight divot.

2A For a skillet Season patties with salt and pepper. Heat oil in 12-inch skillet over medium heat until just smoking. Transfer patties to skillet, divot side up, and cook until well browned on first side, 4 to 6 minutes. Flip patties, top with cheese, if using, and continue to cook until browned on second side and meat registers 160 degrees, 5 to 7 minutes. Transfer burgers to platter and let rest for 5 minutes. Serve burgers on buns.

2B For a charcoal grill Open bottom vent completely. Light large chimney starter filled with charcoal briquettes (6 quarts). When top coals are partially covered with ash, pour evenly over grill. Set cooking grate in place, cover, and open lid vent completely. Heat grill until hot, about 5 minutes. Clean and oil cooking grate. Season patties with salt and pepper. Place patties on grill, divot side up, and cook until well browned on first side and meat easily releases from grill, 4 to 6 minutes. Flip patties, top with cheese, if using, and continue to cook until browned on second side and meat registers 160 degrees, 5 to 7 minutes. Transfer burgers to platter and let rest for 5 minutes. Serve burgers on buns.

2C **For a gas grill** Turn all burners to high, cover, and heat grill until hot, about 15 minutes. Turn all burners to medium. Clean and oil cooking grate. Season patties with salt and pepper. Place patties on grill, divot side up, and cook until well browned on first side and meat easily releases from grill, 4 to 6 minutes. Flip patties, top with cheese, if using, and continue to cook until browned on second side and meat registers 160 degrees, 5 to 7 minutes. Transfer burgers to platter and let rest for 5 minutes. Serve burgers on buns.

ULTIMATE VEGGIE BURGERS

MAKES 12 PATTIES |

Why This Recipe Works The complex, savory flavor and satisfying texture of this homemade vegetarian favorite are well worth the effort, and as an added bonus these burgers can be made ahead and frozen for a quick weeknight meal. An earthy mix of lentils, bulgur, and panko paired with aromatic onions, celery, leek, and garlic gave these burgers a deeply flavorful base. Cremini mushrooms lent meaty flavor, and a surprising addition of ground cashews amplified meatiness even more. Pulsing everything in the food processor made for a cohesive and even-textured mix, and mayonnaise provided necessary fat to bind our burgers. After forming the mixture into patties, we seared them in a skillet to develop a crunchy, browned exterior. Do not confuse bulgur for cracked wheat, which has a much longer cooking time and will not work in this recipe.

¾ cup brown lentils, picked over and rinsed

1 teaspoon table salt, plus salt for cooking lentils and bulgur

¾ cup medium-grind bulgur, rinsed

2 tablespoons vegetable oil, divided, plus extra as needed

2 onions, chopped fine

1 celery rib, chopped fine

1 small leek, white and light green parts only, halved lengthwise, chopped fine, and washed thoroughly

2 garlic cloves, minced

1 pound cremini or white mushrooms, trimmed and sliced ¼ inch thick

1 cup raw cashews

⅓ cup mayonnaise

2 cups panko bread crumbs

4–12 hamburger buns, toasted if desired

1 Bring 3 cups water, lentils, and 1 teaspoon salt to boil in medium saucepan over high heat. Reduce heat to medium-low and simmer gently, stirring occasionally, until lentils are just beginning to fall apart, about 25 minutes. Drain lentils, spread out over paper towel–lined rimmed baking sheet, and pat dry; let cool to room temperature.

2 Bring 2 cups water and ½ teaspoon salt to boil in small saucepan. Off heat, stir in bulgur, cover, and let sit until tender, 15 to 20 minutes. Drain bulgur, pressing with rubber spatula to remove excess moisture, and transfer to large bowl; let cool slightly.

3 Heat 1 tablespoon oil in 12-inch nonstick skillet over medium-high heat until shimmering. Add onions, celery, leek, and garlic and cook, stirring occasionally, until vegetables begin to brown, about 10 minutes. Spread vegetable mixture onto second rimmed baking sheet.

4 Heat remaining 1 tablespoon oil in now-empty skillet over high heat until shimmering. Add mushrooms and cook, stirring occasionally, until golden brown, about 12 minutes; add to baking sheet with other vegetables and let cool to room temperature, about 20 minutes.

5 Pulse cashews in food processor until finely chopped, about 15 pulses. Stir cashews into bulgur, then stir in cooled lentils, vegetable-mushroom mixture, and mayonnaise. Working in 2 batches, pulse mixture in now-empty food processor until coarsely chopped, 15 to 20 pulses (mixture should be cohesive but roughly textured); transfer to clean bowl.

6 Stir in panko and salt. Divide mixture into 12 equal portions (about ½ cup each), then tightly pack each portion into ½-inch-thick patty. (Patties can be refrigerated for up to 3 days or frozen for up to 1 month. To freeze, transfer patties to 2 parchment paper–lined rimmed baking sheets and freeze until firm, about 1 hour. Stack patties, separated by parchment paper, wrap in plastic wrap, and place in zipper-lock freezer bag. Do not thaw patties before cooking.)

TO COOK BURGERS

Heat 2 tablespoons oil in 12-inch nonstick skillet over medium-high heat until shimmering. Place 4 patties in skillet and cook until well browned on first side, about 4 minutes. Using 2 spatulas, gently flip patties and continue to cook until well browned on second side, about 4 minutes, adding extra oil as needed if skillet looks dry. Transfer burgers to platter, wipe skillet clean with paper towels, and repeat with extra oil and remaining patties as desired. (If patties were previously frozen, transfer to wire rack set in rimmed baking sheet and bake in 350-degree oven until heated through, about 10 minutes.) Serve burgers on buns.

GRIND-YOUR-OWN SIRLOIN BURGER BLEND

SERVES 4 |

Why This Recipe Works Although store-bought ground chuck makes a quick and satisfying burger, home-ground meat provides a loose craggy texture and strong beefy flavor that make for a truly superior burger experience. We started with sirloin steak tips—which have good flavor, contain minimal gristly fat, and are available in small quantities—and turned to our trusty food processor to grind them. Butter gave the meat some much-needed moisture and fat for juicy, tender burgers. Freezing the patties prior to grilling helps them hold together. Sirloin steak tips are often sold as flap meat. When trimming the meat, remove any pieces of fat thicker than ⅛ inch along with any silverskin. After trimming, you should have about 1¾ pounds of meat. To double this recipe, spread beef over two baking sheets in step 1 and pulse in food processor in eight batches.

2 pounds sirloin steak tips, trimmed and cut into ½-inch pieces

4 tablespoons unsalted butter, melted and cooled

½ teaspoon table salt

¼ teaspoon pepper

1 teaspoon vegetable oil, if using skillet

1 (13 by 9-inch) disposable aluminum roasting pan, if using charcoal grill

4 slices cheese (4 ounces) (optional)

4 hamburger buns, toasted if desired

1 For the burger blend Arrange beef in single layer on rimmed baking sheet and freeze until very firm and starting to harden around edges but still pliable, 35 to 45 minutes.

2 Working in 4 batches, pulse beef in food processor until finely ground into 1/16-inch pieces, about 20 pulses, stopping to redistribute meat as needed; return to sheet. Spread ground beef over sheet, discarding any long strands of gristle and large chunks of fat. Drizzle with melted butter and gently toss with fork to combine.

TO SHAPE PATTIES

3 Divide beef mixture into 4 lightly packed balls, then gently flatten into ¾-inch-thick patties. Using your fingertips, press center of each patty down until about ½ inch thick, creating slight divot. Cover and refrigerate until ready to cook. (Patties can

be refrigerated for up to 24 hours or frozen for up to 2 weeks. To freeze, stack patties, separated by parchment paper, wrap in plastic wrap, and place in zipper-lock freezer bag.)

TO COOK BURGERS

For a skillet Adjust oven rack to middle position and heat oven to 300 degrees. Season patties with salt and pepper. (If patties were previously frozen, thaw at room temperature for 30 minutes before seasoning and increase baking time to 6 to 12 minutes.) Heat oil in 12-inch skillet over high heat until just smoking. Using spatula, transfer patties to skillet, divot side up, and cook until well browned on first side, 2 to 4 minutes. Gently flip patties and continue to cook until well browned on second side, 2 to 4 minutes. Transfer patties to rimmed baking sheet, divot side down, top with cheese, if using,

and bake until burgers register 120 to 125 degrees (for medium-rare) or 130 to 135 degrees (for medium), 3 to 8 minutes. Transfer burgers to platter and let rest for 5 minutes. Serve burgers on buns.

For a charcoal grill Freeze patties for 30 minutes. (If patties were previously frozen, thaw at room temperature for 30 minutes.) Using skewer, poke 12 holes in bottom of disposable pan. Open bottom vent completely and place prepared pan in center of grill. Light large chimney starter two-thirds filled with charcoal briquettes (4 quarts). When top coals are partially covered with ash, pour into pan. Set cooking grate in place, cover, and open lid vent completely. Heat grill until hot, about 5 minutes. Clean and oil cooking grate. Season patties with salt and pepper. Using spatula, place patties on grill, divot side up, directly over coals. Cook until well browned on first side and meat easily releases from grill, 4 to 7 minutes. Gently flip patties, top with cheese, if using, and continue to cook until well browned on second side and meat registers 120 to 125 degrees (for medium-rare) or 130 to 135 degrees (for medium), 4 to 7 minutes. Transfer burgers to platter and let rest for 5 minutes. Serve burgers on buns.

For a gas grill Freeze patties for 30 minutes. (If patties were previously frozen, thaw at room temperature for 30 minutes.) Turn all burners to high, cover, and heat grill until hot, about 15 minutes. Leave all burners on high. Clean and oil cooking grate. Season patties with salt and pepper. Using spatula, place patties on grill, divot side up, and cook, covered, until well browned on first side and meat easily releases from grill, 4 to 7 minutes. Gently flip patties, top with cheese, if using, and continue to cook until well browned on second side and meat registers 120 to 125 degrees (for medium-rare) or 130 to 135 degrees (for medium), 4 to 7 minutes. Transfer burgers to platter and let rest for 5 minutes. Serve burgers on buns.

GRIND-YOUR-OWN GRASS-FED BEEF BURGER BLEND

SERVES 4 |

Why This Recipe Works Grass-fed beef is all the rage—and for good reason. It has a subtly grassy flavor and a high level of heart-healthy omega-3 fatty acids plus antioxidant vitamins. But because grass-fed meat lacks extensive fat and marbling, it's prone to tasting dry and overcooked. We found that by using grass-fed chuck, which has a high fat-to-protein ratio, and by forming large, thick patties, we were able to produce a burger that stayed juicy and retained its beefy, earthy flavor. When trimming the meat, remove any pieces of fat thicker than ⅛ inch along with any silverskin. After trimming, you should have about 1¾ pounds of meat. To double this recipe, spread beef over two baking sheets in step 1 and pulse in food processor in eight batches.

2 pounds grass-fed bone-less beef chuck-eye roast, trimmed and cut into ½-inch pieces

4 tablespoons unsalted butter, melted and cooled

½ teaspoon table salt

¼ teaspoon pepper

1 teaspoon vegetable oil, if using skillet

1 (13 by 9-inch) disposable aluminum roasting pan, if using charcoal grill

4 slices cheese (4 ounces) (optional)

4 hamburger buns, toasted if desired

1 For the burger blend Arrange beef in single layer on rimmed baking sheet and freeze until very firm and starting to harden around edges but still pliable, 35 to 45 minutes.

2 Working in 4 batches, pulse beef in food processor until finely ground into ¹⁄₁₆-inch pieces, about 20 pulses, stopping to redistribute meat as needed; return to sheet. Spread ground beef over sheet, discarding any long strands of gristle and large chunks of fat. Drizzle with melted butter and gently toss with fork to combine.

TO SHAPE PATTIES

3 Divide beef mixture into 4 lightly packed balls, then gently flatten into ¾-inch-thick patties. Using your fingertips, press center of each patty down until about ½ inch thick, creating slight divot. Cover and refrigerate until ready to cook. (Patties can be refrigerated for up to 24 hours or frozen for up to 2 weeks. To freeze, stack patties, separated by parchment paper, wrap in plastic wrap, and place in zipper-lock freezer bag.)

TO COOK BURGERS

For a skillet Adjust oven rack to middle position and heat oven to 300 degrees. Season patties with salt and pepper. (If patties were previously frozen, thaw at room temperature for 30 minutes before seasoning and increase baking time to 6 to 12 minutes.) Heat oil in 12-inch skillet over high heat until just smoking. Using spatula, transfer patties to skillet, divot side up, and cook until well browned on first side, 2 to 4 minutes. Gently flip patties and continue to cook until well browned on second side, 2 to 4 minutes. Transfer patties to rimmed baking sheet, divot side down, top with cheese, if using, and

bake until burgers register 120 to 125 degrees (for medium-rare) or 130 to 135 degrees (for medium), 3 to 8 minutes. Transfer burgers to platter and let rest for 5 minutes. Serve burgers on buns.

For a charcoal grill Freeze patties for 30 minutes. (If patties were previously frozen, thaw at room temperature for 30 minutes.) Using skewer, poke 12 holes in bottom of disposable pan. Open bottom vent completely and place prepared pan in center of grill. Light large chimney starter two-thirds filled with charcoal briquettes (4 quarts). When top coals are partially covered with ash, pour into pan. Set cooking grate in place, cover, and open lid vent completely.

Heat grill until hot, about 5 minutes. Clean and oil cooking grate. Season patties with salt and pepper. Using spatula, place patties on grill, divot side up, directly over coals. Cook until well browned on first side and meat easily releases from grill, 4 to 7 minutes. Gently flip patties, top with cheese, if using, and continue to cook until well browned on second side and meat registers 120 to 125 degrees (for medium-rare) or 130 to 135 degrees (for medium), 4 to 7 minutes. Transfer burgers to platter and let rest for 5 minutes. Serve burgers on buns.

For a gas grill Freeze patties for 30 minutes. (If patties were previously frozen, thaw at room

temperature for 30 minutes.) Turn all burners to high, cover, and heat grill until hot, about 15 minutes. Leave all burners on high. Clean and oil cooking grate. Season patties with salt and pepper. Using spatula, place patties on grill, divot side up, and cook, covered, until well browned on first side and meat easily releases from grill, 4 to 7 minutes. Gently flip patties, top with cheese, if using, and continue to cook until well browned on second side and meat registers 120 to 125 degrees (for medium-rare) or 130 to 135 degrees (for medium), 4 to 7 minutes. Transfer burgers to platter and let rest for 5 minutes. Serve burgers on buns.

GRIND-YOUR-OWN ULTIMATE BEEF BURGER BLEND

SERVES 4 |

> **Why This Recipe Works** This deluxe, home-ground blend is a perfect combination of intense flavor and rich, tender texture that will instantly elevate your burger into the big leagues. For this particular burger, we were willing to buy and grind several cuts of meat to create the ultimate blend. Skirt steak was a must for its deep, earthy flavor; boneless short ribs offered tender texture; and sirloin steak tips provided the bold beef flavor that we love in a burger. If you can't find skirt steak, you can substitute flank steak, though the flavor will be slightly milder. When trimming the meat, remove any pieces of fat thicker than ⅛ inch along with any silverskin. After trimming, you should have about 1¾ pounds of meat. To double this recipe, spread beef over two baking sheets in step 1 and pulse in food processor in eight batches.

1 pound skirt steak, trimmed and cut into ½-inch pieces

8 ounces boneless beef short ribs, trimmed and cut into ½-inch pieces

8 ounces sirloin steak tips, trimmed and cut into ½-inch pieces

½ teaspoon table salt

¼ teaspoon pepper

1 teaspoon vegetable oil, if using skillet

1 (13 by 9-inch) disposable aluminum roasting pan, if using charcoal grill

4 slices cheese (4 ounces) (optional)

4 hamburger buns, toasted if desired

1 For the burger blend Arrange beef in single layer on rimmed baking sheet and freeze until very firm and starting to harden around edges but still pliable, 35 to 45 minutes.

2 Working in 4 batches, pulse beef in food processor until finely ground into 1/16-inch pieces, about 20 pulses, stopping to redistribute meat as needed; return to sheet. Spread ground beef over sheet, discarding any long strands of gristle and large chunks of fat, and gently toss with fork to combine.

TO SHAPE PATTIES

3 Divide beef mixture into 4 lightly packed balls, then gently flatten into ¾-inch-thick patties. Using your fingertips, press center of each patty down until about ½ inch thick, creating slight divot. Cover and refrigerate until ready to cook. (Patties can be refrigerated for up to 24 hours or frozen for up to 2 weeks. To freeze, stack patties, separated by parchment paper, wrap in plastic wrap, and place in zipper-lock freezer bag.)

TO COOK BURGERS

For a skillet Adjust oven rack to middle position and heat oven to 300 degrees. Season patties with salt and pepper. (If patties were previously frozen, thaw at room temperature for 30 minutes before seasoning and increase baking time to 6 to 12 minutes.) Heat oil in 12-inch skillet over high heat until just smoking. Using spatula, transfer patties to skillet, divot side up; cook until well browned on first side, 2 to 4 minutes. Gently flip patties and cook until well browned on second side,

2 to 4 minutes. Transfer patties to rimmed baking sheet, divot side down, top with cheese, if using, and bake until burgers register 120 to 125 degrees (for medium-rare) or 130 to 135 degrees (for medium), 3 to 8 minutes. Transfer burgers to platter; let rest for 5 minutes. Serve.

For a charcoal grill Freeze patties for 30 minutes. (If patties were previously frozen, thaw at room temperature for 30 minutes.) Using skewer, poke 12 holes in bottom of disposable pan. Open bottom vent completely and place prepared pan in center of grill. Light large chimney starter two-thirds filled with charcoal briquettes (4 quarts). When top coals are partially covered with ash, pour into pan. Set cooking grate in place, cover, and open lid vent completely. Heat grill until hot, about 5 minutes. Clean and oil cooking grate. Season patties with salt and pepper. Using spatula, place patties on grill, divot side up, directly over coals. Cook until well browned on first side and meat easily releases from grill, 4 to 7 minutes. Gently flip patties, top with cheese, if using, and cook until well browned on second side and meat registers 120 to 125 degrees (for medium-rare) or 130 to 135 degrees (for medium), 4 to 7 minutes. Transfer burgers to platter; let rest for 5 minutes. Serve.

For a gas grill Freeze patties for 30 minutes. (If patties were previously frozen, thaw at room temperature for 30 minutes.) Turn all burners to high, cover, and heat grill until hot, about 15 minutes. Leave all burners on high. Clean and oil cooking grate. Season patties with salt and pepper. Using spatula, place patties on grill, divot side up; cook, covered, until well browned on first side and meat easily releases from grill, 4 to 7 minutes. Gently flip patties, top with cheese, if using, and cook until well browned on second side and meat registers 120 to 125 degrees (for medium-rare) or 130 to 135 degrees (for medium), 4 to 7 minutes. Transfer burgers to platter; let rest for 5 minutes. Serve.

GRIND-YOUR-OWN TURKEY BURGER BLEND

SERVES 4 |

> **Why This Recipe Works**   Grinding your own turkey for burgers reaps big rewards when using collagen-rich turkey thighs. To ensure a silky texture and to help the burgers retain moisture, we made a paste with a portion of the ground turkey plus gelatin, soy sauce, and baking soda; mushrooms provided meaty flavor and texture. If you are unable to find boneless, skinless turkey thighs, substitute one 2-pound bone-in thigh, skin and bones removed, trimmed. To double this recipe, spread turkey over two baking sheets in step 1 and pulse in food processor in six batches.

1½   pounds boneless, skinless turkey thighs, trimmed and cut into ½-inch pieces

1   tablespoon unflavored gelatin

3   tablespoons chicken broth

6   ounces white mushrooms, trimmed

1   tablespoon soy sauce

Pinch baking soda

2   tablespoons plus 2 teaspoons vegetable oil, divided

½   teaspoon table salt

¼   teaspoon pepper

4   slices cheese (4 ounces) (optional)

4   hamburger buns, toasted if desired

1   For the burger blend
Arrange turkey in single layer on rimmed baking sheet and freeze until very firm and starting to harden around edges but still pliable, 35 to 45 minutes.

2   Sprinkle gelatin over broth in small bowl and let sit until gelatin softens, about 5 minutes. Pulse mushrooms in food processor until coarsely chopped, about 7 pulses, stopping and redistributing mushrooms as needed; transfer to bowl.

3   Working in 3 batches, pulse turkey in now-empty processor until ground into ⅛-inch pieces, about 20 pulses, stopping to redistribute meat as needed; transfer to separate large bowl.

4   Return ½ cup (about 3 ounces) ground turkey to again-empty processor along with softened gelatin, soy sauce, and baking soda. Process until smooth, about 2 minutes, scraping down sides of bowl as needed. With processor running, slowly add 2 tablespoons oil until incorporated, about 10 seconds. Return mushrooms to processor with paste and pulse to combine, 3 to 5 pulses. Transfer mushroom mixture to bowl with turkey and knead with your hands until combined.

TO SHAPE PATTIES

5   With lightly greased hands, divide turkey mixture into 4 lightly packed balls, then gently flatten into ¾-inch-thick patties. Using your fingertips, press center of each patty down until about ½ inch thick, creating slight divot. Cover and refrigerate until ready to cook. (Patties can be refrigerated for up to 1 hour or frozen for up to 2 weeks. To freeze, stack patties, separated by parchment paper, wrap in plastic wrap, and place in zipper-lock freezer bag.)

TO COOK BURGERS
For a skillet   Adjust oven rack to middle position and heat oven to 300 degrees. Season patties with salt and pepper. (If previously frozen, thaw at room

temperature for 30 minutes before seasoning and increase baking time to 12 to 14 minutes.) Heat remaining 2 teaspoons oil in 12-inch nonstick skillet over high heat until just smoking. Using spatula, transfer patties to skillet, divot side up, and cook until well browned on first side, 2 to 4 minutes. Flip patties and cook until well browned on second side, 2 to 4 minutes. Transfer patties to rimmed baking sheet, divot side down, top with cheese, if using, and bake until burgers register 160 degrees, 6 to 10 minutes. Transfer burgers to platter and let rest for 5 minutes. Serve burgers on buns.

For a charcoal grill Freeze patties for 30 minutes. (If previously frozen, do not thaw.) Open bottom vent completely. Light large chimney starter filled with charcoal briquettes (6 quarts). When top coals are partially covered with ash, pour evenly over half of grill. Set cooking grate in place, cover, and open lid vent completely. Heat grill until hot, about 5 minutes. Clean and oil cooking grate. Brush 1 side of patties with 1 teaspoon oil and season with salt and pepper. Using spatula, gently flip patties, brush with remaining 1 teaspoon oil, and season second side. Place burgers, divot side up, over hotter part of grill and cook until well browned on first side and meat easily releases from grill, 5 to 7 minutes. Flip, top with cheese, if using, and cook until well browned on second side and meat registers 160 degrees, 5 to 7 minutes. Transfer burgers to platter and let rest for 5 minutes. Serve on buns.

For a gas grill Freeze patties for 30 minutes. (If previously frozen, do not thaw.) Turn all burners to high, cover, and heat grill until hot, about 15 minutes. Leave primary burner on high and turn off other burner(s). Clean and oil cooking grate. Brush 1 side of patties with 1 teaspoon oil and season with salt and pepper. Using spatula, flip patties, brush with remaining 1 teaspoon oil, and season second side. Place burgers, divot side up, over hotter part of grill and cook, covered, until well browned and meat easily releases from grill, 5 to 7 minutes. Flip, top with cheese, if using, and cook until well browned on second side and meat registers 160 degrees, 5 to 7 minutes. Transfer burgers to platter and let rest for 5 minutes. Serve on buns.

KETCHUP

MAKES ABOUT 1 CUP

- 1 (6-ounce) can tomato paste
- ½ cup distilled white vinegar
- 6 tablespoons sugar
- ¼ cup water
- 1 teaspoon table salt
- ¼ teaspoon dry mustard
- ¼ teaspoon onion powder
- ⅛ teaspoon garlic powder
- Pinch ground allspice

At its most basic, ketchup is a simple combination of tomatoes, vinegar, sugar, salt, and spices, but this common condiment can add big flavor. We set out to create a homemade, pantry-friendly version that would lend itself to some exciting smoky and spicy variations. When reducing the ketchup, make sure to occasionally scrape the bottom of the saucepan with a rubber spatula to prevent scorching. This recipe can be easily doubled.

1 Whisk all ingredients together in medium saucepan. Bring to gentle simmer over medium-low heat and cook, stirring and scraping bottom of saucepan occasionally, until mixture is thickened and measures about 1 cup, about 10 minutes.

2 Strain ketchup through fine-mesh strainer set over bowl, pressing on solids to extract as much ketchup as possible; discard solids. Let cool to room temperature. (Ketchup can be refrigerated in airtight container for up to 1 week.)

Variations
SMOKY CHIPOTLE KETCHUP
Add 1 tablespoon minced canned chipotle chile in adobo sauce to saucepan with remaining ingredients.

BALSAMIC-SPICE KETCHUP
Substitute ⅓ cup balsamic vinegar for white vinegar and increase water to ½ cup. Add ¼ teaspoon ground cinnamon to saucepan with remaining ingredients.

DIJON MUSTARD
MAKES ABOUT 1 CUP

1⅓ cups water
¾ cup white wine vinegar
½ cup yellow mustard seeds
3 tablespoons dry mustard powder
4 teaspoons onion powder
1 tablespoon table salt
¾ teaspoon garlic powder
¼ teaspoon ground cinnamon
⅛ teaspoon ground turmeric
1⅓ cups dry white wine

Homemade Dijon has unbeatably sharp, intense flavor that gives a burger much bolder bite than store-bought. Passing the mustard through a fine-mesh strainer produced a smooth, velvety texture, and the aging time helped to develop a more balanced flavor. Different brands of mustard powder have different flavors; we had good luck using Colman's mustard powder. The mustard must stand for at least 5 days before using.

1 Combine water, vinegar, mustard seeds, dry mustard, onion powder, salt, garlic powder, cinnamon, and turmeric in bowl. Cover with plastic wrap and let sit at room temperature for at least 8 hours or up to 24 hours.

2 Bring wine to simmer in small saucepan over medium-high heat and cook until reduced to ⅔ cup, 10 to 15 minutes.

3 Process reduced wine and mustard seed mixture in blender until smooth, about 2 minutes, scraping down sides of blender jar as needed. Transfer mixture to now-empty saucepan and cook over medium-low heat, stirring often, until mixture has thickened slightly, 5 to 8 minutes. Strain mustard through fine-mesh strainer set over bowl, pressing firmly on solids with ladle to extract as much mustard as possible; discard solids. Let mustard cool slightly, then transfer to airtight container and refrigerate until flavors mature, at least 5 days or up to 6 months. (Mustard's flavor will deepen over time.)

CLASSIC BURGER SAUCE
MAKES ABOUT 1 CUP

½ cup mayonnaise
¼ cup ketchup
2 teaspoons sweet pickle relish
2 teaspoons sugar
2 teaspoons distilled white vinegar
1 teaspoon pepper

Classic burger sauce, sometimes called "special sauce," takes familiar condiments—ketchup, mayonnaise, and relish—and combines them to create a supercharged sauce that elevates a simple patty from good to great.

Whisk all ingredients together in bowl. (Sauce can be refrigerated in airtight container for up to 4 days; bring to room temperature before serving.)

Variation
MALT VINEGAR–MUSTARD BURGER SAUCE

Omit relish. Substitute whole-grain mustard for ketchup and 1 tablespoon malt vinegar for white vinegar.

PUB BURGER SAUCE

MAKES ABOUT 1 CUP

- ¾ cup mayonnaise
- 2 tablespoons soy sauce
- 1 tablespoon packed dark brown sugar
- 1 tablespoon Worcestershire sauce
- 1 tablespoon minced fresh chives
- 1 garlic clove, minced
- ¾ teaspoon pepper

For a pub-worthy burger sauce with intense salty, sweet, and umami flavors, we swapped out the usual ketchup and relish for flavor-packed Worcestershire and soy sauce. Using mayonnaise for the base ensured a sauce that would be thick enough to spread on toasted burger buns.

Whisk all ingredients together in bowl. (Sauce can be refrigerated in airtight container for up to 4 days; bring to room temperature before serving.)

BARBECUE SAUCE

MAKES ABOUT 2 CUPS

- 1 tablespoon vegetable oil
- 1 onion, chopped fine
  Pinch table salt
- 1 garlic clove, minced
- 1 teaspoon chili powder
- 1¼ cups ketchup
- 6 tablespoons molasses
- 3 tablespoons cider vinegar
- 2 tablespoons Worcestershire sauce
- 2 tablespoons Dijon mustard

Barbecue sauce is an versatile condiment, and making your own opens up a world of sweet, tangy, tomatoey flavors that store-bought bottles can't match. For a thinner, smoother texture, strain the sauce after it has finished cooking.

1 Heat oil in medium saucepan over medium heat until shimmering. Add onion and salt and cook until onion is softened, about 5 minutes. Stir in garlic and chili powder and cook until fragrant, about 30 seconds.

2 Whisk in ketchup, molasses, vinegar, Worcestershire, and mustard. Bring sauce to simmer and cook, stirring occasionally, until thickened and reduced to about 2 cups, about 25 minutes.

3 Let barbecue sauce cool slightly, then transfer to airtight container and let cool to room temperature. (Barbecue sauce can be refrigerated for up to 4 days.)

MAYONNAISE
MAKES ABOUT ¾ CUP

- 2 large egg yolks
- 4 teaspoons lemon juice
- 1 tablespoon water, plus extra as needed
- ¼ teaspoon Dijon mustard
- ¼ teaspoon table salt
- ⅛ teaspoon sugar
- ¾ cup vegetable oil

Creamy, tangy mayonnaise adds fantastic flavor to any burger and is super easy to make from scratch. This versatile spread may seem mysterious, but it's actually made from a simple emulsification of egg yolks and oil. The egg yolks in this recipe are not cooked. If you prefer, ¼ cup Egg Beaters may be substituted.

Process egg yolks, lemon juice, water, mustard, salt, and sugar in blender until combined, about 10 seconds, scraping down sides of blender jar as needed. With blender running, slowly add oil and process until mayonnaise is emulsified, about 2 minutes. Adjust consistency with extra water as needed. Season with salt and pepper to taste. (Mayonnaise can be refrigerated in airtight container for up to 3 days.)

Variations
LEMON-GARLIC MAYONNAISE

Increase lemon juice to 2 table spoons. Add 1 minced garlic clove and ¼ teaspoon lemon zest to blender with egg yolks.

SMOKED PAPRIKA MAYONNAISE

Add 2 teaspoons smoked paprika, 1 minced garlic clove, and pinch cayenne to blender with egg yolks.

HERBED MAYONNAISE

Add 2 tablespoons chopped fresh basil, 1 tablespoon chopped fresh parsley, and 1 tablespoon minced fresh chives to mayonnaise and pulse until combined but not smooth, about 10 pulses.

SPICY CHIPOTLE-LIME MAYONNAISE

Substitute lime juice for lemon juice. Add 1 tablespoon minced canned chipotle chile in adobo sauce and 1 minced garlic clove to blender with egg yolks.

QUICK PICKLED RED ONIONS

MAKES ABOUT 1 CUP

- 1 cup red wine vinegar
- ⅓ cup sugar
- ¼ teaspoon table salt
- 1 red onion, halved and sliced thin through root end

Pickled onions are an absolute breeze to make—just a few minutes of hands-on preparation plus a 30-minute brine bath transform simple slices of red onion into a vibrant topping for burgers. Look for a firm, dry onion with thin, shiny skin and a deep purple color.

Bring vinegar, sugar, and salt to simmer in small saucepan over medium-high heat, stirring occasionally, until sugar has dissolved. Off heat, stir in onion, cover, and let cool to room temperature, about 1 hour. Serve. (Pickled onions can be refrigerated in airtight container for up to 1 week.)

PICKLE RELISH

MAKES ABOUT 2 CUPS

- 1 pound pickling cucumbers, ends trimmed, cut into 1-inch pieces
- ½ green bell pepper, cut into 1-inch pieces
- ½ onion, chopped coarse
- 1½ teaspoons kosher salt
- 1 cup distilled white vinegar
- ½ cup sugar
- 2 teaspoons yellow mustard seeds
- ½ teaspoon celery seeds
- ¼ teaspoon ground turmeric

Great pickle relish has a bright flavor, a little crunch, and a balanced combination of tanginess and sweetness. Our homemade version starts by finely chopping the vegetables in a food processor and then salting them to avoid a watered-down, mushy relish. For a classic relish, we liked the combination of white vinegar, sugar, yellow mustard seeds, and celery seeds; to deepen the flavors we found that a simmer on the stovetop was necessary.

1 Pulse cucumbers in food processor until coarsely chopped into ¼-inch pieces, 8 to 10 pulses; transfer to large bowl. Pulse bell pepper and onion in now-empty food processor until coarsely chopped into ¼-inch pieces, about 6 pulses; transfer to bowl with cucumbers. Stir in salt, cover, and refrigerate for 3 hours.

2 Drain vegetables in colander, transfer to clean dish towel, and squeeze to remove excess liquid. Bring vinegar, sugar, mustard seeds, celery seeds, and turmeric to boil in Dutch oven over medium-high heat. Add vegetables, reduce heat to medium, and simmer until vegetables are translucent and mixture has thickened slightly, 10 to 15 minutes.

3 Let relish cool slightly, then transfer to airtight container and let cool to room temperature. (Relish can be refrigerated for up to 4 months.)

SPICY RED PEPPER RELISH

MAKES ABOUT 1 CUP

- 2 red bell peppers, stemmed, seeded, and cut into 1-inch pieces
- 2 jalapeño chiles, stemmed, seeded, and cut into 1-inch pieces
- 1 small onion, chopped
- 3 garlic cloves, peeled
- ½ cup distilled white vinegar
- ½ cup sugar
- 1 teaspoon yellow mustard seeds
- ½ teaspoon table salt

The irresistible spicy-sweet balance of this relish comes from a combination of sweet red bell peppers and spicy jalapeños. For acidity and added sweetness, we used equal parts white vinegar and sugar, which tempered the chiles' heat. A quick simmer on the stovetop let the sweet and spicy notes of the relish meld.

1 Pulse bell peppers and jalapeños in food processor until coarsely chopped into ¼-inch pieces, 8 to 10 pulses; transfer to large bowl. Pulse onion and garlic in now-empty food processor until coarsely chopped into ¼-inch pieces, about 10 pulses; transfer to bowl with bell pepper mixture.

2 Bring vinegar, sugar, mustard seeds, and salt to boil in Dutch oven over medium-high heat. Add vegetable mixture, reduce heat to medium, and simmer, stirring occasionally, until mixture has thickened, 15 to 18 minutes.

3 Let relish cool slightly, then transfer to airtight container and let cool to room temperature. (Relish can be refrigerated for up to 3 months; flavor will deepen over time.)

QUICK PICKLE CHIPS
MAKES ABOUT 2 CUPS

- ¾ cup seasoned rice vinegar
- 1 garlic clove, peeled and halved
- ¼ teaspoon ground turmeric
- ⅛ teaspoon black peppercorns
- ⅛ teaspoon yellow mustard seeds
- 8 ounces pickling cucumbers, trimmed, sliced ¼ inch thick crosswise
- 2 sprigs fresh dill

Pickles don't have to require days of brining—these classic quick-pickled cucumber slices brighten up any burger after just a few hours of resting. For guaranteed crunch, choose the freshest, firmest pickling cucumbers available; we like Kirby cucumbers. You will need a 1-pint Mason jar with a tight-fitting lid for this recipe. Heating the jar with hot water and then draining it before adding the hot brine ensures that the jar won't crack from the abrupt temperature change. You must refrigerate the pickles for 3 hours before serving.

1 Bring vinegar, ¼ cup water, garlic, turmeric, peppercorns, and mustard seeds to boil in medium saucepan over medium-high heat.

2 Fill one 1-pint jar with hot tap water to warm. Drain jar, then pack with cucumbers and dill sprigs. Using funnel and ladle, pour hot brine over cucumbers to cover. Let cool to room temperature, about 30 minutes. Cover and refrigerate until chilled and flavors meld, about 3 hours. Serve. (Pickles can be refrigerated for up to 6 weeks.)

DILL PICKLE CHIPS

MAKES FOUR 1-PINT JARS

2½ pounds pickling cucumbers, ends trimmed, sliced ¼ inch thick
2 tablespoons kosher salt
2 cups chopped dill plus 4 large sprigs
3 cups cider vinegar
3 cups water
¼ cup sugar
1 tablespoon yellow mustard seeds
2 teaspoons dill seeds
½ teaspoon Ball Pickle Crisp
4 garlic cloves, peeled and quartered

For classic pickle chips, we like Kirby cucumbers. You can omit the Ball Pickle Crisp, but pickles will be less crunchy. You will need four 1-pint Mason jars with tight-fitting lids for this recipe. For pickle spears, quarter the cucumbers lengthwise and pack vertically into jars. You must refrigerate pickles for at least 24 hours before serving.

1 Toss cucumbers with salt in bowl and refrigerate for 3 hours. Drain cucumbers in colander (do not rinse), then pat dry with paper towels.

2 Bundle chopped dill in cheesecloth and secure with kitchen twine. Bring dill sachet, vinegar, water, sugar, mustard seeds, and dill seeds to boil in large saucepan over medium-high heat. Cover, remove from heat, and let steep for 15 minutes; discard sachet.

3 Fill four 1-pint jars with hot tap water to warm. Drain jars, then add ⅛ teaspoon Pickle Crisp to each jar and pack tightly with dill sprigs, garlic, and drained cucumbers.

4 Return brine to brief boil. Using funnel and ladle, pour hot brine over cucumbers to cover, distributing spices evenly and leaving ½ inch headspace. Slide wooden skewer along inside of jar, pressing slightly on vegetables to remove air bubbles, and add extra brine as needed.

5 Let cool to room temperature, cover with lids, and refrigerate for 24 hours before serving. (Pickles can be refrigerated for up to 3 months; flavor will continue to mature over time.)

CARAMELIZED ONION JAM

MAKES ABOUT 1 CUP

- 3 tablespoons extra-virgin olive oil
- 1¼ pounds onions, halved and sliced thin
- 1 bay leaf
- ½ teaspoon minced fresh rosemary
- ½ teaspoon table salt
- ¼ teaspoon pepper
- 2 garlic cloves, peeled and smashed
- ¼ cup balsamic vinegar
- ¼ cup water
- 2 tablespoons sugar

Caramelized onion jam is a test kitchen favorite—its savory sweetness and rich color belie its simplicity, and its versatile flavor and thick, spreadable texture make it a delicious addition to any burger.

1 Heat oil in Dutch oven over medium-high heat until shimmering. Add onions, bay leaf, rosemary, salt, and pepper. Cover and cook, stirring occasionally, until onions have softened, about 10 minutes.

2 Stir in garlic. Reduce heat to medium-low and cook, uncovered, scraping up any browned bits, until onions are golden brown, about 15 minutes.

3 Stir in vinegar, water, and sugar, scraping up any browned bits. Increase heat to medium-high and simmer until mixture is thickened and rubber spatula or wooden spoon leaves distinct trail when dragged across bottom of pot, about 2 minutes.

4 Discard bay leaf. Transfer onion mixture to food processor and pulse to jam-like consistency, about 5 pulses. Transfer onion jam to airtight container and let cool to room temperature. (Onion jam can be refrigerated for up to 4 days.)

TOMATO BUTTER

MAKES ABOUT 2 CUPS

2¾	pounds tomatoes, cored, peeled, seeded, and chopped coarse
1	small onion, chopped
1	cinnamon stick
½	teaspoon table salt
¼	teaspoon ground allspice
1¾	cups packed light brown sugar
¼	cup lemon juice (2 lemons)

This "butter" might be better described as tomato jam. Either way, it's a delicious addition to burgers. To make easy work of peeling the tomatoes, use a vegetable peeler with a serrated blade.

1 Bring tomatoes, onion, cinnamon stick, salt, and allspice to simmer in Dutch oven over medium heat and cook, stirring occasionally, until tomatoes are very soft and beginning to break down, about 20 minutes.

2 Discard cinnamon stick, transfer mixture to food processor, and process until smooth, about 1 minute. Return puree to now-empty pot.

3 Stir in sugar and lemon juice and bring to simmer over medium-low heat, stirring occasionally, until rubber spatula leaves trail when dragged across bottom of pot and mixture measures slightly more than 2 cups, 20 to 30 minutes.

4 just tight container and let cool to room temperature. (Tomato butter can be refrigerated for up to 4 months.)

SAUTÉED MUSHROOM TOPPING

MAKES ABOUT 1½ CUPS

3	tablespoons unsalted butter, divided
1	onion, chopped
1¼	pounds cremini or white mushrooms, trimmed and sliced thin
¼	teaspoon table salt
1	teaspoon minced fresh thyme
2	garlic cloves, minced
¼	cup dry white wine

To turn simple mushrooms into an umami-rich burger topping, we added a good chunk of butter, chopped onion, garlic, fresh thyme, and white wine. Tender mushrooms coated in a creamy sauce pair perfectly with a rich and juicy burger.

1 Melt 2 tablespoons butter in 12-inch skillet over medium heat. Add onion and cook until softened, about 5 minutes. Stir in mushrooms and salt and increase heat to medium-high. Cover and cook, stirring occasionally, until mushrooms have released their moisture, 8 to 10 minutes.

2 Remove lid, add remaining 1 tablespoon butter, and cook, stirring occasionally, until mushrooms are deep golden brown and tender, 8 to 10 minutes. Stir in thyme and garlic and cook until fragrant, about 30 seconds. Stir in wine and cook, scraping up any browned bits, until liquid is nearly evaporated, about 1 minute. Season with salt and pepper to taste. Serve.

SHOESTRING ONIONS
SERVES 4

- 2 quarts peanut or vegetable oil
- 1½ cups all-purpose flour
- 1 teaspoon table salt
- ¾ teaspoon cream of tartar
- ½ teaspoon pepper
- 1 pound onions, sliced into ¼-inch-thick rings
- ½ cup apple juice
- ¼ cup cider vinegar

These shatteringly crisp shoestring onion rings are a guaranteed game-changer when served atop almost any burger. The crispier these onions are, the better, and we found that a combination of apple juice and cider vinegar gave us just the right amount of acid to help the coating crisp up quickly while the onions fried. Use a Dutch oven that holds 6 quarts or more for this recipe. We prefer yellow onions here, but white onions will also work.

1 Adjust oven rack to middle position and heat oven to 200 degrees. Heat oil in Dutch oven over medium-high heat to 350 degrees. Set wire rack in rimmed baking sheet and line with triple layer of paper towels.

2 Meanwhile, combine flour, salt, cream of tartar, and pepper in large bowl. Toss onions with apple juice and vinegar to coat in second large bowl. Drain onions and transfer to flour mixture, tossing to coat.

3 Fry half of onion rings, stirring occasionally, until golden brown and crisp, 3 to 4 minutes. Adjust burner, if necessary, to maintain oil temperature between 325 and 350 degrees. Using wire skimmer or slotted spoon, transfer onion rings to prepared wire rack and keep warm in oven. Return oil to 350 degrees and repeat with remaining onion rings. Season with salt and pepper to taste. Serve.

CRISPY BACON

SERVES 4

6 slices bacon, halved crosswise

While you may be tempted to simply fry up some bacon for your burger, we promise our method, which calls for the simple step of simmering the bacon first, is well worth the extra effort. The addition of water keeps the initial cooking temperature low and gentle, so the bacon retains its moisture and turns out crisp and tender instead of dry and crumbly. You can use thin- or thick-cut bacon here, though the cooking times will vary.

Place bacon in 12-inch skillet and add just enough water to cover (about ½ cup). Bring to simmer over medium-high heat and cook until water has evaporated, about 8 minutes. Lower heat to medium-low and cook bacon until crisp and well browned, 5 to 8 minutes. Transfer bacon to paper towel–lined plate to drain, and serve.

BLACK PEPPER CANDIED BACON

SERVES 4

6 slices center-cut bacon, halved crosswise
2 tablespoons packed light brown sugar
½ teaspoon pepper

It's hard to imagine improving on bacon, but salty, sweet, and crispy bacon candy does just that. Do not use dark brown sugar here. We call for center-cut bacon because we found the strips to be of a more even thickness than regular bacon. The bacon on one tray may cook more quickly than the bacon on the other; if this happens, it's OK to remove one from the oven first. Lining the baking sheets with aluminum foil eases cleanup.

1 Adjust oven rack to middle position and heat oven to 350 degrees. Line rimmed baking sheet with aluminum foil. Arrange bacon slices on prepared sheet.

2 Combine sugar and pepper in bowl. Sprinkle sugar mixture evenly over bacon (do not flip and season second side). Use your finger to evenly spread sugar mixture over each slice.

3 Bake until bacon is dark brown and sugar is bubbling, 20 to 25 minutes, rotating sheet halfway through baking. Transfer bacon to wire rack and let cool for 5 minutes. Serve.

2 WE THE PEOPLE

Classic and Modern Takes on Beef and Poultry Burgers

Double-Decker Drive-Thru Burger

IN THIS CHAPTER

GRIDDLED SMASHED BURGERS

SERVES 4 |

> **Why This Recipe Works** Sometimes it is the simplest burger that proves the most elusive. Take the classic thin, smashed diner burger we all know and love—the one topped with a pile of onions and that "special" sauce. Should be easy to replicate, right? But getting that super crispy exterior while maintaining a tender interior is a challenge. We found that loosely packing and pressing the patties helped create irregular crags at the edges of the burgers and ensured good surface contact with the pan, leading to crispy edges and nicely seared exteriors. After finishing with a little cheese, a soft potato roll, and our special pub burger sauce, we were on our way out of burger-tory and into the beefy embrace of this diner-style classic. You will need a 12-inch skillet with a tight-fitting lid for this recipe.

1 pound 85 percent lean ground beef

½ teaspoon table salt

¼ teaspoon pepper

1 teaspoon vegetable oil

4 slices American cheese (4 ounces), divided

4 hamburger buns, toasted if desired

4 leaves red or green lettuce

1 tomato, cored and sliced thin

¼ cup finely chopped onion, rinsed

¼ cup dill pickle chips

½ cup Pub Burger Sauce (page 30), plus extra for serving

1 Wrap bottom of Dutch oven with aluminum foil. Divide ground beef into 4 lightly packed balls, then gently shape each portion into ¾-inch-thick patty.

2 Season patties with salt and pepper. Heat oil in 12-inch skillet over high heat until just smoking. Transfer 2 patties to skillet. Using prepared pot, press patties until about 4 inches in diameter; set pot aside. Cook burgers, without moving, until well browned on first side, 60 to 90 seconds. Flip patties and top with 1 slice cheese. Cover and continue to cook until browned on second side, about 60 seconds. Transfer burgers to platter and cover to keep warm. Pour off all but 1 teaspoon fat from skillet and repeat with remaining 2 patties and 2 slices cheese.

3 Serve burgers on buns, topped with lettuce, tomato, onion, pickles, and burger sauce, passing extra sauce separately.

GRILLED STEAK BURGERS

SERVES 4 |

Why This Recipe Works We wanted a burger with the big beefy flavor and the crusty char of a grilled steak. Ground sirloin, the most flavorful ground beef, was a natural choice, but unfortunately it's quite lean. A seasoned butter added richness to the sirloin, but something was still missing. Steak sauce! In about five minutes we simmered up our own intensely flavored sauce, which was perfect for serving with the burger, smearing on the bun, and even brushing onto the patties before cooking.

BURGERS

- 8 tablespoons unsalted butter
- 2 garlic cloves, minced
- 2 teaspoons onion powder
- 1 teaspoon pepper
- ½ teaspoon table salt
- 1½ pounds 90 percent lean ground sirloin
- 2 teaspoons soy sauce
- 4 hamburger buns

STEAK SAUCE

- 2 tablespoons tomato paste
- ⅔ cup beef broth
- ⅓ cup raisins
- 2 tablespoons soy sauce
- 2 tablespoons Dijon mustard
- 2 tablespoons balsamic vinegar
- 1 tablespoon Worcestershire sauce

1 For the burgers
Melt butter in 8-inch skillet over medium-low heat. Add garlic, onion powder, pepper, and salt and cook until fragrant, about 1 minute. Pour all but 1 tablespoon butter mixture into bowl and let cool for about 5 minutes.

2 For the steak sauce
Meanwhile, add tomato paste to skillet and cook over medium heat until paste begins to darken, 1 to 2 minutes. Stir in broth, raisins, soy sauce, mustard, vinegar, and Worcestershire and simmer until raisins plump, about 5 minutes. Process sauce in blender until smooth, about 30 seconds; transfer to bowl.

3 Break ground beef into small pieces in large bowl. Add 5 tablespoons cooled butter mixture and soy sauce and gently knead with hands until well combined. Divide beef mixture into 4 equal portions, then gently shape each portion into ¾-inch-thick patty. Using your fingertips, press center of each patty down until about ½ inch thick, creating slight divot. Brush each patty on both sides with 1 tablespoon steak sauce. Combine remaining 2 tablespoons cooled butter mixture with 2 tablespoons steak sauce; set aside.

4A For a charcoal grill
Open bottom vent completely. Light large chimney starter filled with charcoal briquettes (6 quarts). When top coals are partially covered with ash, pour evenly over grill. Set cooking grate in place, cover, and open lid vent completely. Heat grill until hot, about 5 minutes.

4B For a gas grill
Turn all burners to high, cover, and heat grill until hot, about 15 minutes. Leave burners on high.

5 Clean and oil cooking grate. Place patties on grill, divot side up, and cook until well browned on first side, 2 to 4 minutes. Flip patties and continue to cook until browned on second side and meat registers 120 to 125 degrees (for medium-rare) or 130 to 135 degrees (for medium), 3 to 5 minutes. Transfer burgers to platter and let rest for 5 minutes.

6 Brush cut side of buns with butter–steak sauce mixture. Grill buns, cut side down, until golden, about 2 minutes. Serve burgers on buns, topped with remaining steak sauce.

GRILLED WELL-DONE BURGERS

SERVES 4 |

> **Why This Recipe Works** There's nothing worse than checking your burger and finding it has passed medium and hit the dreaded well-done stage—at least, that's what we believed before we perfected the well-done burger. Turns out there are plenty of reasons to opt for a well-done burger: It makes the cooking more hands-off, it requires less precise timing, and if you're trying to please multiple palates it's far easier to cook all of the burgers to the same temperature. Taste tests proved that well-done burgers made from 80 percent lean ground chuck were noticeably moister than burgers made from leaner beef, but they still weren't juicy enough; adding a panade—a paste of bread and milk—ensured the burgers were moist and tender. To punch up the flavor, we added minced garlic and tangy steak sauce. We cooked the burgers over high heat to create a flavorful sear; the panade helped stem moisture loss over the hot fire, leaving us with mouthwatering well-done burgers that would wow even the pickiest burger aficionado. Make sure to use 80 percent lean ground beef; a leaner ground beef will result in a drier burger.

1 slice hearty white sandwich bread, crust removed, torn into 1-inch pieces

2 tablespoons milk

2 teaspoons steak sauce

1 garlic clove, minced

1½ pounds 80 percent lean ground beef

½ teaspoon table salt

¼ teaspoon pepper

4 slices American cheese (4 ounces) (optional)

4 hamburger buns, toasted if desired

1 Using fork, mash bread, milk, steak sauce, and garlic to paste in large bowl. Break ground beef into small pieces and add to bowl with bread mixture. Gently knead with hands until well combined. Divide beef mixture into 4 equal portions, then gently shape each portion into ¾-inch-thick patty. Using your fingertips, press center of each patty down until about ½ inch thick, creating slight divot.

2A For a charcoal grill Open bottom vent completely. Light large chimney starter filled with charcoal briquettes (6 quarts). When top coals are partially covered with ash, pour evenly over grill. Set cooking grate in place, cover, and open lid vent completely. Heat grill until hot, about 5 minutes.

2B For a gas grill Turn all burners to high, cover, and heat grill until hot, about 15 minutes. Leave all burners on high.

3 Clean and oil cooking grate. Season patties with salt and pepper. Place patties on grill, divot side up, and cook (covered if using gas) until well browned on first side, 2 to 4 minutes. Flip patties, top with cheese, if using, and continue to cook until browned on second side and meat registers 140 to 145 degrees (for medium-well) or 150 to 155 degrees (for well-done), 4 to 6 minutes. Transfer burgers to platter and let rest for 5 minutes. Serve burgers on buns.

DOUBLE-DECKER DRIVE-THRU BURGERS

SERVES 4 |

Why This Recipe Works Introduced by a certain fast-food chain, the double-decker—two all-beef patties, special sauce, lettuce, cheese, pickles, and onions on a sesame seed bun—has solidified its place in American pop culture. For our take on this iconic burger, we started with the classic triple bun setup, which we achieved by simply adding another bun bottom to each burger. We knew a large, 12-inch skillet would be essential to cook the eight patties for our double stacks, but we still needed to cook the burgers in two batches to avoid overcrowding the pan, which would cause our patties to steam rather than fry. To keep the thin patties from shrinking too much, we weighted them with a foil-lined pot as they cooked. Once the first set of patties had cooked, we topped each with a slice of cheese and placed them in a warm oven; in the time it took the cheese to melt, the second batch of quick-cooking patties was ready. For this burger's hallmark flavor, we topped them with our Classic Burger Sauce (page 29), along with some shredded lettuce, pickles, and minced onion to re-create this delicious drive-thru classic at home.

1 pound 85 percent lean ground beef

½ teaspoon table salt

¼ teaspoon pepper

1 teaspoon vegetable oil

4 hamburger buns, plus 4 bun bottoms, divided

4 slices American cheese (4 ounces)

½ cup Classic Burger Sauce (page 29), divided, plus extra for serving

2 cups shredded iceberg lettuce, divided

¼ cup finely chopped onion, rinsed

¼ cup dill pickle chips

1. Adjust oven rack to middle position and heat oven to 250 degrees. Wrap bottom of Dutch oven with aluminum foil. Cut sides off 1-quart zipper-lock bag, leaving bottom seam intact.

2. Divide ground beef into eight 2-ounce portions, then roll each portion into balls. Working with 1 ball at a time, enclose in split bag. Using clear pie plate (so you can see size of patty), press ball into even 3½-inch patty. Remove patty from bag and transfer to platter. Season patties with salt and pepper.

3. Heat oil in 12-inch skillet over high heat until just smoking. Place 4 patties in skillet and weight with prepared pot. Cook until well browned on first side, 60 to 90 seconds. Flip patties, return pot, and continue to cook until browned on second side, about 60 seconds. Transfer burgers to rimmed baking sheet, top with cheese, and keep warm in oven. Pour off all but 1 teaspoon fat from skillet and repeat with remaining 4 patties; transfer to sheet.

4. **To assemble** Spread ¼ cup burger sauce over 4 bun bottoms, then top with 1 cup lettuce and cheeseburgers. Spread remaining ¼ cup sauce over remaining 4 buns bottoms, then top with remaining 1 cup lettuce, remaining burgers, onions, and pickle chips. Place second set of burger stacks on top of first and top with bun tops. Serve, passing extra sauce separately.

GRILLED SMOKEHOUSE BARBECUE BURGERS

SERVES 4 |

Why This Recipe Works For burgers infused with the flavor of wood smoke, we added a generous 2 cups of wood chips to our grill for an unmistakable smokiness that thoroughly permeates the meat. Our grilling method uses soaked wood chips to let the smoky flavor infuse the meat without becoming too harsh. Making our patties slightly larger than usual allowed them to absorb more smoke, and incorporating a few tablespoons of bottled barbecue sauce into the ground beef added an extra blast of flavor. Topping the burgers with a sweet and tangy coleslaw combined all the flavors of a smokehouse in one bite. Bull's-Eye is our preferred brand of barbecue sauce, but feel free to use your favorite.

COLESLAW

- 3 cups shredded green cabbage
- 2 tablespoons sugar, plus extra for seasoning
- 1 teaspoon table salt
- 1 carrot, peeled and shredded
- 2 tablespoons cider vinegar, plus extra for seasoning
- 1 tablespoon vegetable oil
- ⅛ teaspoon celery seeds
- ⅛ teaspoon pepper

BURGERS

- 2 pounds 85 percent lean ground beef
- 2 teaspoons garlic powder
- 2 teaspoons onion powder
- 3 tablespoons barbecue sauce, plus extra for serving
- 2 cups wood chips, soaked in water for 15 minutes and drained
- ½ teaspoon table salt
- ¼ teaspoon pepper
- 4 large hamburger buns, toasted if desired

1 For the coleslaw
Toss cabbage with sugar and salt in large bowl. Cover and microwave, stirring occasionally, until cabbage is partially wilted and has reduced in volume by about one-third, about 2 minutes. Transfer cabbage to salad spinner and spin until excess liquid has been removed. Return cabbage to now-empty bowl, add carrot, vinegar, oil, celery seeds, and pepper, and toss to combine. Season with salt and sugar to taste. Refrigerate until well chilled, at least 30 minutes or up to 4 hours.

2 For the burgers
Break ground beef into small pieces and spread into even layer on rimmed baking sheet. Sprinkle with garlic powder and onion powder and drizzle with barbecue sauce. Using 2 forks, gently toss beef mixture to combine. Divide beef mixture into 4 equal portions, then gently shape each portion into 1-inch-thick patty.

Using your fingertips, press center of each patty down until about ½ inch thick, creating slight divot.

3 Using large piece of heavy-duty aluminum foil, wrap soaked chips in 8 by 4½-inch foil packet. (Make sure chips do not poke holes in sides or bottom of packet.) Cut 2 evenly spaced 2-inch slits in top of packet.

4A **For a charcoal grill**
Open bottom vent halfway. Light large chimney starter filled with charcoal briquettes (6 quarts). When top coals are partially covered with ash, pour evenly over grill. Place wood chip packet on coals. Set cooking grate in place, cover, and open lid vent halfway. Heat grill until hot and wood chips are smoking, about 5 minutes.

4B **For a gas grill**
Remove cooking grate and place wood chip packet directly on primary burner. Set grate in place, turn all burners to high, cover, and heat grill until hot and wood chips are smoking, about 15 minutes. Leave all burners on high.

5 Clean and oil cooking grate. Season patties with salt and pepper. Place patties on grill, divot side up, and cook until well browned on first side, 2 to 4 minutes. Flip patties and continue to cook until browned on second side and meat registers 120 to 125 degrees (for medium-rare) or 130 to 135 degrees (for medium), 3 to 5 minutes per side.

6 Transfer burgers to platter and let rest for 5 minutes. Toss coleslaw to recombine. Serve burgers on buns, topped with coleslaw, passing extra barbecue sauce separately.

GRILLED BACON BURGERS WITH CARAMELIZED ONIONS AND BLUE CHEESE

SERVES 4 | 🐄 🔥

Why This Recipe Works Smoky, salty bacon can take any burger to the next level, but burgers with just a few strips on top failed to deliver bold bacon flavor. Our version nixes the strips and mixes bacon directly into the burger for bacony bliss in every bite. Mixing raw bacon with raw ground beef overworked and compressed the patties so that they cooked up tough and dry, and cooked crumbled bacon—though it mixed in better—was too crunchy. For the perfect balance of bacon flavor and juicy texture, we processed raw bacon in the food processor and then cooked it briefly in a skillet. The parcooked pieces incorporated easily into the ground beef and dispersed bacon flavor more evenly throughout while the burgers stayed moist and juicy. Instead of tossing the leftover bacon fat we used it to sauté some onions, which provided salty balance to their sweet flavor. To turn these burgers into a savory showstopper, we topped them with rich and creamy crumbled blue cheese.

8   slices bacon

1   large onion, halved and sliced thin

¼   teaspoon table salt

1½   pounds 85 percent lean ground beef

¼   teaspoon pepper

4   ounces blue cheese, crumbled and chilled (1 cup) (optional)

4   hamburger buns, toasted if desired

1 Process bacon in food processor to smooth paste, about 1 minute, scraping down sides of bowl as needed. Cook bacon in 12-inch nonstick skillet over medium heat, breaking up pieces with wooden spoon, until lightly browned in spots but still pink (do not cook until crisp), about 5 minutes. Drain bacon in fine-mesh strainer set over bowl. Transfer bacon to paper towel–lined plate and let cool completely. Reserve bacon fat.

2 Add 2 tablespoons reserved fat to now-empty skillet and heat over medium heat until shimmering. Add onion and salt and cook until well browned, about 20 minutes. Transfer to bowl and set aside.

3 Break ground beef into small pieces and spread into even layer on rimmed baking sheet. Sprinkle with bacon and gently toss to combine using 2 forks. Divide beef mixture into 4 equal portions, then gently shape each portion into ¾-inch-thick patty. Using your fingertips, press center of each patty down until about ½ inch thick, creating slight divot.

4A **For a charcoal grill** Open bottom vent completely. Light large chimney starter filled with charcoal briquettes (6 quarts). When top coals are partially covered with ash, pour evenly over grill. Set cooking grate in place, cover, and open lid vent completely. Heat grill until hot, about 5 minutes.

4B **For a gas grill** Turn all burners to high, cover, and heat grill until hot, about 15 minutes. Leave all burners on high.

5 Clean and oil cooking grate. Season patties with pepper. Place patties on grill, divot side up, and cook until well browned on first side, 2 to 4 minutes. Flip patties, top with blue cheese, if using, and continue to cook until well browned on second side and meat registers 120 to 125 degrees (for medium-rare) or 130 to 135 degrees (for medium), 3 to 5 minutes. Transfer burgers to platter and let rest for 5 minutes. Serve burgers on buns, topped with onions.

WISCONSIN BUTTER BURGERS

SERVES 4 |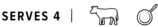

Why This Recipe Works This sumptuous burger—with its thin, crispy patty, stewed onions, and American cheese—gets its name from a surprising topping: a slab of butter slathered on each bun. Putting butter on a burger might sound unusual, but the warm patty melts the butter into an irresistibly creamy, savory sauce that's sure to win over any burger lover. These iconic burgers take their inspiration from a suburban Milwaukee restaurant named Solly's Grille that's considered the gold standard for butter burgers. Despite the short ingredient list, they're packed with rich, complex flavor. Cooking the thin patties quickly in a hot skillet without moving them for the first few minutes ensured that they developed a deeply browned crust with crisp edges to complement the soft textures of the toppings. Slowly stewing our onions in—you guessed it—a little butter contributed even more flavor and allowed them to soften without taking on too much color. American cheese provided a deliciously melty finish to this Midwestern favorite. We prefer salted butter here, but unsalted butter can be substituted by increasing the salt in step 1 to ½ teaspoon.

9 tablespoons salted butter, softened

1 onion, chopped

1 tablespoon water

¾ teaspoon table salt, divided

¼ teaspoon pepper

4 hamburger buns, toasted if desired

1 pound 90 percent lean ground beef

½ teaspoon vegetable oil

4 slices American cheese (4 ounces)

1 Melt 1 tablespoon butter in medium saucepan over medium heat. Add onion, water, and ¼ teaspoon salt; cover; and cook until tender, about 5 minutes. Uncover and continue to cook until onion is translucent and just beginning to brown, about 3 minutes. Remove from heat and cover to keep warm.

2 Spread 2 tablespoons butter onto each bun top; set aside. Divide beef into 4 equal portions, then gently shape each portion into ½-inch-thick patty. Using your fingertips, press center of each patty down until about ¼ inch thick, creating slight divot. Season patties with remaining ½ teaspoon salt and pepper.

3 Heat oil in 12-inch skillet over high heat until just smoking. Transfer patties to skillet, divot side up, and cook until well browned on first side, 2 to 4 minutes. Flip patties and continue to cook until just browned, about 1 minute. Top with cheese and continue to cook until cheese is melted, about 1 minute. Transfer burgers to platter and let rest for 5 minutes. Serve burgers on buns, topped with onions.

GRILLED NEW MEXICAN GREEN CHILE CHEESEBURGERS

SERVES 4 |

Why This Recipe Works This burger turns up the heat with two types of chiles for the ultimate fire-roasted flavor. Our southwestern topping uses both mild Anaheim chiles and hot jalapeños for a complex combination that's slightly sweet and satisfyingly spicy. For intense smoky flavor we roasted the chiles along with an onion on the grill; once they developed a delicious char, we quickly chopped them in the food processor with some garlic to create a chunky chile topping. Pureeing some of the topping and mixing it into the ground beef ensured bold chile flavor throughout. To keep our topping on the burgers—and off our plates—we added some gooey American cheese; layering the cheese on top of the chiles before melting it helped keep the topping in place. Traditional New Mexican chile burgers use Hatch chiles; although they were too difficult for us to track down, you could substitute them for the jalapeños and Anaheims if they are regionally available to you. For more heat, include the jalapeño ribs and seeds.

3 Anaheim chiles, stemmed, halved, and seeded

3 jalapeño chiles, stemmed, halved, and seeded

1 onion, sliced into ½-inch-thick rounds

1 garlic clove, minced

1½ pounds 85 percent lean ground beef

½ teaspoon table salt

¼ teaspoon pepper

4 slices American cheese (4 ounces)

4 hamburger buns, toasted if desired

1A For a charcoal grill Open bottom vent completely. Light large chimney starter filled with charcoal briquettes (6 quarts). When top coals are partially covered with ash, pour evenly over grill. Set cooking grate in place, cover, and open lid vent completely. Heat grill until hot, about 5 minutes.

1B For a gas grill Turn all burners to high, cover, and heat grill until hot, about 15 minutes. Leave all burners on high.

2 Clean and oil cooking grate. Place chiles and onion on grill and cook until vegetables are lightly charred and tender, 2 to 4 minutes per side. Transfer vegetables to bowl, cover, and let sit for 5 minutes. Remove skins from chiles and discard; separate onion rounds into rings.

3 Transfer chiles, onion, and garlic to food processor and pulse until coarsely chopped, about 10 pulses. Transfer all but ¼ cup chopped chile mixture to empty bowl and season with salt and pepper to taste; set aside. Process remaining chile mixture until smooth, scraping down sides of bowl as needed, about 1 minute. (If mixture does not turn smooth, add up to 2 teaspoons water.)

4 Break ground beef into small pieces and add to large bowl with pureed chile mixture. Gently knead with hands until well combined. Divide beef mixture into 4 equal portions, then gently shape each portion into ¾-inch-thick patty. Using your fingertips, press center of each patty down until about ½ inch thick, creating slight divot.

5 Season patties with salt and pepper and place on grill, divot side up. Cook until well browned on first side, 2 to 4 minutes. Flip patties, top with chopped chile mixture and cheese and continue to cook until well browned on second side and meat registers 120 to 125 degrees (for medium-rare) or 130 to 135 degrees (for medium),

3 to 5 minutes. Transfer burgers to platter and let rest for 5 minutes. Serve burgers on buns.

OKLAHOMA FRIED ONION BURGERS

SERVES 4 |

Why This Recipe Works The star of this Oklahoma specialty is its crispy crust of caramelized onions, which is pressed onto a thin patty of ground beef. This exceptional, diner-style burger is traditionally cooked on a large griddle, where chefs press down on the onion-topped patties to seal the components together before serving the burgers on a buttery grilled bun with yellow mustard and dill pickles. For our version, we knew we needed to find a way to get the onions to stay on the burger rather than slide down the sides. Slicing and salting the onions allowed them to release some of their moisture; after the onions rested, we squeezed out their excess liquid to help them brown quickly and stick to the burgers. Instead of layering the onions on top of the patties, we flipped these burgers upside down; starting with individual mounds of onions, we set a ball of meat on top of each and then pressed the patties down onto the onions to help them stick. We placed the burgers in a buttered skillet onion side down to brown the onions and seal them onto the burgers. Cooking the burgers over medium heat allowed the meat and onions to cook together, giving us an onion crust that was caramelized on top and slightly crisp underneath. Finally, we flipped the burgers and turned up the heat to finish cooking and get a nice sear. A mandoline makes quick work of slicing the onion thinly. Squeeze the salted onion slices until they're as dry as possible, or they won't adhere to the patties.

1   large onion, halved and sliced ⅛ inch thick

1½   teaspoons table salt, divided

¾   teaspoon pepper, divided

1   pound 85 percent lean ground beef

1   tablespoon unsalted butter

1   teaspoon vegetable oil

4   slices American cheese (4 ounces)

4   hamburger buns, toasted if desired

1 Toss onion with 1 teaspoon salt in colander and let sit for 30 minutes, tossing occasionally. Transfer onion to clean dish towel, gather edges, and squeeze onion dry. Sprinkle with ½ teaspoon pepper.

2 Divide onion mixture into 4 equal mounds on rimmed baking sheet. Divide ground beef into 4 equal portions, then gently shape into balls. Place beef balls on top of onion mounds and flatten beef firmly so onions adhere and patties measure ¼ inch thick.

3 Season patties with remaining ½ teaspoon salt and ¼ teaspoon pepper. Melt butter and oil in 12-inch nonstick skillet over medium heat. Using spatula, transfer patties to skillet, onion side down, and cook until onion is deep golden brown and beginning to crisp around edges, 8 to 10 minutes. Flip patties, increase heat to high, and continue to cook until well browned on second side, about 2 minutes. Transfer burgers to platter and let rest for 5 minutes. Place 1 slice cheese on each bun bottom. Serve burgers on buns.

GRILLED JUCY LUCY BURGERS

SERVES 4 | 🐄 🍳

> **Why This Recipe Works** For this unique twist on a classic cheeseburger, we switched the cheese from topping to filling for a gooey center surprise. We found a hole in our plan during our first attempts—the cheese melted through the meat, leaving an empty cavern in the burger. We devised a double-patty technique where we wrapped a first small patty around the cheese to create a barrier, and then we molded a second patty around the first so that the center wouldn't ooze out while cooking. Our burgers needed to be cooked to well-done to melt the cheesy center, but this left us with dry, tough burgers. Taking a cue from our Grilled Well-Done Hamburgers (page 46), we added a panade to help keep these burgers tender. Coined the Jucy Lucy in Minneapolis, this tavern offering is sure to become a new cheesy favorite. Buy the American cheese from the deli counter and ask them to slice it into a ½-inch slab from which you can cut four big cubes to fill the center of the burgers. Allow the cooked cheeseburgers to rest for a full 5 minutes before eating them, or the hot, cheesy center will spurt out and could cause burns.

2 slices hearty white sandwich bread, torn into 1-inch pieces

¼ cup milk

1 teaspoon garlic powder

1½ pounds 85 percent lean ground beef

½ teaspoon table salt

¼ teaspoon pepper

1 (½-inch-thick) slice American cheese (4 ounces), quartered

4 hamburger buns, toasted if desired

1 Using fork, mash bread, milk, and garlic powder to paste in large bowl. Break ground beef into small pieces and add to bowl with bread mixture. Gently knead with hands until well combined.

2 Divide beef mixture into 8 equal portions. Encase each cheese piece with one portion of beef mixture to form mini burger patty. Mold second portion of meat around each mini patty and seal edges to form ball. Flatten ball to form ¾-inch-thick patty. Cover and refrigerate patties for at least 30 minutes or up to 24 hours.

3A For a charcoal grill Open bottom vent completely. Light large chimney starter half filled with charcoal briquettes (3 quarts). When top coals are partially covered with ash, pour evenly over grill. Set cooking grate in place, cover, and heat grill until hot, about 5 minutes.

3B For a gas grill Turn all burners to high, cover, and heat grill until hot, about 15 minutes. Turn all burners to medium.

4 Clean and oil cooking grate. Season patties with salt and pepper. Place patties on grill and cook (covered if using gas), without pressing on them, until well browned and cooked through, 6 to 8 minutes per side. Transfer burgers to platter and let rest for 5 minutes. Serve burgers on buns.

1 Using 1 portion of meat, encase cheese to form mini burger patty.

2 Mold second portion of meat around mini patty and seal edges to form ball.

3 Flatten ball with palm of your hand, forming ¾-inch-thick patty.

We the People   **61**

PIMENTO CHEESEBURGERS

SERVES 4 |

Why This Recipe Works Richly textured pimento cheese, sometimes called the caviar of the South, makes for a luxurious burger topping. We wanted to take our burgers one step further and stuff pimento cheese inside the patties as well for a truly decadent experience. We bypassed bland store-bought pimento cheese for our own homemade version. The flavor was an unmistakable hit, but the mixture was too gooey to stuff inside the patties; to fix this, we split the initial mixture in half, swapping out the mayo in our filling mixture for slower-melting cream cheese. To make the filling easier to mold, we shaped it into disks and froze them, then used the double-sealed patty method from our Jucy Lucy Burgers (page 60) to keep the cheese in the center. Allow the cooked cheeseburgers to rest for a full 5 minutes before eating them, or the hot, cheesy center will spurt out and could cause burns. You will need a 12-inch nonstick skillet with a tight-fitting lid for this recipe. For more information on assembling a stuffed burger, see page 61.

PIMENTO CHEESE

- 6 ounces extra-sharp cheddar cheese, shredded (1½ cups)
- ⅓ cup jarred pimentos, chopped fine
- 2 ounces cream cheese, softened
- ½ teaspoon dry mustard
- ⅛ teaspoon cayenne pepper
- 1 tablespoon mayonnaise

HAMBURGERS

- 1½ pounds 85 percent lean ground beef
- 1 tablespoon Worcestershire sauce
- ½ teaspoon table salt
- ¼ teaspoon pepper
- 2 teaspoons vegetable oil
- 4 hamburger buns, toasted if desired

1 For the pimento cheese Mix cheddar, pimentos, cream cheese, mustard, and cayenne in bowl until well combined. Drop four 2-tablespoon portions of cheddar mixture on plate and lightly flatten. Cover and freeze until cheese is firm, about 2 hours. Combine remaining cheddar mixture with mayonnaise, cover, and refrigerate until ready to use.

2 For the hamburgers Break ground beef into small pieces in large bowl. Add Worcestershire and gently knead with hands until well combined. Divide beef mixture into 8 equal portions. Encase each frozen disk of cheese with one portion of beef mixture to form mini burger patty. Mold second portion of meat around each mini patty and seal edges to form ball. Flatten ball to form 1-inch-thick patty.

3 Season patties with salt and pepper. Heat oil in 12-inch nonstick skillet over medium-high heat until just smoking. Cook patties until well browned and cooked through, about 6 minutes per side. Top with cheddar-mayonnaise mixture, cover, and continue to cook until slightly melted, about 1 minute. Transfer burgers to platter and let rest for 5 minutes. Serve burgers on buns.

TEX-MEX QUESO FUNDIDO BURGERS

SERVES 4 |

Why This Recipe Works These burgers put the fun in fundido. *Queso fundido*, which translates to melted cheese, is a molten Mexican cheese dip similar to fondue that gets its signature smoky, spicy flavor from a combination of chorizo sausage and poblano chiles. We used these flavors as the inspiration for a cheeseburger with a little heat and a lot of Tex-Mex flair. To start, we fried our chorizo and poblano in a skillet with some onion and a little water to cook the sausage and vegetables through and allow their flavors to meld. Rather than incorporating our sausage and vegetables into the cheese topping where their flavor could be overpowered, we left them in the skillet, placed our patties on top, and pressed down to create a boldly flavored, caramelized crust. Shredded Colby Jack cheese melted to a gooey, fondue-like consistency and provided a mild flavor that nicely complemented the savory burgers. You will need a 12-inch nonstick skillet with a tight-fitting lid for this recipe.

1½ pounds 85 percent lean ground beef

4 ounces fresh Mexican-style chorizo sausage, casings removed

1 cup water

1 poblano chile, stemmed, seeded, and sliced thin

1 small onion, halved and sliced thin

1 teaspoon table salt, divided

¼ teaspoon pepper

4 ounces Colby Jack cheese, shredded (1 cup)

4 hamburger buns, toasted if desired

1½ cups shredded iceberg lettuce

¼ cup jarred sliced jalapeños

1 Divide beef into 4 equal portions, then gently shape each portion into ¾-inch-thick patty.

2 Combine chorizo, water, poblano, onion, and ½ teaspoon salt in 12-inch nonstick skillet. Cover and cook over high heat, breaking up meat with wooden spoon, until chorizo is cooked through and vegetables are softened, 8 to 10 minutes. Uncover and continue to cook until water is completely evaporated and mixture begins to brown, 1 to 3 minutes.

3 Reduce heat to medium and divide chorizo mixture into 4 even piles in skillet. Season patties with remaining ½ teaspoon salt and pepper and press 1 patty firmly into each pile. Cook until well browned, about 4 minutes. Flip patties and continue to cook until meat registers 120 to 125 degrees (for medium-rare) or 130 to 135 degrees (for medium), 2 to 3 minutes. Top burgers with Colby Jack, cover, and cook until cheese is melted, about 1 minute. Transfer burgers to platter and let rest for 5 minutes. Serve burgers on buns, topped with lettuce and jalapeños.

CONNECTICUT STEAMED CHEESEBURGERS

SERVES 4 |

Why This Recipe Works The unique cooking method for this regional burger, which calls for steaming the patty until perfectly cooked and gently melting the cheese to gooey perfection, promises the perfect no-fuss cheeseburger featuring tender meat smothered in melty cheese and sandwiched in a warm, soft bun. But without the custom-made steam cabinets Connecticut diners traditionally use to cook this burger, we had to devise a way to replicate this cooking environment in a home kitchen. We found the answer with a Dutch oven and steamer basket; the Dutch oven was wide enough to hold four burgers, and the steamer basket held the burgers just above the water. To achieve the savory flavor that other burgers get from browning, we mixed soy sauce, tomato paste, and onion powder into the meat. For a flavorful, evenly melted layer of cheese, we used shredded cheddar and added it off heat so it didn't slide off the burgers. Thirty seconds before serving, we added the buns to the steamer, giving them just enough time to soften and warm through. You will need a collapsible steamer basket for this recipe. The water should not touch the bottom of the steamer basket; adjust the water depth as needed.

1½ pounds 85 percent lean ground beef

2 teaspoons soy sauce

1 teaspoon onion powder

1 teaspoon tomato paste

½ teaspoon table salt

¼ teaspoon pepper

4 ounces sharp cheddar cheese, shredded (1 cup)

4 hamburger buns

1 Break ground beef into small pieces in large bowl. Add soy sauce, onion powder, and tomato paste and gently mix with hands until well combined. Divide beef mixture into 4 equal portions, then gently shape each portion into ¾-inch-thick patty. Using your fingertips, press center of each patty down until about ½ inch thick, creating slight divot.

2 Bring 4 cups water to boil in covered Dutch oven over medium-high heat. Season patties with salt and pepper. Arrange patties in steamer basket, divot side up. Set steamer basket inside Dutch oven, cover, and cook until burgers register 130 to 135 degrees (for medium) or 140 to 145 degrees (for medium-well), 7 to 8 minutes. Off heat, top burgers with cheddar, cover, and let sit until cheese melts, about 2 minutes. Place bun tops on burgers and bun bottoms, cut side up, on top of bun tops. Cover and let sit until buns soften, about 30 seconds. Serve burgers on buns.

EASY BEEF SLIDERS

SERVES 6, MAKES 12 SLIDERS |

Why This Recipe Works Tender, beefy burger? Check. Soft, steamed roll? Check. Gooey melted cheese and sweet browned onions? Check and check. Sliders, the miniature burgers popularized by the White Castle restaurant chain, satisfy meaty cravings in just a few bites. To ensure these small burgers cooked at the same rate, we weighed the meat and then placed individual portions in a zipper-lock bag and used a see-through pie plate to press the patties. Finely chopped onion pressed into the top of the patty at the start of cooking didn't cook quickly enough, and the cheese placed on top at the end didn't have time to melt before the small burgers overcooked. Adding just a little water and covering the skillet with the cheese-and-bun–topped sliders inside not only steamed the top buns to drive-through perfection, but also helped fully soften the onion and melt the cheese while the burgers gently finished cooking. You will need a 12-inch nonstick skillet with a tight-fitting lid for this recipe.

1½ pounds 85 percent lean ground beef

1 recipe Classic Burger Sauce (page 29)

12 slider hamburger buns, divided

6 slices American cheese (6 ounces), divided

½ teaspoon table salt

¼ teaspoon pepper

2 teaspoons vegetable oil, divided

½ cup finely chopped onion, divided

1 Cut sides off 1-quart zipper-lock bag, leaving bottom seam intact. Divide ground beef into twelve 2-ounce portions, then roll each portion into balls. Working with 1 ball at a time, enclose in split bag. Using clear pie plate (so you can see size of patty), press ball into even 4-inch patty. Remove patty from bag and transfer to baking sheet. Cover and refrigerate patties until ready to cook.

2 Divide sauce evenly among bun bottoms and arrange sauce side up on platter; set aside. Stack cheese and cut into quarters (you will have 24 pieces).

3 Season patties with salt and pepper. Heat 1 teaspoon oil in 12-inch skillet over medium heat until just smoking. Using spatula, transfer 6 patties to skillet. Sprinkle ¼ cup onion over top and press firmly into patties with back of spatula.

4 Cook patties, without moving, until browned, about 2 minutes. Flip and top each patty with 2 pieces of cheese and bun tops. Add 2 tablespoons water to skillet (do not wet buns), cover, and cook until cheese is melted, about 2 minutes.

5 Transfer sliders to prepared bun bottoms, tent with aluminum foil, and set aside while cooking remaining patties. Wipe skillet clean with paper towels. Repeat with remaining 1 teaspoon oil, 6 patties, ¼ cup onion, cheese, 6 bun tops, and 2 tablespoons water. Serve.

PATTY MELTS

SERVES 4 |

Why This Recipe Works Whether you call this diner classic a burger or a sandwich is up for debate, but there's no doubting that this crossover between a hamburger and a grilled cheese is the ultimate comfort food. The ground beef patty for patty melts is traditionally cooked twice—browned once in butter and a second time while the sandwich is griddled—so we turned to a panade to help keep our version moist. Rather than use white bread to make our panade, we opted for the same rye bread that we would use to sandwich our patty so that the rye flavor was incorporated throughout. Because this burger would be sitting on a slice of bread instead of a bun, we pressed our patties into ovals rather than circles for a better fit. After cooking the first side of the patties, we pulled them out of the skillet and used some of the remaining fat to soften the onions and give them rich, meaty flavor. We then put the patties back in the pan on top of the onions where they finished cooking together. We found that shredded Swiss cheese gave us the best melty texture, and we put it both under and on top of the patty to envelop this burger in cheesy goodness. After sandwiching the meat, onions, and cheese in rye bread, we put the whole sandwich back in the skillet to develop a toasty brown crust. To make sure the melts hold together, use rye bread that's sliced about ½ inch thick. If your loaf of bread is square rather than oval, shape the patties into 5 by 5-inch squares.

10   slices hearty rye sandwich bread, divided

2   tablespoons milk

¾   teaspoon onion powder

1½   pounds 85 percent lean ground beef

1   teaspoon table salt, divided

¼   teaspoon pepper

3   tablespoons unsalted butter, divided

2   onions, halved and sliced thin

8   ounces Swiss cheese, shredded (2 cups), divided

1 Adjust oven rack to middle position and heat oven to 200 degrees. Set wire rack in rimmed baking sheet. Tear 2 pieces of bread into 1-inch pieces. Using fork, mash torn bread, milk, and onion powder to paste in large bowl. Break ground beef into small pieces and add to bowl with bread mixture. Gently knead with hands until well combined. Divide beef mixture into 4 equal portions, then shape each portion into 6 by 4-inch oval.

2 Season patties with ½ teaspoon salt and pepper. Melt 1 tablespoon butter in 12-inch nonstick skillet over medium-high heat. Transfer 2 patties to skillet and cook, without moving, until well browned on first side, about 5 minutes. Transfer to large plate, browned side up, and repeat with remaining 2 patties.

3 Pour off all but 1 teaspoon fat from skillet. Add onions and remaining ½ teaspoon salt and cook, stirring occasionally, until

softened and lightly browned, 5 to 7 minutes. Arrange patties, browned side up, on top of onions, pouring any accumulated juices into skillet. Reduce heat to medium and cook, shaking skillet occasionally, until onions are tender and meat registers 120 to 125 degrees (for medium-rare) or 130 to 135 degrees (for medium), 3 to 5 minutes.

4 Divide 1 cup cheese among 4 slices bread. Top with patties, onions, remaining cheese, and remaining bread. Wipe skillet clean with paper towels. Melt 1 tablespoon butter in now-empty skillet over medium heat. Transfer 2 sandwiches to skillet and cook until golden brown and cheese is melted, 3 to 4 minutes per side.

5 Transfer to prepared rack and keep warm in oven. Repeat with remaining 1 tablespoon butter and remaining 2 sandwiches. Serve.

CRISPY CALIFORNIA TURKEY BURGERS

SERVES 4 |

Why This Recipe Works California has a reputation for embracing the latest health food crazes, and while we don't usually reach for a burger when we're watching our diet, it's hard to deny that avocado and fresh sprouts make fine burger toppings. For a West Coast–style burger, we paired these toppings with turkey burgers. Mixing some Monterey Jack into the lean turkey meat helped the burgers stay moist during cooking, giving us patties with juicy pockets of fat to yield a melting interior texture; the cheese also crisped around the edges of the burger, creating a pleasantly crunchy crust. We found that adding panko and a little mayonnaise to the turkey mixture kept the burgers from becoming too dense. We loaded the cooked burgers with creamy avocado and tender alfalfa sprouts, and also included some crisp red onion and lettuce for even more freshness. To finish, we slathered some sweet-savory classic burger sauce over simple buns before topping them off. Be sure to use 93 percent lean ground turkey, not 99 percent fat-free ground turkey breast, or the burgers will be tough.

1 pound ground turkey

1 cup panko bread crumbs

2 ounces Monterey Jack cheese, shredded (½ cup)

¼ cup mayonnaise

¼ teaspoon pepper

½ teaspoon table salt

2 teaspoons vegetable oil

½ cup Classic Burger Sauce (page 29), plus extra for serving

4 hamburger buns, toasted if desired

4 leaves Bibb or Boston lettuce

1 tomato, cored and sliced thin

1 ripe avocado, halved, pitted, and sliced ¼ inch thick

¼ cup alfalfa sprouts

½ red onion, sliced thin

1 Break ground turkey into small pieces in large bowl. Add panko, Monterey Jack, mayonnaise, and pepper and gently knead with hands until well combined. Divide turkey mixture into 4 equal portions, then gently shape each portion into ¾-inch-thick patty. Using your fingertips, press center of each patty down until about ½ inch thick, creating slight divot.

2 Season patties with salt. Heat oil in 12-inch nonstick skillet over medium heat until just smoking. Transfer patties to skillet, divot side up, and cook until well browned on first side, 4 to 6 minutes. Flip patties, reduce heat to medium-low, and continue to cook until browned on second side and meat registers 160 degrees, 5 to 7 minutes. Transfer burgers to platter and let rest for 5 minutes.

3 Spread burger sauce over bun tops and arrange lettuce on bun bottoms. Serve burgers on buns, topped with tomato, avocado, alfalfa sprouts, and onion, passing extra burger sauce separately.

GRILLED TURKEY BURGERS WITH SPINACH AND FETA

SERVES 4 |

Why This Recipe Works Ground turkey is a great neutral canvas, making it an ideal choice as the base for a burger with lots of mix-ins. We wanted superflavorful turkey burgers that take full advantage of this fact, but first we had to start by addressing the problems that plague ground turkey. Despite their popularity, turkey burgers are notorious for being bland and/or dry. This is because turkey has a mild flavor, and its leanness means it can easily dry out during cooking. We wanted to reinstate the turkey burger's good reputation with an easy way to crank up the flavor and add some much needed moisture. We boosted the flavor of our patties by stirring some melted butter and feta cheese into the ground meat; these simple additions provided plenty of richness and flavor while also preventing the burgers from drying out. For textural interest, we added fresh baby spinach to the meat mixture. Chopped dill lent a hit of freshness, and minced garlic rounded out the flavors. Be sure to use 93 percent lean ground turkey, not 99 percent fat-free ground turkey breast, or the burgers will be tough.

1¼ pounds ground turkey

2 ounces (2 cups) baby spinach, chopped

2 ounces feta cheese, crumbled (½ cup)

2 tablespoons unsalted butter, melted and cooled

2 teaspoons minced fresh dill

1 garlic clove, minced

¼ teaspoon pepper

½ teaspoon table salt

4 hamburger buns, toasted if desired

1 Break ground turkey into small pieces in large bowl. Add spinach, feta, melted butter, dill, garlic, and pepper and gently knead with hands until well combined. Divide turkey mixture into 4 equal portions, then gently shape each portion into ¾-inch-thick patty. Using your fingertips, press center of each patty down until about ½ inch thick, creating slight divot.

2A **For a charcoal grill** Open bottom vent completely. Light large chimney starter filled with charcoal briquettes (6 quarts). When top coals are partially covered with ash, pour evenly over grill. Set cooking grate in place, cover, and open lid vent completely. Heat grill until hot, about 5 minutes.

2B **For a gas grill** Turn all burners to high, cover, and heat grill until hot, about 15 minutes. Turn all burners to medium.

3 Clean and oil cooking grate. Season patties with salt. Place patties on grill, divot side up, and cook (covered if using gas) until well browned on first side and meat easily releases from grill, 4 to 6 minutes. Flip patties and continue to cook until browned on second side and meat registers 160 degrees, 5 to 7 minutes. Transfer burgers to platter and let rest for 5 minutes. Serve burgers on buns.

Variations

GRILLED TURKEY BURGERS WITH MISO AND GINGER

Omit spinach, feta, salt, and pepper. Whisk 2 tablespoons miso paste and 1 tablespoon water together in bowl until combined. Add miso mixture to turkey with melted butter. Substitute 1 teaspoon grated fresh ginger for dill and 2 minced scallions for garlic.

GRILLED TURKEY BURGERS WITH HERBS AND GOAT CHEESE

Omit spinach and garlic. Substitute ¾ cup crumbled goat cheese for feta. Add 1 large minced shallot and 2 tablespoons minced fresh parsley to turkey with melted butter.

TURKEY-VEGGIE BURGERS WITH LEMON-BASIL SAUCE

SERVES 4 |

Why This Recipe Works Packed with a combo of shredded zucchini and carrot, this great-tasting turkey burger is moist, flavorful, and nutritious. The vegetables didn't require any precooking—adding them raw to the ground turkey gave us the juiciest results. A little grated Parmesan provided a savory balance to the sweetness of the vegetables while an easy, bright sauce made with mayo and yogurt plus lemon and basil added a rich finishing touch. Use the large holes of a box grater to shred the zucchini and carrot. Be sure to use 93 percent lean ground turkey, not 99 percent fat-free ground turkey breast, or the burgers will be tough.

¼ cup mayonnaise

¼ cup plain whole-milk yogurt

2 tablespoons chopped fresh basil

1 tablespoon lemon juice

1 pound ground turkey

1 small zucchini, shredded (1¼ cups)

1 carrot, peeled and shredded (½ cup)

¼ cup grated Parmesan cheese

¼ teaspoon pepper

½ teaspoon table salt

2 teaspoons extra-virgin olive oil

4 hamburger buns, toasted if desired

1 Combine mayonnaise, yogurt, basil, and lemon juice in bowl and season with salt and pepper to taste; cover and refrigerate until ready to serve.

2 Break ground turkey into small pieces in large bowl. Add zucchini, carrot, Parmesan, and pepper and gently knead with hands until well combined. Divide turkey mixture into 4 equal portions, then gently shape each portion into ¾-inch-thick patty. Using your fingertips, press center of each patty down until about ½ inch thick, creating slight divot.

3 Season patties with salt. Heat oil in 12-inch nonstick skillet over medium heat until just smoking. Transfer patties to skillet, divot side up, and cook until well browned on first side, 4 to 6 minutes. Flip patties, reduce heat to medium-low, and continue to cook until browned on second side and meat registers 160 degrees, 5 to 7 minutes. Transfer burgers to platter and let rest for 5 minutes. Serve burgers on buns, dolloped with mayonnaise mixture.

SPICED TURKEY BURGERS WITH MANGO CHUTNEY

SERVES 4 |

Why This Recipe Works Sweet, spicy, fruity, and jammy, mango chutney is a powerhouse ingredient common in Indian cuisine that can liven up even the most mild-mannered of dishes. We first tried packing some chutney into our Classic Turkey Burgers (page 16) by mixing it with the ground turkey, but the chutney's high sugar content caused the patties to burn. Simply moving the chutney from inside the burger to on top of it solved the problem. To complement the chutney we added some garam masala to the ground turkey, as well as a pinch of cayenne for a little fire. Stirring a little melted butter into the turkey mixture prevented the meat from drying out during cooking, and some Worcestershire added extra meaty flavor. A little mayonnaise generally goes a long way on a burger, but we opted for creamy Greek yogurt instead, which nicely complemented the other components. We piled on some crunchy red onion for its savory allium flavor and sprigs of cilantro for a final fresh note. Be sure to use 93 percent lean ground turkey, not 99 percent fat-free ground turkey breast, or the burgers will be tough.

1½ pounds ground turkey

2 tablespoons unsalted butter, melted and cooled

2 teaspoons Worcestershire sauce

1 teaspoon garam masala

⅛ teaspoon cayenne pepper

¼ teaspoon pepper

½ teaspoon table salt

2 teaspoons vegetable oil

¼ cup plain Greek yogurt

4 hamburger buns, toasted if desired

4 leaves Bibb or Boston lettuce

¼ cup mango chutney

½ red onion, sliced thin

12 fresh cilantro sprigs, trimmed and cut into 2-inch pieces

1 Break ground turkey into small pieces in large bowl. Add melted butter, Worcestershire, garam masala, cayenne, and pepper and gently knead with hands until well combined. Divide turkey mixture into 4 equal portions, then gently shape each portion into ¾-inch-thick patty. Using your fingertips, press center of each patty down until about ½ inch thick, creating slight divot.

2 Season patties with salt. Heat oil in 12-inch nonstick skillet over medium heat until shimmering. Transfer patties to skillet, divot side up, and cook until well browned on first side, 4 to 6 minutes. Flip patties, reduce heat to medium-low, and continue to cook until browned on second side and meat registers 160 degrees, 5 to 7 minutes. Transfer burgers to platter and let rest for 5 minutes.

3 Spread yogurt on bun bottoms and arrange lettuce on top. Serve burgers on buns, topped with chutney, onion, and cilantro.

BRIE-STUFFED TURKEY BURGERS WITH RED PEPPER RELISH

SERVES 4 |

Why This Recipe Works There isn't a more indulgent and comforting bistro starter than baked Brie with a sweet conserve, and we thought this combination of flavors and textures could make for a unique and truly decadent stuffed turkey burger. But we soon learned that there were several challenges to pulling off such a feat: namely, getting the cheese to melt enough, but not too much, and distributing it evenly throughout the burger. We first tried simply packing some brie into our turkey patty and found that it melted very quickly, oozing out of the not-yet-cooked patties and leaving us with an empty cavern of departed cheese. Brie melts at around 130 degrees Fahrenheit, but the turkey patties would need to reach 160 degrees before they were fully cooked through. We tried wrapping the cheese in two portions of the burger mixture and refrigerating the patties until the cheese center was fully chilled. This worked perfectly, delaying the cheese's melting long enough for the burgers to cook through. For the sweet-spicy component, we whipped up a red pepper relish. Be sure to use 93 percent lean ground turkey, not 99 percent fat-free ground turkey breast, or the burgers will be tough. For more information on assembling a stuffed burger, see page 61.

4 ounces Brie cheese, rind removed, cut into ½-inch pieces

1½ pounds ground turkey

2 tablespoons unsalted butter, melted and cooled

2 teaspoons Worcestershire sauce

¼ teaspoon pepper

½ teaspoon table salt

2 teaspoons vegetable oil

4 hamburger buns, toasted if desired

½ cup Spicy Red Pepper Relish (page 33)

½ head frisée lettuce (3 ounces), leaves separated

1 Divide Brie into four equal portions; using hands, mash each portion together into rough 2-inch disk.

2 Break ground turkey into small pieces in large bowl. Add melted butter, Worcestershire, and pepper and gently knead with hands until well combined. Divide turkey mixture into 8 equal portions. Encase each disk of cheese with one portion of turkey mixture to form mini burger patty. Mold second portion of turkey around each mini patty and seal edges to form ball. Flatten ball to form ¾-inch-thick patty. Cover and refrigerate patties for at least 30 minutes or up to 24 hours.

3 Season patties with salt. Heat oil in 12-inch nonstick skillet over medium heat until shimmering. Transfer patties to skillet and cook until well browned on first side, 5 to 7 minutes. Flip patties, reduce heat to medium-low, and continue to cook until browned on second side and meat registers 160 degrees, 5 to 7 minutes. Transfer burgers to platter and let rest for 5 minutes. Serve burgers on buns, topped with pepper relish and lettuce.

THAI-STYLE TURKEY SLIDERS

SERVES 6, MAKES 12 SLIDERS |

Why This Recipe Works These sliders may be small in size, but with a creamy peanut sauce and a crunchy cucumber topping they're big on Thai flavors. Lean turkey was the perfect base for these bold mini burgers, and we mixed scallions, cilantro, chili-garlic sauce, and lime right into the patties for a blast of spicy Thai tang. Our simple peanut sauce complements these flavorful burgers with a hint of salt from fish sauce and a touch of sweetness from brown sugar, and using creamy peanut butter makes this traditional sauce easy to replicate at home. For crisp, bright crunch, we created a cucumber salad that makes a perfect topping—as long as you can resist eating it right out of the bowl while the burgers grill. Be sure to use 93 percent lean ground turkey, not 99 percent fat-free ground turkey breast, or the burgers will be tough.

¼ cup creamy peanut butter

2 tablespoons fish sauce, divided

5 teaspoons packed brown sugar, divided

1 teaspoon grated lime zest plus 5 tablespoons juice (3 limes), divided

½ English cucumber, sliced thin

½ red onion, sliced thin

1½ pounds ground turkey

4 scallions, chopped fine

¼ cup chopped fresh cilantro

2 tablespoons unsalted butter, melted and cooled

1 tablespoon Asian chili-garlic sauce

12 slider hamburger buns, toasted if desired

½ teaspoon table salt

¼ teaspoon pepper

2 teaspoons vegetable oil, divided

1 Whisk peanut butter, 4 teaspoons fish sauce, 1 tablespoon sugar, and 3 tablespoons lime juice in bowl until smooth; set aside until ready to serve. (Sauce should have consistency of ketchup; if it seems too thick, add water in small increments as needed to adjust consistency.)

2 Combine cucumber, onion, remaining 2 teaspoons fish sauce, remaining 2 teaspoons sugar, and remaining 2 tablespoons lime juice in second bowl; set aside until ready to serve.

3 Break ground turkey into small pieces in large bowl. Add scallions, cilantro, melted butter, chili-garlic sauce, and lime zest and gently knead with hands until well combined.

4 Cut sides off 1-quart zipper-lock bag, leaving bottom seam intact. Divide turkey mixture into twelve portions (about 2½ ounces each), then roll each portion into balls. Working with 1 ball at a time, enclose in split bag. Using clear pie plate (so you can see size of patty), press ball into even 4-inch patty. Remove patty from bag and transfer to baking sheet. Cover and refrigerate patties until ready to cook.

5 Arrange bun bottoms on platter. Season patties with salt and pepper. Heat 1 teaspoon oil in 12-inch nonstick skillet over medium heat until just smoking. Using spatula, transfer 6 patties to skillet. Cook patties until well browned, 2 to 3 minutes per side. Transfer sliders to prepared bun bottoms, tent with aluminum foil, and set aside while cooking remaining patties. Wipe skillet clean with paper towels. Repeat with remaining 1 teaspoon oil and 6 patties. Top sliders with peanut sauce, cucumber salad, and bun tops. Serve.

CHICKEN BURGERS WITH SUN-DRIED TOMATOES, GOAT CHEESE, AND BALSAMIC GLAZE

SERVES 4 |

Why This Recipe Works Burgers made from ground chicken can easily taste bland. These bright-tasting chicken burgers are infused with deep tomato flavor from sun-dried tomatoes. The tomatoes added umami and sweetness to the delicate chicken with the added benefit of providing a pleasing textural contrast to the meat. Adding some of the oil from the jarred tomatoes, along with a little butter, helped keep the chicken moist while the patties cooked. Minced shallot and some fresh oregano imparted an aromatic depth. At this point, we had the makings of a burger with a delicious Italian flavor profile; with that in mind, we reduced some balsamic vinegar to a concentrated glaze that popped with fruity acidity. The glaze cut through the tang of the creamy goat cheese, which we spread on the burger buns. A final topping of baby arugula added a peppery bite to our elegant-but-easy, full-flavored chicken burgers. Be sure to use ground chicken, not ground chicken breast (also labeled 99 percent fat free), or the burgers will be tough.

⅓ cup balsamic vinegar

1¼ pounds ground chicken

⅓ cup oil-packed sun-dried tomatoes, chopped, plus 1 tablespoon packing oil

1 shallot, minced

2 tablespoons unsalted butter, melted and cooled

1 teaspoon chopped fresh oregano

¼ teaspoon pepper

½ teaspoon table salt

2 teaspoons vegetable oil

2 ounces goat cheese, crumbled (½ cup), room temperature

4 hamburger buns, toasted if desired

1½ ounces (1½ cups) baby arugula

1 Bring vinegar to simmer in small saucepan over medium heat and cook until reduced to 2 tablespoons, 5 to 7 minutes; set aside.

2 Break ground chicken into small pieces in large bowl. Add tomatoes and packing oil, shallot, melted butter, oregano, and pepper and gently knead with hands until well combined. Divide chicken mixture into 4 equal portions, then gently shape each portion into ¾-inch-thick patty. Using your fingertips, press center of each patty down until about ½ inch thick, creating slight divot.

3 Season patties with salt. Heat oil in 12-inch nonstick skillet over medium heat until just smoking. Transfer patties to skillet, divot side up, and cook until well browned on first side, 4 to 6 minutes. Flip patties, reduce heat to medium-low, and continue to cook until browned on second side and meat registers 160 degrees, 5 to 7 minutes. Transfer burgers to platter and let rest for 5 minutes. Spread goat cheese on bun tops. Serve burgers on buns, topped with arugula and drizzled with balsamic reduction.

BUFFALO CHICKEN BURGERS

SERVES 4 |

Why This Recipe Works To translate the popular combination of chicken, Buffalo sauce, and celery into a great burger, we started off with ground chicken and then added some Worcestershire and shallot for umami; melted butter helped keep the patties moist during cooking. Conventional Buffalo sauce is comprised of some combination of butter and hot sauce. For a bold sauce that would be cohesive enough to cling to our patties, we added cornstarch and molasses to the mix. Piling the blue cheese on the burgers while they rested allowed enough time for the cheese to melt before serving. In a nod to the classic Buffalo accompaniment, we topped our burgers with thinly sliced celery along with the delicate leaves, which brought pleasing crispness and refreshing contrast. If the delicate leaves attached to the celery stalks are not available, you can omit them. We prefer a mild blue cheese, such as Gorgonzola, for this recipe. Be sure to use ground chicken, not ground chicken breast (also labeled 99 percent fat free), or the burgers will be tough.

4 tablespoons unsalted butter, plus 2 tablespoons melted and cooled, divided

6 tablespoons hot sauce

1 tablespoon molasses

½ teaspoon cornstarch

1½ pounds ground chicken

1 large shallot, minced

2 teaspoons Worcestershire sauce

¼ teaspoon pepper

½ teaspoon table salt

2 teaspoons vegetable oil

2 ounces mild blue cheese, crumbled (½ cup), room temperature

4 leaves Bibb or Boston lettuce

4 hamburger buns, toasted if desired

1 celery rib, sliced thin on bias, plus ¼ cup celery leaves

1 Microwave 4 tablespoons butter, hot sauce, molasses, and cornstarch in bowl, whisking occasionally, until butter is melted and mixture has thickened slightly, 2 to 3 minutes; cover to keep warm and set aside.

2 Break ground chicken into small pieces in large bowl. Add remaining 2 tablespoons melted butter, shallot, Worcestershire, and pepper and gently knead with hands until well combined. Divide chicken mixture into 4 equal portions, then gently shape each portion into ¾-inch-thick patty. Using your fingertips, press center of each patty down until about ½ inch thick, creating slight divot.

3 Season patties with salt. Heat oil in 12-inch nonstick skillet over medium heat until just smoking. Transfer patties to skillet, divot side up, and cook until well browned on first side, 4 to 6 minutes. Flip patties, reduce heat to medium-low, and continue to cook until browned on second side and meat registers 160 degrees, 5 to 7 minutes. Transfer burgers to platter, brush with half of Buffalo sauce, and let rest for 5 minutes.

4 Arrange lettuce on bun bottoms. Serve burgers on buns, topped with blue cheese, celery, and celery leaves, passing extra Buffalo sauce separately.

3 BEYOND THE BEEF

Inspired Meat and Seafood Burgers to Update Your Routine

Banh Mi Burger

IN THIS CHAPTER

GRILLED BISON BURGERS WITH MEXICAN CORN SALAD

SERVES 4 |

Why This Recipe Works Many opt for bison simply because it's a lower-fat alternative to beef, but we love it for its clean, rich, intensely meaty flavor. Bison's distinct taste translated into patties that needed nothing more than a little salt, pepper, and a few carefully tended moments over the grill. Since we'd already fired up the grill, we decided to also grill some toppings for the ultimate charred, smoky burger. With a Mexican flavor profile in mind, we grilled a few ears of corn and threw together a quick *esquites*—a heady Mexican salad of charred corn slathered in cool, lime-spiked crema and then topped with salty cotija cheese and savory scallions. The balance of sweet and sour, salt and char, and hot and cold was a study in glorious contrasts. We also added some hot chiles; blistering them tamed their heat and emphasized their sweet, smoky characteristics. A mound of cilantro was the perfect finishing touch, its fresh grassiness complementing the smokiness of the salad and chiles. You can substitute 85 percent lean ground beef for the bison and 1 ounce Pecorino Romano for the cotija, if needed. For a spicier burger, use the larger amount of chile powder.

1½ ounces cotija cheese, grated (¾ cup)

3 tablespoons mayonnaise

2 scallions, sliced thin

¼–½ teaspoon chipotle chile powder

¼ teaspoon grated lime zest plus 1 tablespoon juice

3 ears corn, husks and silk removed

4 Fresno or jalapeño chiles, stemmed, halved, and seeded

1 tablespoon vegetable oil

1½ pounds ground bison

½ teaspoon table salt

¼ teaspoon pepper

4 hamburger buns, toasted if desired

12 fresh cilantro sprigs, trimmed and cut into 2-inch pieces

1 Combine cotija, mayonnaise, scallions, chipotle chile powder, and lime zest and juice in bowl; cover and refrigerate until ready to serve.

2 Brush corn and Fresnos with oil. Divide ground bison into 4 equal portions, then gently shape each portion into ¾-inch-thick patty. Using your fingertips, press center of each patty down until about ½ inch thick, creating slight divot.

3A For a charcoal grill Open bottom vent completely. Light large chimney starter filled with charcoal briquettes (6 quarts). When top coals are partially covered with ash, pour evenly over grill. Set cooking grate in place, cover, and open lid vent completely. Heat grill until hot, about 5 minutes.

3B For a gas grill Turn all burners to high, cover, and heat grill until hot, about 15 minutes. Leave burners on high.

4 Clean and oil cooking grate. Place corn and Fresnos on grill and cook (covered if using gas), turning occasionally, until lightly charred on all sides and Fresnos are tender, 10 to 15 minutes. As they finish cooking, transfer corn and Fresnos to platter and tent with aluminum foil.

5 Meanwhile, season patties with salt and pepper. Place patties on grill, divot side up, and cook until well browned, 2 to 4 minutes. Flip patties and continue to cook until browned on second side and meat registers 120 to 125 degrees (for medium-rare) or 130 to 135 (for medium), 3 to 5 minutes. Transfer burgers to platter and let rest for 5 minutes.

6 Transfer corn to cutting board and cut kernels from cobs. Add corn kernels to bowl with cotija mixture and toss to combine. Season with salt and pepper to taste. Serve burgers on buns, topped with corn mixture, Fresnos, and cilantro.

BISON BURGERS WITH PIQUILLO PEPPERS AND CRISPY SERRANO HAM

SERVES 4 |

> **Why This Recipe Works**   These bison burgers are rich, with a faint grassiness, but also intensely meaty. As for complementary toppings, we wanted bold flavors that would enhance but not overpower the meat's distinct taste. A Spanish flavor profile hit the mark. We loved nutty Manchego melted atop the burgers while crisped Serrano ham added concentrated flavor and textural contrast. Jarred piquillo peppers brought a sweet complexity that played off of the savory cheese and ham. To make assembling the burgers easy, we tossed the crisped ham with the chopped peppers and some fresh parsley to make a unified, balanced topping. A smoky, garlicky mayo pulled all the components together. You can substitute 85 percent lean ground beef for the bison.

2 tablespoons extra-virgin olive oil

4 ounces thinly sliced Serrano ham, cut into ½-inch pieces

1½ pounds ground bison

½ teaspoon table salt

¼ teaspoon pepper

3 ounces Manchego cheese, grated (1½ cups)

½ cup jarred piquillo peppers, patted dry and chopped coarse

¼ cup fresh parsley leaves

½ cup Smoked Paprika Mayonnaise (page 31), plus extra for serving

4 hamburger buns, toasted if desired

1 Heat oil in 12-inch nonstick skillet over medium heat until shimmering. Add ham and cook, breaking up pieces with wooden spoon, until crisp, 5 to 8 minutes. Off heat, use slotted spoon to transfer ham to paper towel–lined plate. Pour off all but 1 teaspoon fat from skillet.

2 Divide ground bison into 4 equal portions, then gently shape each portion into ¾-inch-thick patty. Using your fingertips, press center of each patty down until about ½ inch thick, creating slight divot.

3 Season patties with salt and pepper. Heat fat left in skillet over medium heat until just smoking. Transfer patties to skillet, divot side up, and cook until well browned on first side, 2 to 4 minutes. Flip patties, top with Manchego, and continue to cook until browned on second side and meat registers 120 to 125 degrees (for medium-rare) or 130 to 135 (for medium), 3 to 5 minutes. Transfer burgers to platter and let rest for 5 minutes.

4 Combine piquillo peppers, parsley, and ham in bowl. Serve burgers on buns, topped with mayonnaise and piquillo pepper mixture, passing extra mayonnaise separately.

GRILLED MEATLOAF BURGERS

SERVES 4 |

Why This Recipe Works Inspired by traditional meatloaf, we set out to create a burger we could grill that would feature the flavor of meatloaf's tomatoey glaze in every bite. Meatloaf mix—a combination of beef, pork, and veal—offered the best flavor and texture, and we found that just a little bit of thyme and Worcestershire allowed us to successfully re-create the taste of meatloaf with only a few ingredients. An egg was the perfect binder for these meatloaf miniatures and kept them tender and juicy on the grill. As for the glaze, we knew better than to mess with perfection, so we turned to a simple mixture of ketchup, brown sugar, and cider vinegar. We coated our burgers with the glaze twice for maximum flavor—once while the burgers cooked to form the distinctive chewy crust, and again right before serving for a bold hit of flavor. You can substitute equal parts ground beef and ground pork for the meatloaf mix.

½ cup ketchup

2 tablespoons packed brown sugar

2 teaspoons cider vinegar

1½ pounds meatloaf mix

1 large egg

2 teaspoons Worcestershire sauce

1 teaspoon minced fresh thyme

½ teaspoon pepper

½ teaspoon table salt

4 hamburger buns, toasted if desired

1 Whisk ketchup, sugar, and vinegar in bowl until combined; measure out and reserve half of glaze.

2 Break meatloaf mix into small pieces in large bowl. Add egg, Worcestershire, thyme, and pepper and gently knead with hands until well combined. Divide meat mixture into 4 equal portions, then gently shape each portion into ¾-inch-thick patty. Using your fingertips, press center of each patty down until about ½ inch thick, creating slight divot.

3A **For a charcoal grill** Open bottom vent completely. Light large chimney starter filled with charcoal briquettes (6 quarts). When top coals are partially covered with ash, pour evenly over grill. Set cooking grate in place, cover, and open lid vent completely. Heat grill until hot, about 5 minutes.

3B **For a gas grill** Turn all burners to high, cover, and heat grill until hot, about 15 minutes. Turn all burners to medium.

4 Clean and oil cooking grate. Season patties with salt. Place patties on grill, divot side up, and cook (covered if using gas) until well browned, 4 to 6 minutes. Flip patties, brush with remaining glaze, and continue to cook until well browned on second side and meat registers 150 degrees, 5 to 7 minutes. Transfer burgers to platter, brush with reserved glaze, and let rest for 5 minutes. Serve burgers on buns.

BREAKFAST PORK BURGERS

SERVES 4 |

Why This Recipe Works This recipe features everything we love about breakfast in burger form: savory, salty pork with a little maple sweetness, a fresh soft-cooked egg, and a hearty English muffin to mop up any errant, oozing yolk. To keep the patties from drying out during cooking, we relied on the traditional meatball standby of a panade; mixing this paste of mashed bread and milk into the ground pork ensured a juicy patty that stayed tender. A little soy sauce amped up the savoriness of the patty and seasoned it throughout, while fresh sage made the flavors pop. A touch of maple syrup added a rich flavor that was just sweet enough and encouraged beautiful browning. We weren't sure our decadent breakfast burger needed a topping of cheese, but after trying a couple of iterations, we loved how the tang of cheddar offset the burger's ample richness. Look for English muffins that are at least 4 inches in diameter. Serve with hot sauce.

1 slice hearty white sandwich bread, torn into 1-inch pieces

1 shallot, minced

2 tablespoons milk

2 tablespoons maple syrup

4 teaspoons soy sauce

2 teaspoons minced fresh sage

½ teaspoon plus ⅛ teaspoon pepper, divided

1½ pounds ground pork

½ teaspoon plus ⅛ teaspoon table salt, divided

4 teaspoons vegetable oil, divided

4 slices cheddar cheese (4 ounces)

4 large eggs

4 English muffins, toasted

1 Using fork, mash bread, shallot, milk, maple syrup, soy sauce, sage, and ½ teaspoon pepper to paste in large bowl. Break ground pork into small pieces and add to bowl with bread mixture. Gently knead with hands until well combined. Divide pork mixture into 4 equal portions, then gently shape each portion into ¾-inch-thick patty. Using your fingertips, press center of each patty down until about ½ inch thick, creating slight divot.

2 Season patties with ½ teaspoon salt. Heat 1 teaspoon oil in 12-inch nonstick skillet over medium heat until just smoking. Transfer patties to skillet, divot side up, and cook until well browned on first side, 4 to 6 minutes. Flip patties, top with cheddar, and reduce heat to medium-low. Continue to cook until browned on second side

and meat registers 150 degrees, 5 to 7 minutes. Transfer burgers to platter and let rest for 5 minutes. Let skillet cool slightly, then wipe clean with paper towels.

3 Meanwhile, crack eggs into 2 small bowls (2 eggs per bowl) and season with remaining ⅛ teaspoon salt and remaining ⅛ teaspoon pepper. Add remaining 1 tablespoon oil to now-empty skillet and heat over medium-high heat until shimmering. Swirl to coat skillet with oil, then working quickly, pour 1 bowl of eggs in 1 side of skillet and second bowl of eggs in other side. Cover and cook for 1 minute. Remove skillet from burner and let sit, covered, 15 to 45 seconds for runny yolks (white around edge of yolk will be barely opaque), 45 to 60 seconds for soft but set yolks, and about 2 minutes for medium-set yolks. Serve burgers on muffins, topped with eggs.

BANH MI BURGERS

SERVES 4 |

Why This Recipe Works Imagine a stacked burger that takes its cue from the famous Vietnamese sandwich known as *banh mi*, featuring the addictively savory combo of pork and pâté, pickled vegetables, the umami punch of fish sauce, and the crispness of fresh vegetables and herbs. To build the perfect banh mi–inspired burger, we started with the pickles, which are traditionally a simple mix of carrots and radishes. To jazz them up, we passed on standard vinegar and opted instead for lime juice with a touch of sugar. Our pickles were sufficiently bright, but we wanted a bit more depth; a splash of fish sauce provided a savory note to round out the flavors. We let the pickles marinate while we got to work on the meat of the burger. We began with a recipe for classic pork burgers—which uses a panade to keep the burgers moist and meaty—but we wanted to add some complexity in terms of flavor. The solution? You guessed it: more fish sauce, which is packed full of glutamates, making it an umami powerhouse. Mixing the sauce in with the pork blend worked wonders in amping up the burgers' meatiness. For another layer of bold flavor, we smeared decadent chicken liver pâté on a toasted kaiser roll. A simple sriracha mayo and plenty of cucumber, jalapeño, and cilantro completed a classic Vietnamese flavor profile for a burger that was rich, satisfying, crunchy, and refreshing all at the same time. You can find pâté in the gourmet cheese section of most well-stocked supermarkets. Be sure to use a smooth-textured pâté, not a coarse country pâté. Avoid pickling the radishes and carrots for longer than 1 hour; they will begin to turn limp and gray.

PICKLES

1½ teaspoons fish sauce

1½ teaspoons packed dark brown sugar

½ teaspoon grated lime zest plus ¼ cup lime juice (2 limes)

¼ teaspoon table salt

8 ounces daikon radish, peeled and cut into 2-inch-long matchsticks

1 small carrot, peeled and cut into 2-inch-long matchsticks

BURGERS

1 slice hearty white sandwich bread, torn into 1-inch pieces

1 shallot, minced

2 tablespoons milk

1 tablespoon fish sauce

½ teaspoon pepper

1½ pounds ground pork

½ teaspoon table salt

1 teaspoon vegetable oil

½ cup mayonnaise

2 tablespoons sriracha

1½ teaspoons grated lime zest

6 ounces chicken or duck liver pâté

4 kaiser rolls, toasted if desired

¼ English cucumber, halved lengthwise and sliced thin

1 jalapeño chile, stemmed and sliced thin (optional)

12 fresh cilantro sprigs, trimmed and cut into 2-inch pieces

1 **For the pickles** Whisk fish
sauce, sugar, lime zest and
juice, and salt in medium bowl until
sugar and salt have dissolved. Stir
in radish and carrot and refrigerate
for at least 15 minutes or up to
1 hour. Drain vegetables and set
aside for serving.

2 **For the burgers** Using
fork, mash bread, shallot,
milk, fish sauce, and pepper to
paste in large bowl. Break ground
pork into small pieces and add to
bowl with bread mixture. Gently
knead with hands until well

combined. Divide pork mixture
into 4 equal portions, then gently
shape each portion into ¾-inch-
thick patty. Using your fingertips,
press center of each patty down
until about ½ inch thick, creating
slight divot.

3 Season patties with salt.
Heat oil in 12-inch nonstick
skillet over medium heat until just
smoking. Transfer patties to skillet, divot side up, and cook until
well browned on first side, 4 to
6 minutes. Flip patties, reduce
heat to medium-low, and continue

to cook until browned on second side and meat registers
150 degrees, 5 to 7 minutes.
Transfer burgers to platter and
let rest for 5 minutes.

4 Whisk mayonnaise, sriracha,
and lime zest together in
bowl. Spread pâté evenly over
roll tops and bottoms followed
by half of mayonnaise mixture.
Serve burgers on rolls, topped
with pickled vegetables; cucumber; jalapeño, if using; and cilantro
sprigs, passing extra mayonnaise
mixture separately.

ITALIAN PORK BURGERS WITH BROCCOLI RABE

SERVES 4 |

Why This Recipe Works The combination of charred pork, fennel, rosemary, and garlic is a heady one. The succulent meat's flavor is both lightened by this fragrant spice blend and also enhanced by it. We were sure this Italian-inspired combination would translate into burger form; it was just a matter of figuring out the logistics. The patty was the easy part: We took a basic pork burger (which remains juicy thanks to a panade of bread and milk) and stirred in ground fennel and fresh rosemary. Some soy sauce accentuated meatiness. Lettuce was too pallid a partner for this burger, so we tried a cooked green. We loved how the bitterness of sautéed broccoli rabe complemented the seared, herb-infused meat. A little honey balanced any residual bitterness from the rabe and a pinch of red pepper flakes provided a bit of heat. Finally, a bright lemon-garlic mayonnaise pulled the dish together.

1 slice hearty white sandwich bread, torn into 1-inch pieces

1 shallot, minced

2 tablespoons milk

4 teaspoons soy sauce

1 teaspoon ground fennel

1 teaspoon minced fresh rosemary

½ teaspoon pepper

1½ pounds ground pork

4 teaspoons extra-virgin olive oil, divided

2 garlic cloves, sliced thin

8 ounces broccoli rabe, trimmed and cut into ½-inch pieces

1 teaspoon table salt, divided

Pinch red pepper flakes

2 teaspoons honey

4 hamburger buns, toasted if desired

¼ cup Lemon-Garlic Mayonnaise (page 31), plus extra for serving

1 Using fork, mash bread, shallot, milk, soy sauce, fennel, rosemary, and pepper to paste in large bowl. Break ground pork into small pieces and add to bowl with bread mixture. Gently knead with hands until well combined. Divide pork mixture into 4 equal portions, then gently shape each portion into ¾-inch-thick patty. Using your fingertips, press center of each patty down until about ½ inch thick, creating slight divot; set aside.

2 Heat 1 tablespoon oil and garlic in 12-inch nonstick skillet over medium heat until garlic is golden brown and fragrant, 2 to 4 minutes. Add broccoli rabe, ½ teaspoon salt, and pepper flakes and cook, stirring occasionally, until tender, 3 to 5 minutes. Off heat, stir in honey. Transfer to bowl and cover to keep warm. Wipe skillet clean with paper towels.

3 Season patties with remaining ½ teaspoon salt. Heat remaining 1 teaspoon oil in 12-inch nonstick skillet over medium heat until just smoking. Transfer patties to skillet, divot side up, and cook until well browned on first side, 4 to 6 minutes. Flip patties, reduce heat to medium-low, and continue to cook until browned on second side and meat registers 150 degrees, 5 to 7 minutes. Transfer burgers to platter and let rest for 5 minutes. Spread mayonnaise on bun tops. Serve burgers on buns, topped with broccoli rabe, passing extra mayonnaise separately.

GRILLED TERIYAKI PORK BURGERS

SERVES 4 |

Why This Recipe Works The Teri burger, as it's affectionately known in Hawaii, is all about big, bold flavors working in harmony. The main question was whether we wanted an actual sauce, a thick glaze, or a marinade. After trying all three, we found we preferred a glaze to either a marinade (which involved more work) or a sauce (which made the buns soggy). For real clinging power, we added a little cornstarch to the glaze ingredients; briefly heating the mixture in the microwave activated the cornstarch's thickening properties and ensured just the right consistency. As we were grilling the patties, we realized we could easily grill the pineapple as well—the grill accentuated the fruit's sweetness and deepened its flavor with some light carameliza-tion. Hot cherry peppers provided a little heat and tang to round out the burgers' Hawaiian flavor profile. You can substitute regular mayonnaise for the Japanese mayonnaise if desired. We prefer to use fresh pineapple rounds here, but canned pineapple rounds can be substituted.

⅓ cup soy sauce

¼ cup sugar

2 tablespoons mirin

1 tablespoon grated fresh ginger

2 teaspoons cornstarch

1 red onion, sliced into ½-inch-thick rounds

4 (½-inch-thick) pineapple rings

1 tablespoon vegetable oil

1 slice hearty white sandwich bread, torn into 1-inch pieces

2 scallions, sliced thin

2 tablespoons milk

¼ teaspoon pepper

1½ pounds ground pork

¼ cup Japanese-style mayon-naise, such as Kewpie, plus extra for serving

4 Hawaiian sweet rolls, toasted if desired

4 leaves iceberg lettuce

½ cup thinly sliced jarred hot cherry peppers

1 Microwave soy sauce, sugar, mirin, ginger, and cornstarch in bowl, whisking occasionally, until thickened, about 3 minutes. Measure out and reserve half of glaze; cover both portions to keep warm and set aside. Push tooth-pick horizontally through each onion round to keep rings intact while grilling. Brush onion rounds and pineapple rings with oil.

2 Using fork, mash bread, scal-lions, milk, and pepper to paste in large bowl. Break ground pork into small pieces and add to bowl with bread mixture. Gently knead with hands until well com-bined. Divide pork mixture into 4 equal portions, then gently shape each portion into ¾-inch-thick patty. Using your fingertips, press center of each patty down until about ½ inch thick, creating slight divot.

3A **For a charcoal grill** Open bottom vent completely. Light large chimney starter filled with charcoal briquettes (6 quarts). When top coals are partially covered with ash, pour evenly over grill. Set cooking grate in place, cover, and open lid vent completely. Heat grill until hot, about 5 minutes.

3B **For a gas grill** Turn all burners to high, cover, and heat grill until hot, about 15 minutes. Turn all burners to medium.

4 Clean and oil cooking grate. Place onion rounds and pineapple rings on grill and cook (covered if using gas) until softened and lightly charred, 3 to 6 minutes per side. As they finish cooking, transfer onion and pineapple to platter and tent with aluminum foil.

5 Meanwhile, place patties on grill, divot side up, and cook until well browned, 4 to 6 minutes. Flip patties, brush with half of soy mixture, and continue to cook until well browned on

second side and meat registers 150 degrees, 5 to 7 minutes. Transfer burgers to platter, brush with remaining soy mixture, and let rest for 5 minutes.

6 Remove toothpicks from onion rounds and separate into rings. Spread mayonnaise on roll bottoms and top with lettuce. Serve burgers on rolls, topped with pineapple, onion, and cherry peppers, passing extra mayonnaise separately.

GRILLED BAYOU BURGERS WITH SPICY MAYONNAISE

SERVES 4 |

> **Why This Recipe Works** These flavorful pork burgers take a cue from Louisiana cooking by adding smoky, finely chopped andouille sausage to the mix. To make these burgers even more complex, we added mustard and hot sauce to the patties. We recommend serving this burger on onion rolls to complement the flavor of the grilled onion. Our favorite andouille sausage is Jacob's World Famous Andouille, available by mail order.

1 pound ground pork

8 ounces andouille sausage, chopped fine

¼ cup whole-grain mustard, divided

1 tablespoon hot sauce, divided

1 red onion, sliced into ½-inch-thick rounds

1 tablespoon vegetable oil

½ teaspoon table salt

¼ teaspoon pepper

4 slices cheddar cheese (4 ounces)

¼ cup mayonnaise

4 onion rolls, toasted if desired

1 Break ground pork into small pieces in large bowl. Add sausage, 2 tablespoons mustard, and 2 teaspoons hot sauce and gently knead with hands until well combined. Divide meat mixture into 4 equal portions, then gently shape each portion into ¾-inch-thick patty. Using your fingertips, press center of each patty down until about ½ inch thick, creating slight divot.

2 Push toothpick horizontally through each onion round to keep rings intact while grilling. Brush onion rounds with oil.

3A For a charcoal grill Open bottom vent completely. Light large chimney starter filled with charcoal briquettes (6 quarts). When top coals are partially covered with ash, pour evenly over grill. Set cooking grate in place, cover, and open lid vent completely. Heat grill until hot, about 5 minutes.

3B For a gas grill Turn all burners to high, cover, and heat grill until hot, about 15 minutes. Turn all burners to medium.

4 Clean and oil cooking grate. Place onion rounds on grill and cook (covered if using gas) until softened and lightly charred, 3 to 6 minutes per side. As they finish cooking, transfer onion rounds to bowl and cover to keep warm.

5 Meanwhile, season patties with salt and pepper. Place patties on grill, divot side up, and cook (covered if using gas) until well browned, 4 to 6 minutes. Flip patties, top with cheese, and continue to cook until well browned on second side and meat registers 150 degrees, 5 to 7 minutes. Transfer burgers to platter and let rest for 5 minutes.

6 Remove toothpicks from onion rounds and separate into rings. Whisk mayonnaise, remaining 2 tablespoons mustard, and remaining 1 teaspoon hot sauce together in bowl and season with salt and pepper to taste. Spread mayonnaise mixture on bun tops. Serve burgers on buns, topped with onion.

LAMB BURGERS WITH HALLOUMI AND BEET TZATZIKI

SERVES 4 |

Why This Recipe Works   The rich flavor of lamb makes for an exceptional burger experience. We decided to pair delicately spiced ground lamb patties with a colorful beet tzatziki, pan-seared halloumi cheese, and a drizzle of sweet honey for a truly unique burger that could transport us to the Greek islands any night of the week. All that the ground lamb needed was a flavor boost, so we made a warm spice blend of coriander, oregano, and cinnamon. Slabs of firm, salty halloumi cheese developed a beautiful nutty brown crust when seared and offset the richness of the lamb. For a creamy tang, we topped our burgers with a generous dollop of tzatziki, which we spiked with earthy beets to turn it a vivid pink. A drizzle of honey helped pull all the flavors together.

1	beet, peeled and shredded (¾ cup)
¼	English cucumber, shredded
1	teaspoon table salt, divided
½	cup whole Greek yogurt
3	tablespoons plus 1 teaspoon extra-virgin olive oil, divided
1	tablespoon minced fresh mint or dill
1	small garlic clove, minced
1½	pounds ground lamb
1½	teaspoons ground coriander
1½	teaspoons dried oregano
⅛	teaspoon ground cinnamon
½	teaspoon pepper
1	(8-ounce) block halloumi cheese, sliced crosswise into ½-inch-thick slabs
4	hamburger buns, toasted if desired
1½	ounces (1½ cups) baby arugula
1	tablespoon honey

1 Toss beet and cucumber with ½ teaspoon salt in colander set over medium bowl and let sit for 15 minutes. Discard any drained juices and wipe bowl clean with paper towels. Whisk yogurt, 2 tablespoons oil, mint, and garlic together in now-empty bowl, then stir in beet mixture. Cover and refrigerate for at least 1 hour or up to 2 days. Season with salt and pepper to taste.

2 Break ground lamb into small pieces in large bowl. Add coriander, oregano, cinnamon, and pepper and gently knead with hands until well combined. Divide lamb mixture into 4 equal portions, then gently shape each portion into ¾-inch-thick patty. Using your fingertips, press center of each patty down until about ½ inch thick, creating slight divot.

3 Season patties with remaining ½ teaspoon salt. Heat 1 teaspoon oil in 12-inch skillet over medium heat until just smoking. Transfer patties to skillet, divot side up, and cook until well browned on first side, 2 to 4 minutes. Flip patties and continue to cook until browned on second side and meat registers 120 to 125 degrees (for medium-rare) or 130 to 135 (for medium), 3 to 5 minutes. Transfer burgers to platter and let rest for 5 minutes. Wipe skillet clean with paper towels.

4 Pat halloumi dry with paper towels. Heat remaining 1 tablespoon oil in now-empty skillet over medium heat until shimmering. Arrange halloumi in single layer in skillet and cook until golden brown, 2 to 4 minutes per side. Serve burgers on buns, topped with halloumi, tzatziki, and arugula, and drizzled with honey.

GRILLED HARISSA LAMB BURGERS

SERVES 4 |

Why This Recipe Works Harissa is a traditional North African condiment that has an irresistibly complex chile flavor. It pairs perfectly with lamb's earthy taste in this rich, spiced burger. Cool, creamy mayonnaise provides a rich base for our spicy harissa-spiked sauce, and a blast of fresh mint and lemon zest balances out the harissa's heat. You can find harissa in the international aisle of most well-stocked supermarkets.

3 tablespoons mayonnaise

2 tablespoons harissa, divided

1 tablespoon minced fresh mint

1½ teaspoons grated lemon zest, divided

1½ pounds ground lamb

½ teaspoon pepper, divided

1 red onion, sliced into ½-inch-thick rounds

1 tablespoon vegetable oil

½ teaspoon table salt

4 hamburger buns, toasted if desired

1 cup baby arugula

1 Combine mayonnaise, 1 tablespoon harissa, mint, and ½ teaspoon lemon zest in bowl and season with salt and pepper to taste; cover and refrigerate until ready to serve.

2 Break ground lamb into small pieces in large bowl. Add remaining 1 tablespoon harissa, remaining 1 teaspoon lemon zest, and ¼ teaspoon pepper and gently knead with hands until well combined. Divide lamb mixture into 4 equal portions, then gently shape each portion into ¾-inch-thick patty. Using your fingertips, press center of each patty down until about ½ inch thick, creating slight divot.

3 Push toothpick horizontally through each onion round to keep rings intact while grilling. Brush onion rounds with oil.

4A For a charcoal grill Open bottom vent completely. Light large chimney starter filled with charcoal briquettes (6 quarts). When top coals are partially covered with ash, pour evenly over grill. Set cooking grate in place, cover, and open lid vent completely. Heat grill until hot, about 5 minutes.

4B For a gas grill Turn all burners to high, cover, and heat grill until hot, about 15 minutes. Leave all burners on high.

5 Clean and oil cooking grate. Place onion rounds on grill and cook (covered if using gas) until softened and lightly charred, 3 to 6 minutes per side. As they finish cooking, transfer onion rounds to bowl and cover to keep warm.

6 Meanwhile, season patties with salt and remaining ¼ teaspoon pepper. Place patties on grill, divot side up, and cook until well browned on first side, 2 to 4 minutes. Flip patties and continue to cook until browned on second side and meat registers 120 to 125 degrees (for medium-rare) or 130 to 135 (for medium), 3 to 5 minutes. Transfer burgers to platter and let rest for 5 minutes.

7 Remove toothpicks from onion rounds and separate into rings. Spread mayonnaise mixture on bun tops. Serve burgers on buns, topped with onion and arugula.

HOISIN-GLAZED LAMB BURGERS

SERVES 4 |

Why This Recipe Works While we're well acquainted with popular Mediterranean and Middle-Eastern approaches to lamb, we were intrigued by dressing up this bold meat for a burger with Asian flavors. To play up the lamb's intense umami notes, we turned to hoisin sauce. This Chinese powerhouse ingredient packs a spicy, salty, sweet, and savory punch from chiles, garlic, fermented soy, and sugar. For complex flavor throughout, we used it twice, both folded into the ground lamb (along with deeply aromatic five-spice powder) and brushed onto the cooked burgers as they rested, for a beautiful lacquered effect reminiscent of Chinese barbecued meat. The lamb's naturally meaty flavor was both tempered and complemented by these additions, and the burgers were juicier to boot. To round out the Asian flavor profile and add texture to the composed burger, we topped them with some scallions, carrot, and cucumber, all of which we first marinated in rice vinegar. This brought freshness and mellow onion flavor along with some bright color and satisfying crunch. Avoid pickling the cucumber and carrots for longer than 1 hour or they will begin to turn limp and gray.

PICKLES

- 3 tablespoons rice vinegar
- ¼ teaspoon table salt
- ¼ English cucumber, halved lengthwise and sliced thin
- 1 small carrot, peeled and cut into 2-inch-long matchsticks
- 2 scallions, sliced thin on bias

BURGERS

- 1½ pounds ground lamb
- ¼ cup hoisin sauce, divided, plus extra for serving
- 1 teaspoon five-spice powder
- ½ teaspoon table salt
- 1 teaspoon vegetable oil
- 4 hamburger buns, toasted if desired

1 For the pickles Whisk vinegar and salt in medium bowl until salt has dissolved. Stir in cucumber and carrot and refrigerate for at least 15 minutes or up to 1 hour. Drain vegetables, return to now-empty bowl, and stir in scallions; set aside for serving.

2 For the burgers Break ground lamb into small pieces in large bowl. Add 2 tablespoons hoisin and five-spice powder and gently knead with hands until well combined. Divide lamb mixture into 4 equal portions, then gently shape each portion into ¾-inch-thick patty. Using your fingertips, press center of each patty down until about ½ inch thick, creating slight divot.

3 Season patties with salt. Heat oil in 12-inch nonstick skillet over medium heat until just smoking. Transfer patties to skillet, divot side up, and cook until well browned on first side, 2 to 4 minutes. Flip patties, reduce heat to medium-low, and continue to cook until browned on second side and meat registers 120 to 125 degrees (for medium-rare) or 130 to 135 (for medium), 3 to 5 minutes. Transfer burgers to platter, brush with remaining 2 tablespoons hoisin, and let rest for 5 minutes. Serve burgers on buns, topped with pickled vegetables, passing extra hoisin separately.

CRISPY SALMON BURGERS WITH TOMATO CHUTNEY

SERVES 4 |

| Why This Recipe Works For delicious fish burgers with rich, meaty flavor and tender texture, we opted for flavorful salmon patties seared in a skillet to build a crispy crust and then topped them with a sweet-yet-spicy tomato chutney. To make patties that held together, we coarsely chopped chunks of fish in a food processor in three batches. Briefly refrigerating the patties helped them hold their shape when cooked. If using wild salmon, which contains less fat, cook the burgers to 120 degrees (for medium-rare).

1¼ pounds skinless salmon, cut into 1-inch pieces

½ cup panko bread crumbs

½ cup chopped fresh cilantro, divided

8 scallions, minced, divided

3 tablespoons lemon juice, divided

2 tablespoons mayonnaise

½ teaspoon pepper, divided

2 tablespoons vegetable oil, divided

1 tablespoon grated fresh ginger

2 tomatoes, cored, seeded, and chopped

3 tablespoons Asian sweet chili sauce

½ teaspoon table salt

4 leaves Bibb or Boston lettuce

4 hamburger buns, toasted if desired

1 Working in 3 batches, pulse salmon in food processor until coarsely chopped into ¼-inch pieces, about 2 pulses, transferring each batch to large bowl.

2 Add panko, 6 tablespoons cilantro, 3 tablespoons scallions, 1 tablespoon lemon juice, mayonnaise, and ¼ teaspoon pepper to chopped salmon and gently knead with hands until well combined. Using lightly moistened hands, divide salmon mixture into 4 equal portions, then gently shape each portion into 1-inch-thick patty. Place patties on parchment paper–lined rimmed baking sheet and refrigerate for at least 15 minutes or up to 24 hours.

3 Heat 1 tablespoon oil in 12-inch nonstick skillet over medium-high heat until shimmering. Add ginger and remaining scallions and cook until fragrant, about 1 minute. Add tomatoes, chili sauce, and remaining 2 tablespoons lemon juice and cook until mixture is very thick, about 6 minutes. Stir in remaining 2 tablespoons cilantro and season with salt and pepper to taste. Transfer chutney to bowl and wipe out skillet with paper towels.

4 Season patties with salt and remaining ¼ teaspoon pepper. Heat remaining 1 tablespoon oil in now-empty skillet over medium heat until shimmering. Cook patties until browned, centers are still translucent when checked with tip of paring knife, and burgers register 125 degrees (for medium-rare), about 4 minutes per side. Arrange lettuce on bun bottoms. Serve burgers on buns, topped with chutney.

GRILLED SOUTHWESTERN SALMON BURGERS

SERVES 4

Why This Recipe Works These craveworthy, tender salmon burgers feature a creamy Southwestern dressing with citrusy flavor and a kick of chile heat. To prevent the burgers from drying out, we needed to add moisture without overpowering the fish's rich flavor. We hit the jackpot when we added mayonnaise—just 2 tablespoons gave us the creaminess and moisture we were after. Pulsing the salmon in a food processor was easy and left us with a texture good for making cohesive patties. Our creamy dressing has bold bite, with brightness from lime juice and heat from chiles. Chilling the burgers for at least 15 minutes ensures they hold their shape when grilled. If using wild salmon, which contains less fat, cook the burgers to 120 degrees (for medium-rare).

1¼ pounds skinless salmon, cut into 1-inch pieces

½ cup Spicy Chipotle-Lime Mayonnaise (page 31), plus extra for serving

¼ cup chopped fresh parsley

2 tablespoons finely grated onion

2 teaspoons lime juice

½ teaspoon salt

¼ teaspoon pepper

4 hamburger buns, toasted if desired

1 avocado, halved, pitted, and sliced thin

1 tomato, cored and sliced thin

1 Working in 3 batches, pulse salmon in food processor until coarsely chopped into ¼-inch pieces, about 2 pulses, transferring each batch to large bowl.

2 Add 2 tablespoons mayonnaise, parsley, onion, and lime juice to chopped salmon and gently knead with hands until well combined. Using lightly moistened hands, divide salmon mixture into 4 equal portions, then gently shape each portion into 1-inch-thick patty. Place patties on parchment paper–lined rimmed baking sheet and refrigerate for at least 15 minutes or up to 24 hours.

3A **For a charcoal grill** Open bottom vent completely. Light large chimney starter filled with charcoal briquettes (6 quarts). When top coals are partially covered with ash, pour evenly over grill. Set cooking grate in place, cover, and open lid vent completely. Heat grill until hot, about 5 minutes.

3B **For a gas grill** Turn all burners to high, cover, and heat grill until hot, about 15 minutes. Leave burners on high.

4 Clean cooking grate, then repeatedly brush grate with well-oiled paper towels until black and glossy, 5 to 10 times. Season patties with salt and pepper. Using spatula, place patties on grill and cook (covered if using gas) until well browned on first side and patties easily release from grill, 3 to 5 minutes.

5 Gently flip patties and continue to cook until well browned on second side, centers are still translucent when checked with tip of paring knife, and burgers register 125 degrees (for medium-rare), 3 to 5 minutes. Serve burgers on buns, topped with remaining 2 tablespoons of mayonnaise, avocado, and tomato, passing extra mayonnaise separately.

SOUTH CAROLINA SHRIMP BURGERS WITH TARTAR SAUCE

SERVES 4 |

Why This Recipe Works This Southern special features sweet shrimp with a coating that mimics the crunch of fried seafood. We didn't like how dry and rubbery cooked shrimp made our burgers, so we started with raw shrimp for better texture. Pulsing a small amount of shrimp with mayonnaise gave us the perfect binder, and leaving the rest coarsely chopped provided meaty texture. We prefer untreated shrimp—those without added sodium or preservatives like sodium tripolyphosphate (STPP). If you're purchasing peeled and deveined shrimp, you should buy about 1¼ pounds.

TARTAR SAUCE

- ¾ cup mayonnaise
- 3 tablespoons finely chopped dill pickles plus 1 teaspoon brine
- 1 small shallot, minced
- 1 tablespoon capers, rinsed and chopped fine
- ¼ teaspoon pepper

BURGERS

- 1 cup panko bread crumbs
- 1½ pounds large shrimp (26 to 30 per pound), peeled, deveined, and tails removed, divided
- 2 tablespoons mayonnaise
- ½ teaspoon table salt
- ¼ teaspoon pepper
- ⅛ teaspoon cayenne pepper
- 3 scallions, chopped fine
- 3 tablespoons vegetable oil
- 4 leaves Bibb or Boston lettuce
- 4 hamburger buns, toasted if desired

1 **For the tartar sauce** Combine all ingredients in bowl and refrigerate until ready to serve. (Sauce can be refrigerated for up to 3 days.)

2 **For the burgers** Pulse panko in food processor until finely ground, about 15 pulses; transfer to shallow dish. Place one-third of shrimp (1 cup), mayonnaise, salt, pepper, and cayenne in now-empty processor and pulse until shrimp are finely chopped, about 8 pulses. Add remaining shrimp to shrimp mixture in processor and pulse until coarsely chopped, about 4 pulses, scraping down sides of bowl as needed. Transfer shrimp mixture to bowl and stir in scallions.

3 Using lightly moistened hands, divide shrimp mixture into 4 equal portions, then gently shape each portion into ¾-inch-thick patty. Working with 1 patty at a time, dredge both sides in panko, pressing lightly to adhere, and transfer to plate.

4 Heat oil in 12-inch nonstick skillet over medium heat until shimmering. Cook patties until golden brown and register 140 to 145 degrees, 3 to 5 minutes per side. Transfer burgers to paper towel–lined plate and let drain, about 30 seconds per side. Arrange lettuce on bun bottoms. Serve burgers on buns, topped with tartar sauce.

GRILLED TUNA BURGERS WITH WASABI AND PICKLED GINGER

SERVES 4 |

Why This Recipe Works Like salmon burgers, tuna burgers tend to be dry and disappointing. For burgers with good texture and flavor, we hand-chopped the fish and then combined it with a little garlic and ginger. These additions paired well with the tuna's distinctive flavor without overpowering it. The delicate nature of these burgers made them prone to sticking, but wiping the grill grate with well-oiled paper towels multiple times to build up a stick-resistant coating solved this problem. Coating the spatula with vegetable oil spray also helped loosen the burgers from the cooking grate. Tuna is a very lean fish, so to avoid dry burgers we made sure we didn't over-cook them, taking them off the grill when they reached medium-rare. A simple wasabi mayonnaise paired wonderfully with the tuna, and in place of the traditional bun we served these delicate burgers in crisp lettuce wraps along with a few crunchy vegeta-bles. Do not let these burgers overcook; tuna tends to get very dry when cooked for too long.

½ cup mayonnaise

1½ tablespoons wasabi powder

1 teaspoon soy sauce

½ teaspoon water

1¼ pounds tuna steaks

2 teaspoons minced pickled ginger, plus 2 tablespoons pickled ginger, divided

1 garlic clove, minced

½ teaspoon table salt

¼ teaspoon pepper

8 large leaves iceberg lettuce

6 radishes, trimmed and sliced thin

2 scallions, sliced thin on bias

1 Whisk mayonnaise, wasabi, soy sauce, and water together in bowl. Cover and refrigerate for at least 15 minutes or up to 3 days.

2 Chop tuna into ¼-inch pieces. Using rocking motion, continue to chop tuna until it is coarsely chopped into pieces roughly ⅛ inch each; transfer to bowl. Add minced pickled ginger and garlic and gently knead with hands until well combined. Using lightly moistened hands, divide tuna mixture into 4 equal portions, then gently shape each portion into 1-inch-thick patty. Place patties on parchment paper–lined rimmed baking sheet and refriger-ate for at least 15 minutes or up to 24 hours.

3A **For a charcoal grill** Open bottom vent com-pletely. Light large chimney starter filled with charcoal bri-quettes (6 quarts). When top coals are partially covered with ash, pour evenly over grill. Set cooking grate in place, cover, and open lid vent completely. Heat grill until hot, about 5 minutes.

3B **For a gas grill** Turn all burners to high, cover, and heat grill until hot, about 15 minutes. Leave burners on high.

4 Clean cooking grate, then repeatedly brush grate with well-oiled paper towels until black and glossy, 5 to 10 times. Season patties with salt and pepper.

5 Using greased spatula, place patties on grill and cook until well browned on first side and patties easily release from grill, about 3 minutes. Gently flip patties and continue to cook until well browned on second side, centers are still reddish pink when checked with tip of paring knife, and burgers register 125 degrees (for medium-rare), 2 to 3 minutes.

6 Stack lettuce leaves together to create 4 lettuce wraps. Serve burgers on lettuce wraps, topped with wasabi mayonnaise, radishes, scallions, and remaining 2 tablespoons pickled ginger.

Beyond the Beef   119

4 LET'S GO FOR BROKE

Showstopping Stacks for the Burger Enthusiast

Bistro Burger with Pâté, Figs, and Watercress

FRENCH ONION BURGERS

SERVES 4 |

Why This Recipe Works Pairing a burger with the components of classic French onion soup—an abundance of sweet onions and tangy Gruyère cheese—makes a lot of sense given that the soup itself has a deep beefy flavor. But the task proved elusive at first: Sautéing a mound of onions just didn't give us that complex, caramelized onion flavor we were after. Instead, we found that caramelized onion jam—which is packed with savory sweetness and rich color—captured the essence of classic French onion soup far better. A homemade burger blend gave our patties exceptionally big, beefy flavor. To replicate the cheese-smothered crostini that float atop French onion soup, we toasted our burger buns under the broiler, spread the caramelized onion jam over the bun tops, and then piled on a whopping ¾ cup of shredded cheese. We then placed the bun tops back under the broiler until the cheese was melted, bubbly, and caramelized. A few frisée lettuce leaves lent freshness to this rich burger. We prefer to use one of our homemade beef burger blends here; however, you can substitute 1¾ pounds of 85 percent lean ground beef if desired.

1½ teaspoons minced fresh thyme

½ teaspoon table salt

¼ teaspoon pepper

1 recipe Grind-Your-Own Beef Burger Blend (pages 20–25)

1 teaspoon vegetable oil

4 hamburger buns

½ cup Caramelized Onion Jam (page 36)

12 ounces Gruyère cheese, shredded (3 cups)

½ head frisée lettuce (3 ounces), leaves separated

1 Adjust oven rack to middle position and heat oven to 300 degrees. Combine thyme, salt, and pepper in bowl. Divide burger blend into 4 lightly packed balls, then gently flatten into ¾-inch-thick patties. Using your fingertips, press center of each patty down until about ½ inch thick, creating slight divot.

2 Season patties with thyme mixture. Heat oil in 12-inch skillet over high heat until just smoking. Using spatula, transfer patties to skillet, divot side up, and cook until well browned on first side, 2 to 4 minutes. Gently flip patties and continue to cook until well browned on second side, 2 to 4 minutes. Transfer patties to rimmed baking sheet, divot side down, and bake until burgers register 120 to 125 degrees (for medium-rare) or 130 to 135 degrees (for medium), 3 to 8 minutes. Transfer burgers to platter and let rest for 5 minutes.

3 Meanwhile, adjust oven rack 6 inches from broiler element and heat broiler. Arrange buns on clean rimmed baking sheet, cut sides up, and broil until lightly toasted, about 1 minute. Transfer bun bottoms to plate. Spread onion jam over bun tops, then top evenly with Gruyère. Broil until Gruyère is melted and bubbly, about 2 minutes. Serve burgers on buns, topped with frisée.

REUBEN BURGERS

SERVES 4 |

Why This Recipe Works Sauerkraut, pastrami, Swiss cheese, caraway seeds, and a tangy sauce transform an ordinary burger into a satisfying spin on the Reuben sandwich. We started by making a classic sauce of mayo, ketchup, and sweet pickle relish. Next, we turned to the burgers: Rich patties made from one of our own burger blends were the perfect complement to the leaner pastrami. After cooking the burgers, we sautéed the pastrami and sauerkraut to drive off moisture and added caraway seeds for classic Reuben flavor. We separated the pastrami and sauerkraut mixture into four portions, mounding them to form little piles in the still-hot skillet. We topped these mounds with Swiss cheese and covered the skillet to melt the cheese. Finally, we assembled our burgers, first stacking the pastrami mounds on top of the patties and then adding our burger sauce. Eden Organic Sauerkraut is the test kitchen's favorite sauerkraut. We prefer to use one of our homemade beef burger blends here; however, you can substitute 1¾ pounds of 85 percent lean ground beef if desired.

1 recipe Grind-Your-Own Beef Burger Blend (pages 20–25)

½ teaspoon table salt

¼ teaspoon pepper

1 teaspoon vegetable oil, plus extra as needed

6 ounces thinly sliced deli pastrami

1½ cups sauerkraut, drained and pressed dry

1 teaspoon caraway seeds, toasted

4 slices deli Swiss cheese (4 ounces)

4 hamburger buns, toasted if desired

½ cup Classic Burger Sauce (page 29), plus extra for serving

1 Adjust oven rack to middle position and heat oven to 300 degrees. Divide burger blend into 4 lightly packed balls, then gently flatten into ¾-inch-thick patties. Using your fingertips, press center of each patty down until about ½ inch thick, creating slight divot.

2 Season patties with salt and pepper. Heat oil in 12-inch skillet over high heat until just smoking. Using spatula, transfer patties to skillet, divot side up, and cook until well browned on first side, 2 to 4 minutes. Gently flip patties and continue to cook until well browned on second side, 2 to 4 minutes. Transfer patties to rimmed baking sheet, divot side down, and bake until burgers register 120 to 125 degrees (for medium-rare) or 130 to 135 degrees (for medium), 3 to 8 minutes. Transfer burgers to platter and let rest while making topping.

3 Pour off all but 1 tablespoon fat from skillet. (If necessary, add extra oil as needed to equal 1 tablespoon.) Add pastrami and cook over medium-high heat, breaking up pieces with wooden spoon, until beginning to brown, about 1 minute. Stir in sauerkraut and caraway seeds and cook until heated through, about 1 minute. Off heat, separate pastrami mixture into 4 portions in skillet, then top each portion with Swiss. Cover and let sit until cheese has melted, about 3 minutes. Serve burgers on buns, topped with pastrami mixture and burger sauce, passing extra burger sauce separately.

GRILLED WILD MUSHROOM BURGERS

SERVES 4 |

Why This Recipe Works The earthy flavor and hearty texture of wild mushrooms make them an ideal topping for a grilled beef burger. For perfectly cooked mushrooms, we first cooked them covered until they released their moisture. Next, we uncovered the mushrooms and cooked them until golden brown and tender, which fortified their umami-rich flavor without making them chewy. Aromatics provided another layer of flavor and parsley leaves added freshness. Grilling our burgers over a blazing-hot fire ensured a well-browned exterior. We finished by spreading tangy goat cheese over the bun tops, which provided a pleasing contrast to the rich flavor of the mushrooms. Although we prefer a mix of wild mushrooms, you can use 12 ounces of just one type if you'd like. We prefer to use one of our homemade beef burger blends here; however, you can substitute 1¾ pounds of 85 percent lean ground beef if desired.

1 recipe Grind-Your-Own Beef Burger Blend (pages 20–25)

3 tablespoons unsalted butter, divided

1 onion, chopped

12 ounces chanterelle, shiitake, and oyster mushrooms, trimmed and cut into 1-inch pieces

¾ teaspoon table salt, divided

2 garlic cloves, minced

1 teaspoon minced fresh thyme or ¼ teaspoon dried

¼ cup dry white wine

1 (13 by 9-inch) disposable aluminum roasting pan, if using charcoal grill

¼ teaspoon pepper

⅓ cup fresh parsley leaves

4 ounces goat cheese, room temperature

4 hamburger buns, toasted if desired

1 Divide burger blend into 4 lightly packed balls, then gently flatten into ¾-inch-thick patties. Using your fingertips, press center of each patty down until about ½ inch thick, creating slight divot. Freeze patties for 30 minutes.

2 Melt 2 tablespoons butter in 12-inch skillet over medium heat. Add onion and cook until softened, about 5 minutes. Stir in mushrooms and ¼ teaspoon salt, cover, and cook until mushrooms have released their moisture, about 3 minutes. Add remaining 1 tablespoon butter and cook, uncovered, until mushrooms are deep golden brown and tender, 5 to 7 minutes. Stir in garlic and thyme and cook until fragrant, about 30 seconds. Stir in wine and cook, scraping up any browned bits, until liquid is nearly evaporated, about 30 seconds. Remove from heat and cover to keep warm.

3A **For a charcoal grill** Using skewer, poke 12 holes in bottom of disposable pan. Open bottom vent completely and place prepared pan in center of grill. Light large chimney starter two-thirds filled with charcoal briquettes (4 quarts). When top coals are partially covered with ash, pour into pan. Set cooking grate in place, cover, and open lid vent completely. Heat grill until hot, about 5 minutes.

3B **For a gas grill** Turn all burners to high, cover, and heat grill until hot, about 15 minutes. Leave all burners on high.

4 Clean and oil cooking grate. Season patties with remaining ½ teaspoon salt and pepper. Using spatula, place patties on grill, divot side up, directly over coals. Cook (covered if using

gas) until well browned on first side and meat easily releases from grill, 4 to 7 minutes. Gently flip patties and continue to cook until well browned on second side and meat registers 120 to 125 degrees (for medium-rare or 130 to 135 degrees (for medium), 4 to 7 minutes. Transfer burgers to platter and let rest for 5 minutes.

5 Stir parsley into mushroom mixture and season with salt and pepper to taste. Spread goat cheese on bun tops. Serve burgers on buns, topped with mushroom mixture.

BISTRO BURGERS WITH PÂTÉ, FIGS, AND WATERCRESS

SERVES 4 |

Why This Recipe Works You could say that pairing a rich home-ground burger with pâté and a fig salad is gilding the lily, but this is truly an extraordinary burger, dressed to impress. Pâté—a spread more often found on menus of ritzy restaurants than atop a burger—is a rich, umami-dense paste generally made from duck or chicken liver. The beauty of pâté is that it adds intensely rich flavor but requires no prep beyond spreading a thick layer on the bun. The combined richness of the pâté and burger was a bit much on its own, so we knew we needed some fresh, bright ingredients for balance. We created a quick salad by tossing figs with honey to bring out their natural sweetness, balsamic for sweet tang, and shallot for a sharp counterpoint. Watercress, which needed no embellishment, lent texture and a pleasant vegetal flavor. We prefer to use one of our homemade beef burger blends here; however, you can substitute 1¾ pounds of 85 percent lean ground beef if desired. You can find pâté in the gourmet cheese section of most well-stocked supermarkets. Be sure to use a smooth-textured pâté, not a coarse country pâté.

8 ounces figs, stemmed and sliced thin

1 small shallot, halved and sliced thin

2 teaspoons balsamic vinegar

1 teaspoon honey

1 recipe Grind-Your-Own Beef Burger Blend (pages 20–25)

½ teaspoon table salt

¼ teaspoon pepper

1 teaspoon vegetable oil

6 ounces chicken or duck liver pâté

4 hamburger buns, toasted if desired

2 ounces (2 cups) watercress

1 Adjust oven rack to middle position and heat oven to 300 degrees. Combine figs, shallot, vinegar, and honey in bowl; set aside for serving.

2 Divide burger blend into 4 lightly packed balls, then gently flatten into ¾-inch-thick patties. Using your fingertips, press center of each patty down until about ½ inch thick, creating slight divot.

3 Season patties with salt and pepper. Heat oil in 12-inch skillet over high heat until just smoking. Using spatula, transfer patties to skillet, divot side up, and cook until well browned on first side, 2 to 4 minutes. Gently flip patties and continue to cook until well browned on second side, 2 to 4 minutes. Transfer patties to rimmed baking sheet, divot side down, and bake until burgers register 120 to 125 degrees (for medium-rare) or 130 to 135 degrees (for medium), 3 to 8 minutes. Transfer burgers to platter and let rest for 5 minutes.

4 Spread pâté evenly over bun tops. Serve burgers on buns, topped with fig mixture and watercress.

GRILLED CRISPY ONION–RANCH BURGERS

SERVES 4

Why This Recipe Works Add ranch dressing to a burger with crisp onion rings, lettuce, and tomato and you have an irresistible combination of flavors and textures. To start, we combined mayonnaise, sour cream, fresh dill, shallot, and white wine vinegar to make our own homemade weeknight-friendly ranch dressing. Opting for sour cream over the classic buttermilk ensured our dressing was thick enough to stay on the burgers. For the onion rings, we used our recipe for Shoestring Onions (page 38), which can be made ahead of time and kept hot and crisp in the oven. We prefer to use one of our homemade beef burger blends here; however, you can substitute 1¾ pounds of 85 percent lean ground beef if desired.

¼ cup mayonnaise

¼ cup sour cream

1 tablespoon minced fresh dill

2 teaspoons minced shallot

1½ teaspoons white wine vinegar

½ teaspoon table salt

¼ teaspoon pepper

1 recipe Grind-Your-Own Beef Burger Blend (pages 20–25)

1 (13 by 9-inch) disposable aluminum roasting pan, if using charcoal grill

4 hamburger buns, toasted if desired

4 leaves red or green lettuce

1 tomato, cored and sliced thin

1 recipe Shoestring Onions (page 38)

1 Whisk mayonnaise, sour cream, dill, shallot, and vinegar together in bowl. Season with salt and pepper to taste. Refrigerate until ready to serve.

2 Divide burger blend into 4 lightly packed balls, then gently flatten into ¾-inch-thick patties. Using your fingertips, press center of each patty down until about ½ inch thick, creating slight divot. Freeze patties for 30 minutes.

3A For a charcoal grill Using skewer, poke 12 holes in bottom of disposable pan. Open bottom vent completely and place prepared pan in center of grill. Light large chimney starter two-thirds filled with charcoal briquettes (4 quarts). When top coals are partially covered with ash, pour into pan. Set cooking grate in place, cover, and open lid vent completely. Heat grill until hot, about 5 minutes.

3B For a gas grill Turn all burners to high, cover, and heat grill until hot, about 15 minutes. Leave all burners on high.

4 Clean and oil cooking grate. Season patties with salt and pepper. Using spatula, place patties on grill, divot side up, directly over coals. Cook (covered if using gas) until well browned on first side and meat easily releases from grill, 4 to 7 minutes. Gently flip patties and continue to cook until well browned on second side and meat registers 120 to 125 degrees (for medium-rare) or 130 to 135 degrees (for medium), 4 to 7 minutes. Transfer burgers to platter and let rest for 5 minutes.

5 Spread mayonnaise mixture over bun tops. Serve burgers on buns, topped with lettuce, tomato, and shoestring onions.

LOADED NACHO BURGERS

SERVES 4 |

Why This Recipe Works We wanted to find a way to incorporate our favorite elements of nachos into a burger without resulting in a soggy mess. The burger part was easy—we opted for home-ground beef burgers that we seared in a skillet before finishing in the oven to a perfect medium-rare. Next, we set our sights on the nacho component. Nachos are all about layering, so we started by assembling four distinct piles of chips on a rimmed baking sheet, consisting of just a few chips each. We covered the chips with an abundant amount of cheese and added some jalapeños and beans. After repeating this layering once more, we baked our nacho piles until the chips were super crunchy and the melted cheese bound the elements together. To finish, we slid the nacho piles onto the burgers and topped them with shredded lettuce, a dollop of sour cream, and fresh salsa. We prefer to use one of our homemade beef burger blends here; however, you can substitute 1¾ pounds of 85 percent lean ground beef if desired.

1 small tomato, cored and chopped

1 tablespoon minced shallot

2 teaspoons minced jarred jalapeños, plus extra for serving

¾ teaspoon table salt, divided

4 ounces tortilla chips

8 ounces Colby Jack cheese, shredded (2 cups)

1 recipe Grind-Your-Own Beef Burger Blend (pages 20–25)

¼ teaspoon pepper

1 teaspoon vegetable oil

2 tablespoons chopped fresh cilantro

1 teaspoon lime juice

¼ cup sour cream

4 hamburger buns, toasted if desired

1 cup shredded iceberg lettuce

1 Combine tomato, shallot, jalapeños, and ¼ teaspoon salt in bowl. Transfer salsa to fine-mesh strainer set over bowl and let sit for 30 minutes. Discard accumulate juices and return salsa to now-empty bowl; set aside for serving.

2 Divide half of tortilla chips into four equal mounds (about 4 inches in diameter) on rimmed baking sheet and top with 1 cup Colby Jack. Repeat layering with remaining chips and Colby Jack; set aside.

3 Adjust oven rack to middle position and heat oven to 300 degrees. Divide burger blend into 4 lightly packed balls, then gently flatten into ¾-inch-thick patties. Using your fingertips, press center of each patty down until about ½ inch thick, creating slight divot.

4 Season patties with remaining ½ teaspoon salt and pepper. Heat oil in 12-inch skillet over high heat until just smoking. Using spatula, transfer patties to skillet, divot side up, and cook until well browned on first side, 2 to 4 minutes. Gently flip patties and continue to cook until well browned on second side, 2 to 4 minutes. Transfer patties to second rimmed baking sheet, divot side down, and bake until burgers register 120 to 125 degrees (for medium-rare) or 130 to 135 degrees (for medium), 3 to 8 minutes. Transfer burgers to platter and let rest while finishing nachos and salsa.

5 Bake nachos until cheese has melted, about 5 minutes. Stir cilantro and lime juice into salsa and season with salt and pepper to taste.

6 Spread sour cream over bun tops. Serve burgers on buns, topped with nachos, lettuce, salsa, and extra jalapeños.

BURGERS AU POIVRE

SERVES 4 |

Why This Recipe Works For this burger we were inspired by the bistro favorite steak au poivre, which translates to "peppered steak." We swapped out the expensive cut of meat for a beef burger patty, but kept the requisite black pepper crust and silky, fragrant cream sauce for a burger that would satisfy even the most refined palate. We started by coating our burgers with Dijon, which added a pungent kick and helped the coarsely ground pepper adhere. We seared the burgers quickly to build a good crust and then moved them to the oven to finish. While our burgers rested we made a pan sauce with chicken broth, red wine, heavy cream, and brandy, reducing it on the stovetop to concentrate flavors. A sprinkling of spicy arugula lent the burger a pop of freshness. We prefer to use one of our homemade beef burger blends here; however, you can substitute 1¾ pounds of 85 percent lean ground beef if desired. Serve with cornichons or dill pickles.

1 recipe Grind-your-Own Beef Burger Blend (pages 20–25)

½ teaspoon table salt

3 tablespoons Dijon mustard, divided

4½ teaspoons coarsely ground pepper, divided

1 teaspoon vegetable oil

½ cup chicken broth

¼ cup dry red wine

½ cup heavy cream

2 tablespoons brandy

4 hamburger buns, toasted if desired

1 cup baby arugula

1 Adjust oven rack to middle position and heat oven to 300 degrees. Divide burger blend into 4 lightly packed balls, then gently flatten into ¾-inch-thick patties. Using your fingertips, press center of each patty down until about ½ inch thick, creating slight divot.

2 Season patties with salt, then brush 1 side of each patty with 1 teaspoon mustard and sprinkle with ½ teaspoon pepper, pressing to adhere. Flip patties and repeat with 4 teaspoons mustard and 2 teaspoons pepper.

3 Heat oil in 12-inch skillet over high heat until just smoking. Using spatula, transfer patties to skillet, divot side up, and cook until well browned on first side, 2 to 4 minutes. Gently flip patties and continue to cook until well browned on second side, 2 to 4 minutes. Transfer patties to rimmed baking sheet, divot side down, and bake until burgers register 120 to 125 degrees (for medium-rare) or 130 to 135 degrees (for medium), 3 to 8 minutes. Transfer burgers to platter and let rest while making sauce.

4 Pour off fat from skillet and add broth and wine. Bring to boil over medium-high heat and cook, scraping up any browned bits, until reduced to ¼ cup, about 4 minutes. Stir in cream and brandy, return to boil, and cook until reduced to ¼ cup, 3 to 5 minutes. Off heat, whisk in remaining 1 teaspoon mustard and remaining ½ teaspoon pepper. Season with salt to taste. Serve burgers on buns, topped with sauce and arugula.

DONUT SHOP BURGERS

SERVES 4 |

Why This Recipe Works This unusual burger, served on a halved, vanilla-glazed donut, is certain to turn a few heads at first; but after one bite, the combo of salty bacon, melted cheese, juicy beef burger patty, and sweet donut is sure to instantly win over the skeptics. We started by searing our burgers in a skillet to develop a well-browned crust before finishing them gently in the oven for a perfectly cooked interior. For the bacon, we used our Black Pepper Candied Bacon (page 39); slicing each bacon strip in half created more burger-friendly and manageable pieces, and rubbing them with a combination of black pepper and brown sugar before baking created a mildly spicy and pleasantly caramelized exterior. Once cooled, the sugar solidified to form a crunchy coating, adding pleasant texture to our burger. For the glazed donut bun, we found that premium donuts from a local bakery were less sweet and a much better choice than those from a fast-food chain. We prefer to use one of our home-made beef burger blends here; however, you can substitute 1¾ pounds of 85 percent lean ground beef if desired.

1 recipe Grind-Your-Own Beef Burger Blend (pages 20–25)

½ teaspoon table salt

¼ teaspoon pepper

1 teaspoon vegetable oil

4 slices American cheese (4 ounces)

4 (4-inch) vanilla glazed donuts, split crosswise

1 recipe Black Pepper Candied Bacon (page 39)

1   Adjust oven rack to middle position and heat oven to 300 degrees. Divide burger blend into 4 lightly packed balls, then gently flatten into ¾-inch-thick patties. Using your fingertips, press center of each patty down until about ½ inch thick, creating slight divot.

2   Season patties with salt and pepper. Heat oil in 12-inch skillet over high heat until just smoking. Using spatula, transfer patties to skillet, divot side up, and cook until well browned on first side, 2 to 4 minutes. Gently flip patties, top with cheese, and continue to cook until well browned on second side, 2 to 4 minutes. Transfer patties to rimmed baking sheet, divot side down, and bake until burgers register 120 to 125 degrees (for medium-rare) or 130 to 135 degrees (for medium), 3 to 8 minutes. Transfer burgers to platter and let rest for 5 minutes. Serve burgers on donuts, topped with bacon.

MASCARPONE BURGERS WITH WILTED RADICCHIO AND PEAR

SERVES 4 |

Why This Recipe Works Here we transform a simple beef burger into something unexpected by topping it with the unique combination of hearty radicchio, tender pear, and creamy mascarpone. For the burgers, we found using one of our grind-at-home blends was optimal; the big beefy flavor of a homemade blend was well-suited to the bold flavors of our toppings. Briefly sautéing the radicchio tamed its bitterness, while a spoonful of Dijon mustard emphasized its spiciness. A pear, cut into thin matchsticks, provided a sweet, crunchy counterpoint. Finally, we thought a creamy element would be a welcome accompaniment. We first tried ricotta but it proved too grainy, while tangy goat cheese clashed with the Dijon. We found mascarpone to be the perfect addition as it lent a silky creaminess to round out this unexpected and delicious burger. We prefer to use one of our homemade beef burger blends here; however, you can substitute 1¾ pounds of 85 percent lean ground beef if desired.

---

1 recipe Grind-Your-Own Beef Burger Blend (pages 20–25)

¾ teaspoon table salt, divided

½ teaspoon pepper, divided

1 teaspoon vegetable oil, plus extra as needed

1 small head radicchio, halved and sliced into ¼-inch-thick ribbons (2½ cups)

1 teaspoon minced fresh thyme or ¼ teaspoon dried

1 tablespoon Dijon mustard

2 teaspoons honey

1 ripe but firm pear, halved, cored, and cut into 2-inch-long matchsticks

4 ounces mascarpone cheese (½ cup)

4 hamburger buns, toasted if desired

1 Adjust oven rack to middle position and heat oven to 300 degrees. Divide burger blend into 4 lightly packed balls, then gently flatten into ¾-inch-thick patties. Using your fingertips, press center of each patty down until about ½ inch thick, creating slight divot.

2 Season patties with ½ teaspoon salt and ¼ teaspoon pepper. Heat oil in 12-inch skillet over high heat until just smoking. Using spatula, transfer patties to skillet, divot side up, and cook until well browned on first side, 2 to 4 minutes. Gently flip patties and continue to cook until well browned on second side, 2 to 4 minutes. Transfer patties to rimmed baking sheet, divot side down, and bake until burgers register 120 to 125 degrees (for medium-rare) or 130 to 135 degrees (for medium), 3 to 8 minutes. Transfer burgers to platter and let rest while making topping.

3 Pour off all but 2 teaspoons fat from skillet. (If necessary, add extra oil as needed to equal 2 teaspoons.) Add radicchio, thyme, remaining ¼ teaspoon salt, and remaining ¼ teaspoon pepper and cook over medium-high heat, stirring occasionally, until radicchio is slightly wilted, about 2 minutes. Off heat, stir in mustard and honey, then add pear and gently toss to combine.

4 Spread mascarpone on bun tops. Serve burgers on buns, topped with radicchio-pear mixture.

GRILLED BLUE CHEESE BURGERS WITH BACON AND TOMATO RELISH

SERVES 4 |

Why This Recipe Works This substantial burger is inspired by a perennial steakhouse favorite: the wedge salad. Using one of our homemade burger blends as the base, we pile it high with freshly made chunky blue cheese dressing, tomatoes, and bacon. Sliced tomatoes have a tendency to slide off burgers, so instead we created a savory relish that would stay put. We cooked cherry tomatoes with some balsamic vinegar for extra tang and a bit of sugar to bring out the tomatoes' natural sweetness. A ½ cup of crumbled blue cheese added plenty of salty, cheesy punch. As for the bacon, we used our simple recipe for Crispy Bacon (page 39), cutting each bacon strip in half to create burger-friendly pieces. We prefer to use one of our homemade beef burger blends here; however, you can substitute 1¾ pounds of 85 percent lean ground beef if desired.

1 teaspoon extra-virgin olive oil

8 ounces cherry tomatoes, halved

2 teaspoons balsamic vinegar

¼ teaspoon sugar

1 recipe Grind-Your-Own Beef Burger Blend (pages 20–25)

1 (13 by 9-inch) disposable aluminum roasting pan, if using charcoal grill

½ teaspoon table salt

¼ teaspoon pepper

4 hamburger buns, toasted if desired

1 recipe Crispy Bacon (page 39)

2 ounces blue cheese, crumbled (½ cup)

1 Heat oil in medium saucepan over medium-high heat until shimmering. Add tomatoes and cook, stirring occasionally, until softened and beginning to break down, 1 to 2 minutes. Stir in vinegar and sugar and cook for 1 minute. Off heat, season with salt and pepper to taste. Cover to keep warm.

2 Divide burger blend into 4 lightly packed balls, then gently flatten into ¾-inch-thick patties. Using your fingertips, press center of each patty down until about ½ inch thick, creating slight divot. Freeze patties for 30 minutes.

3A **For a charcoal grill** Using skewer, poke 12 holes in bottom of disposable pan. Open bottom vent completely and place prepared pan in center of grill. Light large chimney starter two-thirds filled with charcoal briquettes (4 quarts). When top coals are partially covered with ash, pour into pan. Set cooking grate in place, cover, and open lid vent completely. Heat grill until hot, about 5 minutes.

3B **For a gas grill** Turn all burners to high, cover, and heat grill until hot, about 15 minutes. Leave all burners on high.

4 Clean and oil cooking grate. Season patties with salt and pepper. Using spatula, place patties on grill, divot side up, directly over coals. Cook (covered if using gas) until well browned on first side and meat easily releases from grill, 4 to 7 minutes. Gently flip patties and continue to cook until well browned on second side and meat registers 120 to 125 degrees (for medium-rare) or 130 to 135 degrees (for medium), 4 to 7 minutes. Transfer burgers to platter and let rest for 5 minutes. Serve burgers on buns, topped with bacon, tomatoes, and blue cheese.

Let's Go for Broke 141

BIBIMBAP BURGERS

SERVES 4 |

Why This Recipe Works This inspired burger incorporates many of the elements of *dolsot bibimbap*, a Korean rice bowl that boasts a variety of flavors, colors, and textures. Bibimbap features rice with a crisp crust, sautéed leafy greens, pickles, Korean chili sauce (*gochujang*), and a fried egg—all of which make stellar burger toppings. First up were the easy-to-make pickled bean sprouts, which needed only a brief time to ferment. Next we used leftover rice to create crispy "chips" of rice that added a surprising yet satisfying texture to the burger. For the remainder of the topping, we sautéed shiitake mushrooms and spinach with aromatic scallion and garlic, along with a little soy sauce. While our burgers cooked, we fried four eggs to serve as the crowning touch. We prefer to use one of our homemade beef burger blends here; however, you can substitute 1¾ pounds of 85 percent lean ground beef if desired.

½ cup cider vinegar

4 teaspoons sugar, divided

1¼ teaspoons table salt, divided

4 ounces (2 cups) bean sprouts

1 recipe Grind-Your-Own Beef Burger Blend (pages 20–25)

3 tablespoons plus 1 teaspoon vegetable oil, divided

1 cup cooked white rice

4 ounces shiitake mushrooms, stemmed and sliced thin

5 ounces curly-leaf spinach, stemmed and chopped coarse

1 scallion, minced

1 tablespoon soy sauce

1 garlic clove, minced

1 teaspoon toasted sesame oil

4 large eggs

3 tablespoons gochujang, plus extra for serving

4 hamburger buns, toasted if desired

1 Whisk vinegar, 1 tablespoon sugar, and ¾ teaspoon salt together in medium bowl. Stir in bean sprouts, gently pressing on them to submerge; set aside.

2 Adjust oven rack to middle position and heat oven to 300 degrees. Divide burger blend into 4 lightly packed balls, then gently flatten into ¾-inch-thick patties. Using your fingertips, press center of each patty down until ½ inch thick, creating slight divot. Cover and refrigerate until ready to cook.

3 Heat 1 tablespoon vegetable oil in 12-inch nonstick skillet over high heat until shimmering. Add rice and press into even layer. Cover and cook, without stirring, until rice begins to form crust on bottom of skillet, 1 to 2 minutes. Uncover, reduce heat to medium, and continue to cook until crust

has fully formed, 4 to 6 minutes. Break rice into 1-inch pieces and transfer to bowl; set aside. Wipe skillet clean with paper towels.

4 Heat 1 tablespoon vegetable oil in now-empty skillet over high heat until shimmering. Add mushrooms and cook, stirring often, until mushrooms begin to brown, about 2 minutes. Add spinach, scallion, soy sauce, garlic, and remaining 1 teaspoon sugar. Cover and cook until spinach begins to wilt, about 1 minute. Uncover and continue to cook until spinach is fully wilted, 1 to 2 minutes. Transfer spinach mixture to small bowl and stir in sesame oil; cover to keep warm. Wipe skillet clean with paper towels.

5 Season patties with remaining ½ teaspoon salt. Heat 1 teaspoon oil in 12-inch skillet

over high heat until just smoking. Using spatula, transfer patties to skillet, divot side up, and cook until well browned on first side, 2 to 4 minutes. Gently flip patties and continue to cook until well browned on second side, 2 to 4 minutes. Transfer patties to rimmed baking sheet, divot side down, and bake until burgers register 120 to 125 degrees (for medium-rare) or 130 to 135 degrees (for medium), 3 to 8 minutes. Transfer burgers to platter and let rest while cooking eggs.

6 Crack eggs into 2 small bowls (2 eggs per bowl). Add remaining 1 tablespoon vegetable oil to now-empty skillet and heat over medium-high heat until shimmering. Swirl to coat skillet with oil, then working quickly, pour 1 bowl of eggs in 1 side of skillet and second bowl of eggs in other side. Cover and cook for 1 minute. Remove skillet from burner and let sit, covered, 15 to 45 seconds for runny yolks (white around edge of yolk will be barely opaque), 45 to 60 seconds for soft but set yolks, or about 2 minutes for medium-set yolks.

7 Drain bean sprouts and stir into spinach mixture. Spread gochujang on bun tops. Serve burgers on buns, topped with spinach mixture, rice, and eggs, passing extra gochujang separately.

SURF AND TURF BURGERS

SERVES 4 |

Why This Recipe Works Classic steak Oscar features filet mignon topped with asparagus and chunks of fresh crabmeat, all drizzled with a tarragon-infused béarnaise sauce. Our goal was to translate its components into a rich, elegant burger. To keep our recipe streamlined (we were making a burger after all), we decided to make a cheater's béarnaise by combining mayonnaise, lemon juice, fresh tarragon, and a bit of Dijon; mixing our béarnaise with the fresh crabmeat made for a cohesive topping. While our burgers cooked, we trimmed and halved asparagus spears and seared them until they just developed flavorful browning but were still crisp-tender. We placed the asparagus on top of the beef patties and topped it with our crabmeat mixture, which held the asparagus in place. The result was a sumptuous steakhouse meal on a bun. We prefer to use one of our homemade beef burger blends here; however, you can substitute 1¾ pounds of 85 percent lean ground beef if desired.

---

8   ounces lump crabmeat, picked over for shells

¼   cup mayonnaise

1   tablespoon minced fresh tarragon

2   teaspoons Dijon mustard

¾   teaspoon table salt, divided

½   teaspoon grated lemon zest plus 1 tablespoon juice

    Pinch cayenne pepper

1   recipe Grind-Your-Own Beef Burger Blend (pages 20–25)

¼   teaspoon pepper

1   teaspoon vegetable oil, plus extra as needed

8   ounces thin asparagus, trimmed and halved

4   hamburger buns, toasted if desired

1 Adjust oven rack to middle position and heat oven to 300 degrees. Combine crab, mayonnaise, tarragon, mustard, ¼ teaspoon salt, lemon zest and juice, and cayenne in bowl. Season with salt to taste. Set aside until ready to serve.

2 Divide burger blend into 4 lightly packed balls, then gently flatten into ¾-inch-thick patties. Using your fingertips, press center of each patty down until about ½ inch thick, creating slight divot.

3 Season patties with remaining ½ teaspoon salt and pepper. Heat oil in 12-inch skillet over high heat until just smoking. Using spatula, transfer patties to skillet, divot side up, and cook until well browned on first side, 2 to 4 minutes. Gently flip patties and continue to cook until well browned on second side, 2 to 4 minutes. Transfer patties to rimmed baking sheet, divot side down, and bake until burgers register 120 to 125 degrees (for medium-rare) or 130 to 135 degrees (for medium), 3 to 8 minutes. Transfer burgers to platter and let rest while cooking asparagus.

4 Pour off all but 1 teaspoon fat from skillet. (If necessary, add extra oil as needed to equal 1 teaspoon.) Add asparagus and cook over medium-high heat, stirring occasionally, until just tender and spotty brown, 4 to 6 minutes. Serve burgers on buns, topped with asparagus and crab mixture.

TURKEY BURGERS WITH CRANBERRY RELISH AND SMOKED GOUDA

SERVES 4 |

Why This Recipe Works When a craving for the flavors of Thanksgiving strikes, this turkey burger is sure to satisfy with its homemade cranberry relish, rich gouda cheese, and toasted bun slathered with flavored butter. We started by making a simple cranberry relish, simmering the cranberries with water and sugar until a good portion of the berries burst and the mixture thickened. Next we cooked our turkey burgers, which we seared in a pan before adding smoked gouda and finishing them in a low oven. While the burgers rested, we bloomed dried sage, garlic, and celery seeds in butter and then brushed this mixture over the toasted buns. We prefer to use our homemade turkey burger blend here; however, you can substitute 1¾ pounds of ground turkey tossed with 2 tablespoons melted butter if desired. Avoid ground turkey breast (also labeled 99 percent fat-free).

⅓ cup sugar

¼ cup water

4 ounces (1 cup) fresh or frozen cranberries

1 recipe Grind-Your-Own Turkey Burger Blend (page 26)

¾ teaspoon table salt, divided

¼ teaspoon pepper

2 teaspoons vegetable oil

4 ounces smoked gouda cheese, shredded (1 cup)

6 tablespoons unsalted butter

1 teaspoon dried sage

1 garlic clove, minced

¼ teaspoon celery seeds

4 hamburger buns, toasted

4 leaves red or green lettuce

1 Bring sugar and water to boil in medium saucepan over medium-high heat, stirring occasionally to dissolve sugar. Stir in cranberries, bring to simmer, and cook until slightly thickened and about two-thirds of berries have popped open, 3 to 5 minutes; transfer to bowl and let cool to room temperature. Season with salt and pepper to taste.

2 Adjust oven rack to middle position and heat oven to 300 degrees. With lightly greased hands, divide burger blend into 4 lightly packed balls, then gently flatten into ¾-inch-thick patties. Using your fingertips, press center of each patty down until about ½ inch thick, creating slight divot.

3 Season patties with ½ teaspoon salt and pepper. Heat oil in 12-inch nonstick skillet over high heat until just smoking. Using spatula, transfer patties to skillet, divot side up, and cook until well browned on first side, 2 to 4 minutes. Gently flip patties and continue to cook until well browned on second side, 2 to 4 minutes. Transfer patties to rimmed baking sheet, divot side down, and top with gouda. Bake until burgers register 160 degrees, 6 to 10 minutes. Transfer burgers to platter and let rest for 5 minutes.

4 Microwave butter, sage, garlic, celery seeds, and remaining ¼ teaspoon salt in small bowl, stirring occasionally, until butter is melted and mixture is fragrant, about 2 minutes. Brush bun tops with butter mixture and arrange lettuce on bun bottoms. Serve burgers on buns, topped with cranberry relish.

MEDITERRANEAN TURKEY BURGERS WITH SHAVED ZUCCHINI SALAD AND RICOTTA

SERVES 4 |

Why This Recipe Works A great turkey burger deserves some special fixings as much as any other burger, and in keeping with turkey's leaner profile we decided to top it with delicate shaved zucchini tossed with a little olive oil, lemon juice, garlic, and red pepper flakes. Not only was this simple zucchini salad delicious, keeping the zucchini raw added a pleasant crunch to our burgers. A sprinkling of basil and toasted pine nuts added further interest. We wanted a creamy element for our burger, and thought ricotta cheese would complement the zucchini. We whisked it until it was light and fluffy and then added a little olive oil and some lemon zest for brightness. Slathered onto each bun, this ricotta spread took our burger to the next level. We prefer to use our homemade turkey burger blend here; however, you can substitute 1¾ pounds of ground turkey tossed with 2 tablespoons melted butter if desired. Avoid ground turkey breast (also labeled 99 percent fat-free). Look for small zucchini; they will have fewer seeds. Use a vegetable peeler to slice the zucchini into very thin ribbons.

1 recipe Grind-Your-Own Turkey Burger Blend (page 26)

¾ teaspoon table salt, divided

½ teaspoon pepper, divided

2 teaspoons plus 2 tablespoons extra-virgin olive oil, divided

4 ounces (½ cup) whole-milk ricotta cheese

½ teaspoon grated lemon zest plus 1 tablespoon juice

1 pound small zucchini, trimmed and sliced lengthwise into ribbons

¼ cup chopped fresh basil

2 tablespoons pine nuts, toasted

1 small garlic clove, minced

¼ teaspoon red pepper flakes

4 hamburger buns, toasted if desired

1 Adjust oven rack to middle position and heat oven to 300 degrees. With lightly greased hands, divide burger blend into 4 lightly packed balls, then gently flatten into ¾-inch-thick patties. Using your fingertips, press center of each patty down until about ½ inch thick, creating slight divot.

2 Season patties with ½ teaspoon salt and ¼ teaspoon pepper. Heat 2 teaspoons oil in 12-inch nonstick skillet over high heat until just smoking. Using spatula, transfer patties to skillet, divot side up, and cook until well browned on first side, 2 to 4 minutes. Gently flip patties and continue to cook until well browned on second side, 2 to 4 minutes. Transfer patties to rimmed baking sheet, divot side down, and bake until burgers register 160 degrees, 6 to 10 minutes. Transfer burgers to platter and let rest while preparing toppings.

3 Whisk ricotta, lemon zest, 1 tablespoon oil, remaining ¼ teaspoon salt, and remaining ¼ teaspoon pepper together in bowl. Toss zucchini with remaining 1 tablespoon oil, lemon juice, basil, pine nuts, garlic, and pepper flakes in separate bowl. Spread ricotta mixture over bun tops. Serve burgers on buns, topped with zucchini salad.

GRILLED TURKEY CAESAR BURGERS

SERVES 4 |

Why This Recipe Works Here creamy Caesar dressing and crisp romaine meet rich and meaty turkey burgers for a new classic. After making our Caesar dressing—the real deal, nothing light—we dressed our salad and mounded it on our deeply flavored grilled turkey patties before topping them with additional whole anchovies and a final drizzle of dressing. Toasting the rolls until golden and crisp and then rubbing them with a piece of garlic replicated the crunch and flavor of croutons. We prefer to use our homemade turkey burger blend here; however, you can substitute 1¾ pounds of ground turkey tossed with 2 tablespoons melted butter if desired. Avoid ground turkey breast (also labeled 99 percent fat-free).

1 recipe Grind-Your-Own Turkey Burger Blend (page 26)

½ cup mayonnaise

1 ounce Parmesan cheese, ½ ounce grated (¼ cup) and ½ ounce shredded (3 tablespoons)

4 teaspoons lemon juice

3 anchovy fillets, rinsed and minced, plus extra fillets for serving (optional)

2 small garlic cloves (1 minced to paste, 1 whole)

¼ teaspoon Worcestershire sauce

2 teaspoons vegetable oil, divided

½ teaspoon table salt

¼ teaspoon pepper

4 ciabatta rolls, toasted

1 small romaine heart (6 ounces), cut into 1½-inch pieces

1 With lightly greased hands, divide burger blend into 4 lightly packed balls, then gently flatten into ¾-inch-thick patties. Using your fingertips, press center of each patty down until about ½ inch thick, creating slight divot. Freeze patties for 30 minutes. Whisk mayonnaise, grated Parmesan, lemon juice, anchovies, minced garlic, and Worcestershire together in bowl; set aside.

2A For a charcoal grill Open bottom vent completely. Light large chimney starter filled with charcoal briquettes (6 quarts). When top coals are partially covered with ash, pour evenly over half of grill. Set cooking grate in place, cover, and open lid vent completely. Heat grill until hot, about 5 minutes.

2B Turn all burners to high, cover, and heat grill until hot, about 15 minutes. Leave primary burner on high and turn off other burner(s).

3 Clean and oil cooking grate. Brush 1 side of patties with 1 teaspoon oil and season with ¼ teaspoon salt and ⅛ teaspoon pepper. Using spatula, gently flip patties, brush with remaining 1 teaspoon oil, and season with remaining ¼ teaspoon salt and ⅛ teaspoon pepper. Place burgers, divot side up, over hotter part of grill and cook (covered if using gas) until well browned and meat easily releases from grill, 5 to 7 minutes. Gently flip patties and continue to cook until well browned on second side and meat registers 160 degrees, 5 to 7 minutes. Transfer burgers to platter and let rest while preparing toppings.

4 Rub toasted rolls with whole garlic. Toss romaine with 4 tablespoons dressing and shredded Parmesan in bowl until combined. Season with salt and pepper to taste. Serve burgers on buns, topped with romaine mixture and extra anchovies, if using, passing remaining dressing separately.

JERK SPICE–RUBBED TURKEY BURGERS WITH FRIED GREEN TOMATOES

SERVES 4 |

Why This Recipe Works This mouthwatering burger features the sweet, spicy, and bold elements of jerk seasoning to give mild turkey a serious flavor boost. To create an authentic jerk-style spice rub we started by combining ground allspice berries, black peppercorns, and dried thyme; for heat and depth we added garlic powder, dry mustard, and cayenne. When it came time to top our burgers we chose fried green tomatoes; these cornmeal-crusted tomatoes lent freshness and crunch to each bite. For a creamy element we created a quick aioli and stirred in some habanero for a little extra spice. We prefer to use our homemade turkey burger blend here; however, you can substitute 1¾ pounds of ground turkey tossed with 2 tablespoons melted butter if desired. Avoid ground turkey breast (also labeled 99 percent fat-free). If green tomatoes are unavailable, you can substitute 2 plum tomatoes. Be sure to wear gloves when mincing the habanero.

1 green tomato, cored and sliced ¼ inch thick

½ cup mayonnaise

1 habanero chile, stemmed, seeds and ribs removed, and minced

½ teaspoon grated lime zest plus 1 tablespoon juice

1¼ teaspoons table salt, divided

2½ teaspoons pepper, divided

½ cup cornmeal

¼ cup all-purpose flour

⅔ cup buttermilk

1 large egg

2 tablespoons packed brown sugar

2 teaspoons garlic powder

2 teaspoons ground allspice

1½ teaspoons dry mustard

1½ teaspoons dried thyme

1 teaspoon cayenne pepper

1 recipe Grind-Your-Own Turkey Burger Blend (page 26)

2 teaspoons vegetable oil, plus ½ cup oil for frying

4 hamburger buns, toasted if desired

4 leaves red or green lettuce

2 scallions, sliced thin on bias

1 Place tomato on paper towel–lined plate. Cover with more paper towels and let sit for 20 minutes. Combine mayonnaise, habanero, lime zest and juice, ¼ teaspoon salt, and ¼ teaspoon pepper in bowl; refrigerate until ready to serve.

2 Combine cornmeal, flour, ¼ teaspoon salt, and ¼ teaspoon pepper in shallow dish. Whisk buttermilk and egg together in second shallow dish. Pat tomatoes dry. Working with one tomato slice at a time, dip in buttermilk mixture, letting excess drip off, then dredge in cornmeal mixture, pressing firmly to adhere; transfer to clean baking sheet and set aside.

3 Adjust oven rack to middle position and heat oven to 300 degrees. Whisk sugar, garlic powder, allspice, dry mustard, thyme, cayenne, remaining ¾ teaspoon salt, and remaining 2 teaspoons pepper together in bowl. With lightly greased hands, divide burger blend into 4 lightly packed balls, then gently flatten into ¾-inch-thick patties. Using your fingertips, press center of each patty down until about ½ inch thick, creating slight divot.

4 Sprinkle patties with brown sugar mixture, pressing gently to adhere. Heat 2 teaspoons oil in 12-inch nonstick skillet over medium heat until shimmering. Using spatula, transfer patties to skillet, divot side up, and cook until well browned on first side, 2 to 4 minutes. Gently flip patties and continue to cook until well browned on second side, 2 to 4 minutes. Transfer patties to rimmed baking sheet, divot side down, and bake until burgers register 160 degrees, 6 to 10 minutes.

Transfer burgers to platter and let rest while finishing tomatoes. Wipe skillet clean with paper towels.

5 Heat remaining ½ cup oil in now-empty skillet over medium-high heat until shimmering. Cook tomato until golden brown, 2 to 3 minutes per side. Transfer to paper towel–lined plate, let drain briefly, then season with salt and pepper to taste. Spread mayonnaise mixture on bun tops and arrange lettuce on bottoms. Serve burgers on buns, topped with fried tomatoes and scallions.

Let's Go for Broke

5 FROM THE FIELD AND GARDEN

Crave-Worthy Vegetarian and Vegan Burgers

**Southwestern Black Bean Burgers
with Chipotle Sauce**

IN THIS CHAPTER

ULTIMATE VEGGIE BURGERS WITH SWEET AND TANGY NAPA SLAW

SERVES 4

Why This Recipe Works Our earthy Ultimate Veggie Burgers (page 18) deserved some delectable toppings and this impressive burger delivers with a crisp slaw and a flavorful mayo. We wilted the cabbage in the microwave to avoid a watery slaw and whirled it dry in a salad spinner. Celery and apple added crunch and sweetness. Mayonnaise mixed with rich apple butter, garlic, and vinegar made a quick but complex spread. (Vegan mayonnaise can be substituted.) If cooking the patties from frozen in step 3, transfer browned patties to wire rack set in rimmed baking sheet and bake in a 350-degree oven until heated through, about 10 minutes, before serving.

3   cups shredded napa cabbage

½   teaspoon sugar, plus extra for seasoning

1   teaspoon table salt

1   Fuji, Gala, or Golden Delicious apple, peeled and shredded

1   celery rib, sliced thin on bias

1   tablespoon cider vinegar, divided

2½   tablespoons vegetable oil, divided, plus extra as needed

⅛   teaspoon pepper

3   tablespoons mayonnaise

1   tablespoon apple butter

1   garlic clove, minced

1   tablespoon minced fresh chives

4   Ultimate Veggie Burgers patties (page 18)

4   hamburger buns, toasted if desired

1 Toss cabbage with sugar and salt in large bowl. Cover and microwave, stirring occasionally, until cabbage is partially wilted and has reduced in volume by about one-third, about 2 minutes. Transfer cabbage to salad spinner and spin until excess liquid has been removed; wipe bowl clean with paper towels. Return cabbage to now-empty bowl, add apple, celery, 2½ teaspoons vinegar, 1½ teaspoons oil, and pepper and toss to combine. Refrigerate until well chilled, at least 30 minutes or up to 4 hours.

2 Combine mayonnaise, apple butter, garlic, and remaining ½ teaspoon vinegar in small bowl; refrigerate until ready to serve.

3 Heat remaining 2 tablespoons oil in 12-inch nonstick skillet over medium-high heat until shimmering. Place patties in skillet and cook until well browned on first side, about 4 minutes.

Using 2 spatulas, gently flip patties and continue to cook until well browned on second side, about 4 minutes, adding extra oil as needed if skillet looks dry; transfer to plate. Add chives to coleslaw and toss to recombine. Season with salt and extra sugar to taste. Spread mayonnaise mixture over bun tops. Place burgers on bun bottoms and top with coleslaw and bun tops. Serve.

FLIPPING A DELICATE BURGER

To flip delicate burger, slide one spatula under patty and use second spatula to support and guide patty as you flip it.

VEGAN PINTO BEAN AND BEET BURGERS

SERVES 8 |

> **Why This Recipe Works** This modern twist on the typical bean burger combines starchy pinto beans, vibrant beet, and wholesome bulgur for a patty rich with both protein and flavor. Meatless burgers are prone to crumbling and although bread crumbs helped to bind the patties, they weren't enough to stop these burgers from falling apart. We discovered a surprisingly perfect vegan binder—carrot baby food, which added tackiness to help the burgers hold their shape and lent a subtle sweetness that heightened the flavor of the beet. When shopping, don't confuse bulgur with cracked wheat, which has a much longer cooking time and will not work in this recipe. Use a coarse grater or the shredding disk of a food processor to shred the beet.

1½ teaspoons table salt, plus salt for cooking bulgur

⅔ cup medium-grind bulgur, rinsed

1 large beet (9 ounces), peeled and shredded

¾ cup walnuts

½ cup fresh basil leaves

2 garlic cloves, minced

1 (15-ounce) can pinto beans, rinsed

1 (4-ounce) jar carrot baby food

1 tablespoon whole-grain mustard

½ teaspoon pepper

1½ cups panko bread crumbs

6 tablespoons vegetable oil, divided, plus extra as needed

8 hamburger buns, toasted if desired

1 Bring 1½ cups water and ½ teaspoon salt to boil in small saucepan. Off heat, stir in bulgur, cover, and let sit until tender, 15 to 20 minutes. Drain bulgur, spread onto rimmed baking sheet, and let cool slightly.

2 Pulse beet, walnuts, basil, and garlic in food processor until finely chopped, about 12 pulses, scraping down sides of bowl as needed. Add beans, carrot baby food, 2 tablespoons water, mustard, salt, and pepper and pulse until well combined, about 8 pulses. Transfer mixture to large bowl and stir in panko and cooled bulgur.

3 Divide beet-bulgur mixture into 8 equal portions, then tightly pack each portion into ¾-inch-thick patty. (Patties can be refrigerated for up to 3 days. To freeze, transfer patties to parchment paper–lined rimmed baking sheet, cover with plastic wrap, and freeze until firm, about 1 hour. Stack patties, separated by parchment paper, wrap in plastic wrap, and place in zipper-lock freezer bag. Do not thaw patties before cooking.)

4 Adjust oven rack to middle position and heat oven to 200 degrees. Set wire rack in rimmed baking sheet. Heat 3 tablespoons oil in 12-inch non-stick skillet over medium-high heat until shimmering. Place 4 patties in skillet and cook until well browned and crisp on first side, about 4 minutes. Using 2 spatulas, gently flip patties and continue to cook until well browned and crisp on second side, about 4 minutes, adding extra oil as needed if skillet looks dry. Transfer burgers to prepared rack and keep warm in oven. Wipe skillet clean with paper towels and repeat with remaining 3 tablespoons oil and remaining 4 patties. Serve burgers on buns.

SOUTHWESTERN BLACK BEAN BURGERS WITH CHIPOTLE SAUCE

SERVES 6 |

> **Why This Recipe Works** For an easy route to tasty veggie burgers on a busy weeknight, canned black beans are the ultimate shortcut. But who hasn't eaten a black bean burger where the texture of the burger is disconcertingly similar to that of the bun? To avoid an overly soft, mealy texture, we used ground tortilla chips to bind our spice-infused burgers, which added both flavor and an appealing texture. Thoroughly drying the beans and grinding them coarsely helped prevent pasty, soggy patties. We reinforced the Southwestern flavor profile of our burgers with a creamy chipotle sauce for a blast of smoky spice. When forming the patties, it's important to pack them together firmly. Our favorite canned black beans are Bush's Best.

CHIPOTLE SAUCE

- ¼ cup mayonnaise
- ¼ cup sour cream
- 1 tablespoon lime juice
- 1 tablespoon minced canned chipotle chile in adobo sauce
- 1 garlic clove, minced

BURGERS

- 2 (15-ounce) cans black beans, rinsed
- 2 large eggs
- 2 tablespoons all-purpose flour
- 4 scallions, minced
- 3 tablespoons minced fresh cilantro, plus 1 cup leaves, divided

- 2 garlic cloves, minced
- 1 teaspoon hot sauce
- 1 teaspoon ground cumin
- ½ teaspoon ground coriander
- ¼ teaspoon table salt
- 1 ounce tortilla chips, crushed coarse (½ cup)
- 8 teaspoons vegetable oil, divided
- 6 hamburger buns, toasted if desired
- 2 avocados, halved, pitted, and sliced thin
- ½ cup Quick Pickled Red Onions (page 32)

1 **For the chipotle sauce** Combine all ingredients in small bowl; refrigerate until ready to serve. (Sauce can be refrigerated for up to 4 days.)

2 **For the burgers** Spread beans onto rimmed baking sheet lined with triple layer of paper towels and let drain for 15 minutes. In large bowl, whisk eggs and flour into uniform paste, then stir in scallions, minced cilantro, garlic, hot sauce, cumin, coriander, and salt.

3 Process tortilla chips in food processor until finely ground, about 30 seconds. Add black beans and pulse until beans are roughly broken down, about 5 pulses. Stir processed bean mixture into egg mixture until well combined. Cover and refrigerate for at least 1 hour or up to 24 hours.

4 Divide bean mixture into 6 equal portions. Using lightly moistened hands, tightly pack each portion into ½-inch-thick patty. (Patties can be frozen for up to 1 month. To freeze, transfer patties to parchment paper–lined rimmed baking sheet, cover with plastic wrap, and freeze until firm, about 1 hour. Stack patties, separated by parchment paper; wrap in plastic wrap; and place in zipper-lock freezer bag. Thaw patties completely before cooking.)

5 Adjust oven rack to middle position and heat oven to 200 degrees. Set wire rack in rimmed baking sheet. Heat 2 teaspoons oil in 12-inch non-stick skillet over medium heat until shimmering. Place 3 patties in skillet and cook until well browned and crisp on first side, about 5 minutes. Using 2 spatulas, gently flip patties, add 2 teaspoons oil to skillet, and cook until well browned and crisp on second side, 3 to 5 minutes. Transfer burgers to prepared rack and keep warm in oven. Repeat with remaining 4 teaspoons oil and remaining 3 patties. Spread chipotle sauce over bun bottoms. Serve burgers on buns, topped with avocados, pickled onions, and remaining 1 cup cilantro leaves.

SPICY BROWN RICE–EDAMAME BURGERS

SERVES 4 |

Why This Recipe Works No one will miss the meat when they take their first bite of these ultrasavory, Japanese-inspired rice burgers packed with edamame and infused with fresh ginger, sesame, and the distinct taste of nori, a type of dried seaweed. For a burger with edamame in every bite, we pulsed it—along with some fresh spinach—with the rice in the food processor. This enabled us to incorporate far more filling into each burger, and slightly processing the rice released more starch, making the patties easier to shape. We topped our burgers with flavorful sriracha mayonnaise and a medley of matchstick carrots, bean sprouts, and thinly sliced radishes for lively crunch. Swapping out the traditional burger bun in favor of iceberg lettuce leaves gave our burgers a lighter, fresher taste. To make these burgers vegan, substitute vegan mayonnaise.

1 cup short-grain brown rice

1 cup baby spinach

¾ cup frozen shelled edamame beans, thawed and patted dry

2 (8 by 7 ½-inch) sheets nori, crumbled

2 teaspoons toasted sesame oil

2 teaspoons grated fresh ginger

½ teaspoon table salt

2 tablespoons vegetable oil

½ cup mayonnaise

2 tablespoons sriracha

8 large leaves iceberg lettuce

1 carrot, peeled and cut into 2-inch-long matchsticks

3 ounces (1½ cups) bean sprouts

2 radishes, trimmed, halved, and sliced thin

1 Bring 1¾ cups water and rice to simmer in large saucepan over medium-high heat. Reduce heat to low, cover, and simmer gently until rice is tender and water is fully absorbed, 40 to 45 minutes. Off heat, lay clean dish towel underneath lid, and let sit for 10 minutes. Fluff rice with fork and cover.

2 Pulse spinach, edamame, nori, sesame oil, ginger, and salt in food processor until mixture is finely ground (it should not be smooth), about 10 pulses, scraping down sides of bowl as needed. Add rice and pulse until rice is coarsely chopped and mixture is well combined, about 8 pulses.

3 Divide rice mixture into 4 equal portions. Using lightly moistened hands, tightly pack each portion into ¾-inch-thick patty. (Patties can be refrigerated for up to 24 hours.) Heat vegetable oil in 12-inch nonstick skillet over medium heat until shimmering. Place patties in skillet and cook until golden brown and crisp on first side, 5 to 7 minutes. Using 2 spatulas, gently flip patties and cook until browned and crisp on second side, 5 to 7 minutes.

4 Whisk mayonnaise and sriracha together in bowl. Stack lettuce leaves together to create 4 lettuce wraps. Serve burgers on lettuce wraps, topped with sriracha mayonnaise, carrot, bean sprouts, and radishes.

QUINOA BURGERS WITH SPINACH, SUN-DRIED TOMATOES, AND MARINATED FETA

SERVES 4 |

Why This Recipe Works Quinoa's unique texture makes for a hearty burger, and its nutty yet neutral flavor benefits from bold and exciting flavors. For fantastic quinoa burgers we used white quinoa, which softened enough for us to shape. We found that the usual toasting step caused the grains to separate, so we skipped it. For patties that stayed together in the pan, we used a combination of bread and egg as a binder and also added some Parmesan cheese, which not only helped with binding but also contributed rich flavor. Chilling the patties before cooking further ensured they held their shape. Cooking the patties on the stovetop over medium-low heat created a crisp, flavorful crust on the outside but kept the interior moist. For bright, fresh flavor, we mixed in chopped sun-dried tomatoes, scallions, delicate baby spinach, and a little lemon zest and juice. Feta cheese was the perfect topping for these Mediterranean-inspired patties, and a quick marinade allowed the cheese to soak up the flavor of fragrant oregano, the citrusy bouquet of fresh lemon zest, and the spicy heat of red pepper flakes. Chopped parsley stirred into the marinated cheese just before serving added a final burst of freshness to these super-satisfying vegetable burgers.

⅓ cup plus 2 tablespoons extra-virgin olive oil, divided

5 garlic cloves (4 minced, 1 sliced thin)

½ teaspoon minced fresh oregano

1 teaspoon grated lemon zest, divided, plus 2 teaspoons juice

⅛ teaspoon red pepper flakes

4 ounces feta cheese, crumbled (1 cup)

¼ cup oil-packed sun-dried tomatoes, chopped coarse, plus 1 tablespoon packing oil

4 scallions, chopped fine

2 cups water

1 cup prewashed white quinoa, rinsed

1 teaspoon table salt

2 slices hearty white sandwich bread, torn into pieces

1 large egg plus 1 large yolk, lightly beaten

2 ounces (2 cups) baby spinach, chopped

2 ounces Parmesan cheese, grated (1 cup)

1 tablespoon chopped fresh parsley

8 large leaves iceberg lettuce

½ cup Quick Pickled Red Onions (page 32)

1 Microwave ⅓ cup olive oil, sliced garlic, oregano, ½ teaspoon lemon zest, and pepper flakes until garlic is softened and fragrant, about 1 minute. Gently stir in feta and refrigerate until ready to serve. (Feta mixture can be refrigerated for up to 24 hours.)

2 Line rimmed baking sheet with parchment paper. Heat tomato oil in large saucepan over medium heat until shimmering. Add scallions and cook until softened, 3 to 5 minutes. Stir in minced garlic and cook until fragrant, about 30 seconds. Stir in water, quinoa, and salt and bring to simmer. Cover, reduce heat to medium-low, and simmer until

quinoa is tender, 16 to 18 minutes. Off heat, let quinoa sit, covered, until liquid is fully absorbed, about 10 minutes.

3 Pulse bread in food processor until coarsely ground, about 10 pulses. Add egg and yolk and remaining ½ teaspoon lemon zest and pulse until mixture comes together, about 5 pulses. Stir bread mixture, tomatoes, spinach, Parmesan, and lemon juice into cooled quinoa until

thoroughly combined. Divide quinoa mixture into 4 equal portions. Using lightly moistened hands, tightly pack each portion into ¾-inch-thick patty and place on prepared sheet. Re-shape patties as needed. Cover and refrigerate patties until chilled and firm, at least 30 minutes or up to 24 hours.

4 Heat remaining 2 tablespoons olive oil in 12-inch nonstick skillet over medium-low

heat until shimmering. Place patties in skillet and cook until golden brown and crisp on first side, 5 to 7 minutes. Using 2 spatulas, gently flip patties and cook until browned and crisp on second side, 5 to 7 minutes.

5 Stir parsley into feta mixture. Stack lettuce leaves together to create 4 lettuce wraps. Serve burgers on lettuce wraps, topped with feta mixture and pickled onions.

CURRIED MILLET BURGERS WITH PEACH-GINGER CHUTNEY

SERVES 4 |

Why This Recipe Works Millet might not be the first grain you think of to use as the base for veggie burgers, but its nutty, corn-like flavor is the perfect foil for a variety of seasonings; and since it releases a sticky starch as it cooks, it makes for perfectly cohesive burgers. Here we combined millet with colorful baby spinach and shredded carrot for patties with bright vegetable flavor, while some minced shallot provided aromatic balance. Creamy yogurt and an egg added moisture and richness and also served as a binder. Curry powder gave our burgers an Indian-inspired flavor profile, which perfectly complemented a topping of sweet-savory peach chutney; using readily available frozen peaches made the chutney a snap to assemble. Pan-frying the patties created a flavorful crust on the exterior while maintaining a moist interior. A dollop of cooling plain yogurt tempered the chutney's heat. Tasters found burger buns to be a bit much with these dense burgers, so we ditched the bread in favor of the lighter freshness of lettuce leaves.

PEACH-GINGER CHUTNEY

- 1 shallot, minced
- 1 tablespoon vegetable oil
- 1 teaspoon grated fresh ginger
- ⅛ teaspoon table salt
  Pinch red pepper flakes
- 1½ cups thawed frozen peaches, cut into ½-inch pieces
- 2 tablespoons packed light brown sugar
- 2 tablespoons cider vinegar

BURGERS

- 1 cup millet, rinsed
- 2 cups water
- ½ teaspoon table salt, plus salt for cooking millet
- 3 tablespoons vegetable oil, divided
- 1 shallot, minced
- 6 ounces (6 cups) baby spinach, chopped
- 2 carrots, peeled and shredded
- 2 teaspoons curry powder
- ¼ teaspoon pepper
- ½ cup plain yogurt, divided
- 1 large egg, lightly beaten
- 2 tablespoons minced fresh cilantro
- 8 large leaves iceberg lettuce

1 For the chutney Microwave shallot, oil, ginger salt, and pepper flakes in small bowl, stirring occasionally, until shallot has softened, about 1 minute. Stir in peaches, sugar, and vinegar and microwave until peaches have softened and mixture has thickened, 6 to 8 minutes, stirring once halfway through microwaving. Set aside to cool to room temperature. (Chutney can be refrigerated for up to 3 days; let come to room temperature before serving.)

2 For the burgers Line rimmed baking sheet with parchment paper. Combine millet, water, and ½ teaspoon salt in medium saucepan and bring to simmer over medium-high heat.

Reduce heat to low, cover, and simmer gently until millet is tender, 15 to 20 minutes. Off heat, let millet sit, covered, until liquid is fully absorbed, about 10 minutes. Transfer millet to large bowl and let cool for 15 minutes.

3 Heat 1 tablespoon oil in 12-inch nonstick skillet over medium heat until shimmering. Add shallot and cook until softened, about 3 minutes. Stir in spinach and carrots and cook until spinach is wilted, about 2 minutes. Stir in curry powder, salt, and pepper and cook until fragrant, about 30 seconds; transfer to bowl with millet. Wipe skillet clean with paper towels.

4 Stir ¼ cup yogurt, egg, and cilantro into millet mixture until well combined. Divide mixture into 4 equal portions. Using lightly moistened hands, firmly pack each portion into ¾-inch-thick patty and place on prepared sheet. Re-shape patties as needed. Cover and refrigerate patties until chilled and firm, at least 30 minutes or up to 24 hours.

5 Heat remaining 2 tablespoons oil in now-empty skillet over medium-low heat until shimmering. Place patties in skillet and cook until golden brown and crisp on first side, 5 to 7 minutes. Using 2 spatulas, gently flip patties and cook until browned and crisp on second side, 5 to 7 minutes.

6 Stack lettuce leaves together to create 4 lettuce wraps. Serve burgers on lettuce wraps, topped with remaining ¼ cup yogurt and peach chutney.

FALAFEL BURGERS WITH TAHINI-YOGURT SAUCE

SERVES 4 | 🥕 🍳

> **Why This Recipe Works** Falafel are crispy on the outside, soft on the inside, packed with seasoning, and utterly irresistible. Here we essentially supersize these chickpea fritters to make a uniquely delicious burger. We started by soaking dried chickpeas overnight to soften before grinding them into coarse bits along with onion, herbs, garlic, and spices. Traditional falafel recipes use flour and chickpeas for a dough-like texture, but uncooked flour yielded patties that were dry and bready; instead, we used a microwaved flour paste to add moisture and create a soft interior. To ensure burger-size falafel, we used a dry measuring cup and dropped scoops of the falafel mixture into a heated skillet and then used the back of a spoon to press each portion into a ¾-inch-thick patty. To top off our burgers, we created a sauce featuring tahini, Greek yogurt, and lemon juice and also added sliced cucumber and quick pickled red onions for a burger so flavorful we may never go back to falafel wrapped in pita bread.

8   ounces dried chickpeas, picked over and rinsed

⅓   cup tahini

⅓   cup plain Greek yogurt

3   tablespoons lemon juice, plus extra for seasoning

¾   cup fresh cilantro leaves and stems

¾   cup fresh parsley leaves

½   onion, chopped fine

2   garlic cloves, minced

1½   teaspoons ground coriander

1   teaspoon ground cumin

1   teaspoon table salt

¼   teaspoon cayenne pepper

¼   cup all-purpose flour

2   teaspoons baking powder

2   tablespoons vegetable oil, plus extra as needed

4   hamburger buns, toasted if desired

¼   English cucumber, sliced thin

½   cup Quick Pickled Red Onions (page 32)

1 Place chickpeas in large container and cover with water by 2 to 3 inches. Soak at room temperature for at least 8 hours or up to 24 hours. Drain well.

2 Whisk tahini, yogurt, and lemon juice in medium bowl until smooth. Season with salt and extra lemon juice to taste; set aside. (Sauce can be refrigerated for up to 4 days; let come to room temperature and stir to recombine before serving.)

3 Process cilantro, parsley, onion, garlic, coriander, cumin, salt, and cayenne in food processor until mixture is finely ground, about 30 seconds, scraping down sides of bowl as needed. Add chickpeas and pulse 6 times.

Continue to pulse until chickpeas are coarsely chopped and resemble sesame seeds, about 6 more pulses. Transfer mixture to large bowl and set aside.

4 Whisk flour and ⅓ cup water in bowl until no lumps remain. Microwave, whisking every 10 seconds, until mixture thickens to stiff, smooth, pudding-like consistency that forms mound when dropped from end of whisk into bowl, 40 to 80 seconds. Stir baking powder into flour paste. Add flour paste to chickpea mixture and, using rubber spatula, mix until fully incorporated. (Falafel mixture can be refrigerated for up to 2 hours.)

5 Heat oil in 12-inch nonstick skillet over medium heat until shimmering. Using 1 cup measure, drop 4 even portions (about ¾ cup each) into skillet, then press each portion into ¾-inch-thick patty with back of spoon. Cook until golden brown and crisp on first side, 4 to 6 minutes. Using 2 spatulas, gently flip patties and cook until well browned and crisp on second side, 4 to 6 minutes, adding extra oil as needed if skillet looks dry. Serve burgers on buns, topped with cucumber, pickled onions, and tahini-yogurt sauce.

VEGAN GRILLED BARBECUED TEMPEH BURGERS WITH SPICY PICKLED JÍCAMA

SERVES 4 |

Why This Recipe Works For a grilled veggie burger with rich, smoky flavor we turned to tempeh, which is made from fermented soybeans and a mix of grains. Instead of making patties, we halved two tempeh pieces crosswise to create four planks that would serve as our "meat." Marinating the tempeh in a mixture of barbecue sauce and water infused it with flavor, and patting it dry before grilling ensured a crispy edge. For an extra boost of barbecue flavor, we brushed both sides of each plank with additional sauce during the last few minutes of grilling. To add a layer of crunch and liveliness, we paired the burgers with sweet, spicy pickled jícama. We prefer to use our homemade Barbecue Sauce (page 30) here, but feel free to use your favorite store-bought brand.

1 cup cider vinegar

⅓ cup sugar

¼ teaspoon table salt

6 ounces jícama, peeled and cut into 2-inch matchsticks (1½ cups)

1 jalapeño chile, stemmed, seeded, and sliced into thin rings

1½ cups barbecue sauce, divided, plus extra for serving

¼ cup water

2 (8-ounce) packages tempeh, cut in half crosswise

4 hamburger buns, toasted if desired

1 cup baby arugula

1 Bring vinegar, sugar, and salt to simmer in small saucepan over medium-high heat, stirring occasionally, until sugar has dissolved. Off heat, stir in jícama and jalapeño, cover, and let cool to room temperature, about 1 hour. (Pickled jícama can be refrigerated in airtight container for up to 1 week.)

2 Whisk 1 cup barbecue sauce and water together in small bowl, then transfer to 1-gallon zipper-lock bag. Add tempeh patties, press out air, seal, and toss gently to coat. Refrigerate for at least 1 hour, flipping bag occasionally. Remove patties from marinade and pat dry with paper towels.

3A **For a charcoal grill** Open bottom vent completely. Light large chimney starter filled with charcoal briquettes (6 quarts). When top coals are partially covered with ash, pour evenly over grill. Set cooking grate in place, cover, and open lid vent completely. Heat grill until hot, about 5 minutes.

3B **For a gas grill** Turn all burners to high, cover, and heat grill until hot, about 15 minutes. Leave all burners on high.

4 Clean and oil cooking grate. Place tempeh patties on grill and cook (covered if using gas), turning as needed, until well browned, 8 to 12 minutes. Brush patties with ¼ cup barbecue sauce, flip, and continue to cook until sizzling and well browned, about 1 minute. Brush second side of patties with remaining ¼ cup sauce, flip, and continue to cook until well browned, about 1 minute. Serve burgers on buns, topped with pickled jícama and arugula, passing extra barbecue sauce separately.

GRILLED PORTOBELLO BURGERS WITH GOAT CHEESE AND ARUGULA

SERVES 4 |

> **Why This Recipe Works** When the king of mushrooms meets the grill, magic happens as its texture softens and its earthy, rich flavor deepens. Layer this portobello burger with melty goat cheese and peppery arugula, top it off with a tomato slice and smoky grilled onion, and you have a meatless burger featuring an irresistible combination of flavors and textures. Mushroom gills can have an off-tasting flavor, so we scraped them out to avoid a muddy taste. Before cooking, we lightly scored the smooth side of the mushroom with a crosshatch pattern to expedite the release of moisture and give the caps a more tender texture.

- 4 **portobello mushroom caps (4 to 5 inches in diameter), gills removed**
- 1 **large red onion, sliced into ½-inch-thick rounds (do not separate rings)**
- 3 **tablespoons plus 1 teaspoon extra-virgin olive oil, divided**
- 2 **garlic cloves, minced**
- 2 **teaspoons minced fresh thyme**
- ¼ **teaspoon table salt**
- ¼ **teaspoon pepper**
- 2 **ounces goat cheese, crumbled (½ cup)**
- 1 **cup baby arugula**
- ¼ **teaspoon balsamic vinegar**
- 4 **hamburger buns, toasted if desired**
- 1 **tomato, cored and sliced thin**

1 Cut ¹⁄₁₆-inch-deep slits on top side of mushroom caps, spaced ½ inch apart, in crosshatch pattern. Brush onion with 1 tablespoon oil and season with salt and pepper. Combine garlic, thyme, salt, pepper, and 2 tablespoons oil in bowl.

2A **For a charcoal grill** Open bottom vent completely. Light large chimney starter three-quarters filled with charcoal briquettes (4½ quarts). When top coals are partially covered with ash, pour evenly over grill. Set cooking grate in place, cover, and open lid vent completely. Heat grill until hot, about 5 minutes.

2B **For a gas grill** Turn all burners to high, cover, and heat grill until hot, about 15 minutes. Turn all burners to medium-high.

3 Clean and oil cooking grate. Place mushrooms, gill side down, and onion on grill. Cook mushrooms (covered if using gas) until lightly charred and beginning to soften on gill side, 4 to 6 minutes. Flip mushrooms, brush with oil-garlic mixture, and cook until tender and browned on second side, 4 to 6 minutes. Sprinkle with goat cheese and let cheese melt, about 2 minutes.

4 Meanwhile, cook onion, turning as needed, until lightly charred on both sides, 8 to 12 minutes. As they finish cooking, transfer mushrooms and onion to platter and tent with aluminum foil.

5 Toss arugula with vinegar and remaining 1 teaspoon oil in bowl and season with salt and pepper to taste. Separate onion rings. Place arugula and mushroom caps on bun bottoms. Top with tomato, onion, and bun tops. Serve.

SPICED CAULIFLOWER BURGERS WITH YOGURT SAUCE

SERVES 4 |

> **Why This Recipe Works** These North African–inspired cauliflower burgers are bursting with complex flavor, and we love the contrast between their creamy, nutty interiors and crunchy, well-browned exteriors. We found the trick was to first roast the cauliflower, which takes less than 30 minutes; this intensified its flavor and made it easy to mash the florets. Before roasting, we tossed the florets with oil, cumin, and paprika. After roasting and mashing the cauliflower, we simply added panko (it worked far better than flour) and an egg for binding and absorbing excess moisture, along with shredded carrots and golden raisins. Peppery baby arugula and herbed yogurt sauce provided a fresh burst of flavor, and toasted sliced almonds sprinkled over the top added textural interest. Use the large holes of a box grater to shred the carrot.

YOGURT SAUCE

- ¼ cup plain Greek yogurt
- 1 tablespoon minced fresh cilantro
- 1 scallion, sliced thin
- 1 tablespoon lemon juice
- ¼ teaspoon table salt

BURGERS

- 1 head cauliflower (2 pounds), cored and cut into 1-inch florets
- 3 tablespoons extra-virgin olive oil, divided
- ½ teaspoon ground cumin
- ½ teaspoon paprika
- ½ teaspoon table salt
- ⅛ teaspoon pepper
- ½ cup panko bread crumbs
- 1 small carrot, peeled and shredded
- ⅓ cup golden raisins, chopped
- 1 large egg, lightly beaten
- 4 hamburger buns, toasted if desired
- 3 tablespoons sliced almonds, toasted
- 1 cup baby arugula

1 **For the yogurt sauce** Combine all ingredients in bowl; cover and refrigerate until ready to serve. (Sauce can be refrigerated for up to 4 days.)

2 **For the burgers** Adjust oven rack to middle position and heat oven to 450 degrees. Toss cauliflower with 1 tablespoon oil, cumin, paprika, salt, and pepper. Spread cauliflower evenly over aluminum foil–lined rimmed baking sheet and roast until well browned and tender, 20 to 25 minutes. Let cool slightly, then transfer to large bowl.

3 Line clean rimmed baking sheet with parchment paper. Using potato masher, mash cauliflower until broken down into rough ½-inch pieces. Stir in panko, carrot, raisins, and egg until well combined. Divide cauliflower mixture into 4 equal

portions. Using lightly moistened hands, tightly pack each portion into ¾-inch-thick patty and place on prepared sheet. Cover and refrigerate patties until chilled and firm, at least 30 minutes or up to 24 hours.

4 Heat remaining 2 tablespoons oil in 12-inch nonstick skillet over medium heat until shimmering. Using spatula, place patties in skillet and cook until deep golden brown and crisp on first side, 3 to 5 minutes. Using 2 spatulas, gently flip patties and cook until browned and crisp on second side, 3 to 5 minutes. Serve burgers on buns, topped with yogurt sauce, almonds, and arugula.

6 YOU WANT FRIES WITH THAT?

Classic Sides and Drinks to Complete the Meal

Easier French Fries

IN THIS CHAPTER

EASIER FRENCH FRIES

SERVES 4

Why This Recipe Works It's almost impossible to picture the ultimate burger without a side of classic, golden French fries, with their mouthwateringly crispy outsides and creamy, potato-y centers. For crispy fries with tender interiors and lots of potato flavor, the key was to submerge low-starch Yukon Gold potatoes in room-temperature oil before frying them over high heat until browned. This gave the potatoes' interiors time to soften and cook through before the exteriors started to crisp. We prefer peanut oil for frying, but vegetable or canola oil can be substituted. This recipe will not work with russets or sweet potatoes. Use a Dutch oven that holds 6 quarts or more for this recipe.

2½ pounds Yukon Gold potatoes, unpeeled

6 cups peanut or vegetable oil

1 Using chef's knife, square off sides of potatoes. Cut potatoes lengthwise into ¼-inch planks, then slice each plank into ¼-inch-thick fries.

2 Line rimmed baking sheet with triple layer of paper towels. Combine potatoes and oil in large Dutch oven. Cook over high heat until oil has reached rolling boil, about 5 minutes. Once boiling, continue to cook, without stirring, until potatoes are limp but exteriors are beginning to firm, about 15 minutes.

3 Using tongs, stir potatoes, gently scraping up any that stick, and continue to cook, stirring occasionally, until golden and crisp, 5 to 10 minutes. Using wire skimmer or slotted spoon, transfer fries to prepared sheet. Season with salt and serve.

CHIVE AND BLACK PEPPER DIPPING SAUCE
Makes about ½ cup

5 tablespoons mayonnaise

3 tablespoons sour cream

2 tablespoons minced fresh chives

1½ teaspoons lemon juice

¼ teaspoon table salt

¼ teaspoon pepper

Whisk all ingredients together in small bowl. (Sauce can be refrigerated for up to 2 days.)

BELGIAN-STYLE DIPPING SAUCE
Makes about ½ cup

5 tablespoons mayonnaise

3 tablespoons ketchup

1 garlic clove, minced

½ teaspoon hot sauce

¼ teaspoon table salt

Whisk all ingredients together in small bowl. (Sauce can be refrigerated for up to 2 days.)

THICK-CUT OVEN FRIES

SERVES 4

Why This Recipe Works We love a perfectly crunchy French fry but often the time and cleanup involved in deep-frying feels daunting, so we set out to create a recipe for thick-cut, golden fries using the oven. During the traditional frying process water is rapidly driven out of the starch cells at the surface of the potato, leaving behind tiny cavities that create a delicate, crispy crust. Since oven fries don't heat fast enough for air pockets to form, we coated the potato planks in a cornstarch slurry; this formed a crust around the potatoes and allowed them to crisp up like a deep-fried fry. We then arranged the planks on a rimmed baked sheet that we coated with both vegetable oil spray and vegetable oil; the spray prevented the oil from pooling and kept the potatoes from sticking, which meant we needed only a modest 3 tablespoons of oil to evenly coat the fries. Covering the baking sheet with aluminum foil for the first half of cooking ensured that the potatoes were fully tender by the time they were browned. Choose potatoes that are 4 to 6 inches in length to ensure well-proportioned fries. A heavy-duty rimmed baking sheet that will not warp in the heat of the oven is essential to the success of this recipe. The rate at which the potatoes brown will depend on your baking sheet and oven; after removing the foil from the baking sheet in step 5, monitor the color of the potatoes carefully to prevent scorching.

3 tablespoons vegetable oil

2 pounds Yukon Gold potatoes, unpeeled

3 tablespoons cornstarch

1 Adjust oven rack to lowest position and heat oven to 425 degrees. Generously spray rimmed baking sheet with vegetable oil spray. Pour oil into prepared sheet and tilt sheet until surface is evenly coated with oil.

2 Halve potatoes lengthwise and turn halves cut sides down on cutting board. Trim thin slice from both long sides of each potato half; discard trimmings. Slice potatoes lengthwise into ⅓- to ½-inch-thick planks.

3 Combine ¾ cup water and cornstarch in large bowl, making sure no lumps of cornstarch remain on bottom of bowl. Microwave, stirring every 20 seconds, until mixture begins to thicken, 1 to 3 minutes. Remove from microwave and continue to stir until mixture thickens to pudding-like consistency. (If necessary, add up to 2 tablespoons water to achieve correct consistency.)

4 Transfer potatoes to bowl with cornstarch mixture and toss until each plank is evenly coated. Arrange planks on prepared sheet, leaving small gaps between planks. (Some cornstarch mixture will remain in bowl.) Cover sheet tightly with lightly greased aluminum foil and bake for 12 minutes.

5 Remove foil from sheet and bake until bottom of each fry is golden brown, 10 to 18 minutes. Remove sheet from oven and, using thin metal spatula, carefully flip each fry. Return sheet to oven and continue to bake until second sides are golden brown, 10 to 18 minutes. Transfer fries to paper towel–lined plate and season with salt to taste. Serve.

SWEET POTATO FRIES

SERVES 4 TO 6

Why This Recipe Works Despite their name, sweet potatoes have little in common with russet potatoes—for one thing, they're much lower in starch, which means getting crispy exteriors can be a challenge. To make up for the sweet potatoes' lack of starch, we started by blanching them in a Dutch oven in water spiked with salt and baking soda. This seasoned the potatoes throughout and softened their exteriors. When we transferred the potatoes to a cornstarch slurry, the outer layer of the parcooked potatoes sloughed off, creating a substantial, pleasingly orange crust. Our Dutch oven then pulled double duty as our frying vessel, minimizing splatter and sticking. If your sweet potatoes are shorter than 4 inches in length, do not cut the wedges crosswise. Use a Dutch oven that holds 6 quarts or more for this recipe.

½   cup cornstarch

    Table salt for blanching potatoes

1   teaspoon baking soda

3   pounds sweet potatoes, peeled and cut into ¾-inch-thick wedges, wedges cut in half crosswise, divided

1   quart peanut or vegetable oil

1 Adjust oven rack to middle position and heat oven to 200 degrees. Set wire rack in rimmed baking sheet. Whisk cornstarch and ½ cup cold water together in large bowl.

2 Bring 2 quarts water, 2 tablespoons salt, and baking soda to boil in Dutch oven. Add potatoes and return to boil. Reduce heat to simmer and cook until exteriors turn slightly mushy (centers will remain firm), 3 to 5 minutes. Whisk cornstarch slurry to recombine. Using wire skimmer or slotted spoon, transfer potatoes to bowl with slurry. Discard cooking water and wipe out Dutch oven with paper towels.

3 Using rubber spatula, fold potatoes with slurry until slurry turns light orange, thickens to paste, and clings to potatoes.

4 Add oil to Dutch oven until it measures ¾ inch deep and heat over high heat to 325 degrees. Using tongs, carefully add one-third of potatoes to oil, making sure that potatoes aren't touching one another. Fry until crispy and lightly browned, 7 to 10 minutes, using tongs to flip potatoes halfway through frying. Adjust burner, if necessary, to maintain oil temperature between 280 and 300 degrees. Using wire skimmer or slotted spoon, transfer fries to prepared wire rack (fries that stick together can be separated with tongs or forks). Season with salt to taste and keep warm in oven. Return oil to 325 degrees and repeat with remaining potatoes in 2 batches. Serve immediately.

KETTLE CHIPS

SERVES 4 TO 6

Why This Recipe Works Good kettle chips are salty and supremely crunchy, making them the perfect foil to a rich, juicy burger. Best of all, it's surprisingly easy to make a version of this beloved snack food at home that's less greasy than store-bought bags. We chose Yukon Gold potatoes for their superior flavor, and the food processor gave us even and consistent ⅛-inch slices, which were thick enough to hold their shape during frying, yet thin enough to cook up crisp and crunchy. Our first frying attempts resulted in dark brown, bitter chips, but we soon realized that the amount of starch in the potatoes was the source of our troubles. Rinsing the potato slices washed away exterior starch, and parboiling jump-started the cooking and further reduced the amount of starch. Frying the potatoes in batches ensured that the oil temperature didn't drop too much and that the chips weren't greasy. It was a bit of extra work, but the reward of fresh, golden homemade potato chips was well worth it. It is important to slice the potatoes no more than ⅛ inch thick. Use a mandoline slicer or V-slicer to slice the potatoes uniformly thin. Use a Dutch oven that holds 6 quarts or more for this recipe. These chips are best enjoyed the day they are made.

2 pounds Yukon Gold potatoes, unpeeled, sliced ⅛ inch thick, divided

2 quarts vegetable oil

1 Cover potatoes with cold water in large bowl and gently swirl to rinse off starch. Drain potatoes and repeat swirling with cold water until water no longer turns cloudy, about 5 rinses.

2 Line rimmed baking sheet with clean dish towel. Bring 2 quarts water to boil in large saucepan over high heat. Add potatoes, return to simmer, and cook until just beginning to soften, about 3 minutes. Gently drain potatoes and spread into even layer in prepared sheet. Top with another clean dish towel and press gently on potatoes to dry thoroughly.

3 Set wire rack in rimmed baking sheet and line with triple layer of paper towels. Add oil to large Dutch oven until it measures about 1½ inches deep and heat over medium-high heat to 350 degrees. Carefully add one-third of potatoes to oil and fry, stirring frequently to separate chips, until golden and crisp, 12 to 18 minutes. Adjust burner, if necessary, to maintain oil temperature of about 325 degrees. Using skimmer or slotted spoon, transfer chips to prepared sheet as they finish cooking and season with salt and pepper to taste. Let chips cool completely. Return oil to 350 degrees and repeat with remaining potatoes in 2 batches. Serve.

BEER-BATTERED ONION RINGS

SERVES 4 TO 6

Why This Recipe Works What could possibly make thick-cut onions fried to a delicious golden-brown even better? Beer. Beer's hoppy flavor lends a distinctively yeasty and uniquely delicious undertone to the batter. To infuse our onions with even more flavor, we soaked them in a mixture of beer, malt vinegar, and salt. As a bonus, the salty soak helped soften the onions, ensuring that they wouldn't remain crunchy and raw after frying. Although the carbonation from the beer added some lift, we found that our batter was still too dense and doughy. A little baking powder lightened the batter while keeping it thick enough to coat the rings. To ensure that the rings didn't stick together, we added them to the oil one by one and fried them in three batches. Do not soak the onion rounds for longer than 2 hours in step 1 or they will become too soft and saturated to crisp properly. We prefer to use sweet onions, such as Vidalia, here, but ordinary large yellow onions will produce acceptable rings. Use a Dutch oven that holds 6 quarts or more for this recipe.

2   sweet onions, sliced into ½-inch-thick rounds

3   cups full-bodied lager, such as Sam Adams, divided

2   teaspoons malt or cider vinegar

1   teaspoon table salt, divided

¾   teaspoon pepper, divided

2   quarts peanut or vegetable oil

¾   cup all-purpose flour

¾   cup cornstarch

1   teaspoon baking powder

1 Place onion rounds, 2 cups beer, vinegar, ½ teaspoon salt, and ½ teaspoon pepper in 1-gallon zipper-lock bag. Refrigerate for at least 30 minutes or up to 2 hours.

2 Adjust oven rack to middle position and heat oven to 200 degrees. Line rimmed baking sheet with triple layer of paper towels. Add oil to Dutch oven until it measures about 1½ inches deep and heat over medium-high heat to 350 degrees. Combine flour, cornstarch, baking powder, remaining ½ teaspoon salt, and remaining ¼ teaspoon pepper in large bowl. Whisk in ¾ cup beer until just combined (some lumps will remain). Whisk in remaining beer as needed, 1 tablespoon at a time, until batter falls from whisk in steady stream and leaves faint trail across surface of batter.

3 Remove onions from bag and discard liquid. Pat onion rounds dry with paper towels and separate into rings. Transfer one-third of rings to batter. Using fork, remove 1 ring at a time from batter, allowing excess batter to drip back into bowl, and add to hot oil, briefly dragging ring along surface of oil to prevent sticking. Fry until rings are golden brown and crisp, about 5 minutes, flipping halfway through frying. Using wire skimmer or slotted spoon, transfer rings to prepared sheet, season with salt and pepper to taste, and keep warm in oven. Return oil to 350 degrees and repeat with remaining onion rings and batter in 2 batches. Serve.

CLASSIC POTATO SALAD

SERVES 4 TO 6

> **Why This Recipe Works** All-American potato salad conjures visions of lazy picnics and summertime grilling, and our rich, flavorful version will have you loading your plate with this homey classic (just be sure to leave room for your burger). Potatoes absorb moisture right after they cook, which means that adding the mayonnaise too early can lead to a dry, disappointing salad. To avoid this pitfall, we waited to add the mayonnaise but drizzled our just-cooked potatoes with a tangy, briny mixture of pickle juice and mustard. After the potatoes cooled, we added our creamy dressing, onion, celery, and pickles. Though it's controversial, we love the flavor of hard-cooked egg. Make sure not to overcook the potatoes. Keep the water at a gentle simmer and use the tip of a paring knife to judge the doneness of the potatoes. If the knife inserts easily into the potato pieces, they are done. This recipe can be easily doubled; use a large Dutch oven to cook the potatoes in step 1.

2 pounds Yukon Gold potatoes, unpeeled, cut into ¾-inch pieces

½ teaspoon table salt, plus salt for cooking potatoes

¼ cup finely chopped dill pickles, plus 3 tablespoons brine, divided

1 tablespoon yellow mustard

¾ cup mayonnaise

½ cup finely chopped red onion

1 celery rib, minced

2 tablespoons distilled white vinegar, plus extra for seasoning

½ teaspoon celery seeds

¼ teaspoon pepper

2 hard-cooked large eggs, chopped (optional)

1 Place potatoes and 1 teaspoon salt in large saucepan and cover with cold water by 1 inch. Bring to simmer over medium-high heat and cook until potatoes are tender, 10 to 15 minutes.

2 Drain potatoes thoroughly in colander, then spread out on rimmed baking sheet. Mix 2 tablespoons pickle brine and mustard together in bowl, then drizzle over potatoes, gently tossing until evenly coated. Refrigerate potato mixture until cooled slightly, about 15 minutes.

3 Combine mayonnaise, onion, celery, vinegar, celery seeds, pickles, remaining 1 tablespoon pickle brine, salt, and pepper in large bowl. Add cooled potato mixture and toss to combine. Cover and refrigerate until well chilled, about 30 minutes. (Salad can be refrigerated for up to 2 days.) Gently fold in eggs, if using. Season with extra vinegar, salt, and pepper to taste before serving.

Variations

GREEN GODDESS POTATO SALAD

Add ¼ cup chopped fresh chives, ¼ cup chopped fresh parsley, 2 tablespoons chopped fresh tarragon, and 1 minced garlic clove to mayonnaise mixture.

HORSERADISH POTATO SALAD

Buy refrigerated prepared horseradish, not the shelf-stable kind, which contains preservatives and additives.

Add ¼ cup drained prepared horseradish to mayonnaise mixture.

SMOKY GRILLED POTATO SALAD

SERVES 4 TO 6

Why This Recipe Works Creamy potato salad may be the classic, but we wanted a modern, summery option that could cook on the grill from start to finish right alongside some of our delectably charred burgers. For smoky potatoes with tender insides and crispy, grilled outsides, we started with halved, unpeeled red potatoes. Leaving the skins on helped the potatoes stay intact, as their firm, waxy texture stood up to the heat of the grill. Crumbled bacon was an obvious choice to add smokiness, and we found that we could infuse our salad with even more savory bacon flavor by reserving some of the fat and coating the potatoes with it before grilling. Grilling our onions with the potatoes gave them a beautiful char that heightened their flavor. Instead of a thick dressing that would hide the spectacular grill marks on our potatoes, we opted for a bold vinaigrette with a kick of chipotle to add even more smoky depth. Halving our potatoes after they cooled exposed their creamy center and allowed them to soak up the spicy, tangy flavors of the dressing. Use small red potatoes 1½ to 2 inches in diameter. If you don't have 2 tablespoons of fat in the skillet after frying the bacon, add olive oil to make up the difference.

4   slices bacon

2   tablespoons red wine vinegar

1½ tablespoons mayonnaise

1½ teaspoons minced canned chipotle chile in adobo sauce

½   teaspoon table salt, divided

¼   teaspoon pepper

2   tablespoons extra-virgin olive oil, plus extra for brushing

2   pounds small red potatoes, unpeeled, halved

1   onion, sliced into ½-inch-thick rounds

3   scallions, sliced thin

1 Cook bacon in 12-inch skillet over medium heat until crisp, 7 to 9 minutes. Using slotted spoon, transfer bacon to paper towel–lined plate. When cool enough to handle, crumble bacon and set aside. Reserve 2 tablespoons bacon fat. (If necessary, add olive oil to equal 2 tablespoons.) Whisk vinegar, mayonnaise, chipotle, ¼ teaspoon salt, and pepper together in large bowl. Slowly whisk in oil until combined; set aside.

2A **For a charcoal grill** Open bottom vent completely. Light large chimney starter three-quarters filled with charcoal briquettes (4½ quarts). When top coals are partially covered with ash, pour evenly over grill. Set cooking grate in place, cover, and open lid vent completely. Heat grill until hot, about 5 minutes.

2B **For a gas grill** Turn all burners to high, cover, and heat grill until hot, about 15 minutes. Turn all burners to medium.

3 Clean and oil cooking grate. Toss potatoes with reserved bacon fat and remaining ¼ teaspoon salt in bowl. Push toothpick horizontally through each onion round to keep rings intact while grilling. Brush onion rounds lightly with oil and season with salt and pepper. Place potatoes, cut side down, and onion rounds on grill and cook, covered, until charred on first side, 10 to 14 minutes.

4 Flip potatoes and onion rounds and continue to cook, covered, until well browned all over and potatoes are tender, 10 to 16 minutes. Transfer potatoes and onion rounds to rimmed baking sheet and let cool slightly.

5 When cool enough to handle, halve potatoes. Remove toothpicks and coarsely chop onion rounds.

6 Add potatoes, onion, scallions, and bacon to dressing and toss to combine. Season with salt and pepper to taste. Serve warm or at room temperature.

COOL AND CREAMY MACARONI SALAD

SERVES 4 TO 6

Why This Recipe Works It's easy to see why macaroni salad is a block party and barbecue favorite: Pasta is mixed with crunchy onion and celery and dressed with seasoned tangy mayonnaise for a cool and refreshing side that complements the flavors of even the boldest burgers. The biggest challenge with macaroni salad is keeping the pasta from absorbing too much mayonnaise, which causes it to turn into a dry, flavorless blob. We had learned from our Classic Potato Salad (page 188) that adding the mayonnaise to a warm salad will cause the potatoes to soak up all of the mayo's moisture, so for our macaroni salad we cooked the pasta until tender, and then rinsed and drained it so that there was still a little moisture remaining. Next we mixed in all of the ingredients except our mayonnaise and let the mixture sit so that the pasta could absorb not just the water, but also the flavors of the seasonings so that everything melded together. We prefer garlic powder to fresh garlic here because its flavor isn't as sharp and the powder dissolves into the smooth dressing. Cooking the pasta until it is completely tender and leaving it slightly wet after rinsing are important for the texture of the finished salad. This recipe can be easily doubled.

8 ounces (2 cups) elbow macaroni

Table salt for cooking pasta

¼ cup finely chopped red onion

¼ cup finely chopped celery

2 tablespoons minced fresh parsley

1 tablespoon lemon juice

1½ teaspoons Dijon mustard

Pinch garlic powder

Pinch cayenne pepper

¾ cup mayonnaise

1 Bring 4 quarts water to boil in large pot. Add macaroni and 1 tablespoon salt and cook, stirring often, until tender. Drain macaroni, rinse with cold water, and drain again, leaving macaroni slightly wet.

2 Toss macaroni, onion, celery, parsley, lemon juice, mustard, garlic powder, and cayenne together in large bowl and let sit until flavors are absorbed, about 2 minutes. Stir in mayonnaise and let sit until salad is no longer watery, 5 to 10 minutes. (Salad can be refrigerated for up to 2 days; adjust consistency with hot water as needed.) Season with salt and pepper to taste before serving.

Variations

COOL AND CREAMY MACARONI SALAD WITH CURRY, APPLE, AND GOLDEN RAISINS

Increase cayenne to ⅛ teaspoon and add 1 small Granny Smith apple, cored and chopped, ½ cup golden raisins, ¼ cup mango chutney, and 1 teaspoon curry powder to macaroni with onion.

COOL AND CREAMY MACARONI SALAD WITH ROASTED RED PEPPERS AND CAPERS

Add ½ cup jarred roasted red peppers, chopped, and 3 tablespoons drained capers, chopped, to macaroni with onion.

BUTTERMILK COLESLAW

SERVES 4 TO 6

Why This Recipe Works The cool, tangy crunch of coleslaw provides an ideal foil for rich, juicy burgers, and our version of this classic adds buttermilk to the dressing for a slaw that is decadently rich and creamy. To avoid a watery slaw with dressing pooled at the bottom of the bowl, we salted and drained our shredded cabbage so that it released some of its moisture and wilted to a pickle-crisp texture our dressing could cling to. For extra crunch and a lightly sweet flavor, we added bright shredded carrot to our cabbage. Buttermilk alone was too thin to really coat the slaw, but combining buttermilk, mayonnaise, and sour cream gave us a base that was both creamy and tangy. Vinegar and sugar rounded out the flavors of our dressing while Dijon added a subtle kick and shallot and parsley provided aromatic freshness. This recipe can be easily doubled.

½ head red or green cabbage, cored, quartered, and shredded (6 cups)

1¼ teaspoons table salt, divided

1 carrot, peeled and shredded

½ cup buttermilk

2 tablespoons mayonnaise

2 tablespoons sour cream

1 small shallot, minced

2 tablespoons minced fresh parsley

½ teaspoon cider vinegar, plus extra for seasoning

½ teaspoon sugar

¼ teaspoon Dijon mustard

⅛ teaspoon pepper

1 Toss cabbage and 1 teaspoon salt in colander set over large bowl and let sit until wilted, at least 1 hour or up to 4 hours. Rinse cabbage under cold running water. Press, but do not squeeze, to drain, and blot dry with paper towels.

2 Combine wilted cabbage and carrot in large bowl. In separate bowl, whisk buttermilk, mayonnaise, sour cream, shallot, parsley, vinegar, sugar, mustard, pepper, and remaining ¼ teaspoon salt together. Pour dressing over cabbage mixture and toss to combine. Refrigerate until chilled, about 30 minutes. (Coleslaw can be refrigerated for up to 3 days.) Season with extra vinegar, salt, and pepper to taste before serving.

Variations

BUTTERMILK COLESLAW WITH SCALLIONS AND CILANTRO
Omit mustard. Substitute 1 tablespoon minced fresh cilantro for parsley and 1 teaspoon lime juice for cider vinegar. Add 2 thinly sliced scallions to dressing.

LEMONY BUTTERMILK COLESLAW
Substitute 1 teaspoon lemon juice for cider vinegar. Add 1 teaspoon minced fresh thyme and 1 tablespoon minced fresh chives to dressing.

CARROT, RADISH, AND ASIAN PEAR SLAW

SERVES 4 TO 6

Why This Recipe Works This modern take on classic coleslaw pairs earthy carrots, peppery radish, and sweet pears for a light, fresh, and crunchy side dish. In an attempt to avoid watery dressing, we took a cue from our Buttermilk Coleslaw (page 194) and tossed our shredded carrots with salt to draw out some of their moisture. Inspired by the sweetness of the carrots, we balanced the salt with some sugar—which also extracts liquid from vegetables—and let the mixture rest to allow the carrots a chance to soften. Because there was still liquid pooling in the bottom of the bowl, we put our carrots in a salad spinner and gave them a quick spin to remove the extra moisture. To complement the crunch of the carrots and radishes, we added Asian pears; their lighter, airier texture gave the salad some lift. For a simple but flavorful dressing, we combined olive oil, rice vinegar, Dijon, and sesame oil and finished our slaw with a bit of bite from thinly sliced scallions. To save time, we recommend shredding the carrots with the shredding disk of a food processor.

1½ pounds carrots, trimmed, peeled, and shredded

¼ cup sugar, plus extra for seasoning

1½ teaspoons table salt, divided

½ cup extra-virgin olive oil

3 tablespoons rice vinegar, plus extra for seasoning

2 tablespoons Dijon mustard

1 tablespoon toasted sesame oil

½ teaspoon pepper

2 Asian pears, peeled, halved, cored, and cut into ⅛-inch matchsticks

12 ounces radishes, trimmed, halved, and sliced thin

10 scallions, green parts only, sliced thin on bias

1 Toss carrots with sugar and 1 teaspoon salt in large bowl and let sit until partially wilted and reduced in volume by one-third, about 15 minutes.

2 Meanwhile, whisk olive oil, vinegar, mustard, sesame oil, pepper, and remaining ½ teaspoon salt in large bowl until combined.

3 Transfer carrots to salad spinner and spin until excess water is removed, 10 to 20 seconds. Transfer carrots to bowl with dressing. Add pears, radishes, and scallions to bowl with carrots and toss to combine. Season with salt, pepper, extra sugar, and/or extra vinegar to taste. Serve immediately.

BROCCOLI SALAD WITH RAISINS AND WALNUTS

SERVES 4 TO 6

Why This Recipe Works A crisp broccoli salad makes a nice foil to a loaded burger—and just might make you a feel a bit better about slathering that burger with cheese and sauce. But most recipes for this classic fall short right from the start by using raw broccoli, which gives the salad an unappealing bitter, woody taste. By quickly blanching the broccoli and then dunking it in an ice bath, we were able to eliminate its raw taste while retaining the broccoli's crisp crunch. We found that the stalks needed a bit longer to cook than the florets, so we added the stalks to the pot first to give them a head start. To make sure our creamy dressing coated every piece and didn't slide off, we gave the blanched broccoli a quick spin in a salad spinner to remove any water remaining on the surface. For the perfect balance of crunchy and chewy textures, we added earthy toasted walnuts and sweet golden raisins, which we softened and plumped by letting them sit for a few minutes in boiling water to rehydrate. When prepping the broccoli, keep the stalks and florets separate. If you don't own a salad spinner, lay the broccoli on a clean dish towel to dry in step 2.

½ cup golden raisins

1½ pounds broccoli, florets cut into 1-inch pieces, stalks peeled and sliced ¼ inch thick

½ cup mayonnaise

1 tablespoon balsamic vinegar

½ teaspoon table salt

¼ teaspoon pepper

½ cup walnuts, toasted and chopped coarse

1 large shallot, minced

1 Bring 3 quarts water to boil in Dutch oven. Fill large bowl halfway with ice and water. Combine ½ cup of boiling water and raisins in small bowl, cover, and let sit for 5 minutes; drain and set aside.

2 Add broccoli stalks to pot of boiling water and cook for 1 minute. Add florets and cook until slightly tender, about 1 minute. Drain broccoli, then transfer to bowl of ice water and let sit until chilled, about 5 minutes. Drain again, transfer broccoli to salad spinner, and spin dry.

3 Whisk mayonnaise, vinegar, salt, and pepper together in large bowl. Add broccoli, raisins, walnuts, and shallot and toss to combine. (Dressed salad can be refrigerated for up to 2 hours.) Season with salt and pepper to taste before serving.

FRESH CORN AND TOMATO SALAD

SERVES 4 TO 6

Why This Recipe Works While corn on the cob is certainly a simple, crowd-pleasing summertime side, we were looking for a fresh alternative to accompany our burgers. This bright, seasonal salad pairing corn and tomatoes fits the bill, and as a bonus it can be made a few hours ahead. Initially a recipe featuring vibrant corn tossed with juicy tomatoes and an easy vinaigrette seemed straightforward, but bland corn, limp tomatoes, and watery dressing all proved problematic. Salting and draining the tomatoes helped remove some of the excess moisture so that their juices wouldn't flood and dilute the dressing. Toasting the corn in a skillet brought out a delicious nutty depth while still allowing the kernels to keep some of their snappy bite, and adding the dressing and scallions while the kernels were still warm gave the corn a chance to soak up even more flavor. To give the flavors a chance to meld, we stirred in the remaining ingredients once the corn had cooled and allowed the salad to rest. Don't add the tomatoes to the toasted corn until it is cool, as the heat from the corn will partially cook the tomatoes.

2 tomatoes, cored and cut into ½-inch pieces

1¼ teaspoons table salt, divided

2½ tablespoons extra-virgin olive oil, divided

5 ears corn, kernels cut from cobs (about 5 cups)

2 scallions, sliced thin

1½ tablespoons white wine vinegar

½ teaspoon pepper

¼ cup minced fresh parsley

1 Toss tomatoes with ½ teaspoon salt in colander set over bowl and let drain for 30 minutes.

2 Meanwhile, heat 1 tablespoon oil in 12-inch nonstick skillet over medium-high heat until shimmering. Add corn and cook, stirring occasionally, until spotty brown, 5 to 7 minutes. Transfer to large bowl and stir in scallions, vinegar, pepper, remaining ¾ teaspoon salt, and remaining 1½ tablespoons oil. Let cool to room temperature, about 20 minutes.

3 Stir in drained tomatoes and parsley. Let sit until flavors meld, about 30 minutes. (Dressed salad can be refrigerated for up to 2 hours.) Season with salt and pepper to taste before serving.

Variations

FRESH CORN AND TOMATO SALAD WITH ARUGULA AND GOAT CHEESE

Omit parsley. Substitute lemon juice for white wine vinegar. Stir in 2 ounces chopped baby arugula and 4 ounces crumbled goat cheese with tomatoes.

FRESH CORN AND TOMATO SALAD WITH WHITE BEANS AND BASIL

Substitute red wine vinegar for white wine vinegar. Toss 1 (15-ounce) can rinsed cannellini beans with vinaigrette and hot corn. Substitute 2 tablespoons chopped fresh basil for parsley.

WATERMELON SALAD WITH BASIL AND FETA

SERVES 4 TO 6

Why This Recipe Works Watermelon's sweet, juicy flavor takes center stage in this surprisingly savory twist on a fruit salad, which makes a delicious accompaniment to a stacked burger. Salty feta, briny olives, and aromatic basil work in tandem with the sweet watermelon for a salad full of contrasting flavors and textures. We started by macerating the fresh melon in sugar for 30 minutes; this easy step drove off excess moisture and prevented a watery salad. A simple dressing of white wine vinegar and olive oil allowed the bold flavors of the salad to shine, and soaking sliced shallot in the vinegar before tossing it in the bowl tamed its bite and infused the vinegar with plenty of flavor. Mild, chopped cucumber added fresh crunch, and some red pepper flakes contributed a kick of heat to round out the flavors of our dressing. Letting the dressed watermelon and olives rest in the fridge chilled the salad and allowed the sweet and salty flavors to meld, and finishing with some basil and feta just before serving added a burst of freshness.

6 cups seedless watermelon, cut into 1-inch pieces

1½ teaspoons sugar, divided

1 shallot, sliced into thin rings

3 tablespoons white wine vinegar

¼ teaspoon red pepper flakes

½ teaspoon table salt, divided

1 English cucumber, peeled, quartered lengthwise, seeded, and cut into ½-inch pieces

½ teaspoon pepper

3 tablespoons extra-virgin olive oil

½ cup pitted kalamata olives, chopped coarse

½ cup fresh basil leaves, torn into bite-size pieces

3 ounces feta cheese, crumbled (¾ cup)

1 Toss watermelon with 1 teaspoon sugar in colander set over large bowl and let drain for 30 minutes. Combine shallot, vinegar, pepper flakes, ¼ teaspoon salt, and remaining ½ teaspoon sugar in separate bowl and let sit while watermelon drains. Discard watermelon juice and wipe bowl clean with paper towels.

2 Pat cucumber and drained watermelon dry with paper towels and transfer to now-empty bowl. Using fork, remove shallot from vinegar mixture and add to bowl with watermelon. Add pepper and remaining ¼ teaspoon salt to vinegar mixture and slowly whisk in oil until incorporated. Add dressing and olives to bowl with watermelon and toss to combine. Refrigerate for at least 30 minutes or up to 4 hours.

3 Add basil to salad and toss to combine. Season with salt and pepper to taste. Transfer to serving platter and sprinkle with feta. Serve.

VANILLA MILKSHAKES

SERVES 2

Why This Recipe Works Milkshakes are a perennial favorite, and it's no wonder: After all, a thick, creamy milkshake is an indulgent treat for kids and adults alike. Hoping to re-create a classic diner shake at home, we turned to our trusty food processor. Unlike a narrow blender, the larger bowl of the food processor exposed more of the ice cream mixture to air and to the walls of the workbowl, resulting in a lighter, frothier shake that was easy to sip through a straw. Additionally, the slightly higher heat generated by the food processor's blade caused more of the ice cream's tiny crystals to melt slightly, creating a smooth milkshake that remained cold but fluid. To amp up the vanilla flavor in our milkshake, we added a pinch of salt, which also offset the sweetness. For a chocolate version, we turned to cocoa powder (chocolate sauce was much too sweet), and added malted milk powder for complex, well-rounded flavor. A little extra salt along with some caramel sauce gave us a tasty salted caramel milkshake, while thawed frozen strawberries made for a vibrant strawberry shake. Serving these milkshakes in chilled glasses helps them stay colder longer. Our favorite vanilla ice cream is Ben & Jerry's Vanilla.

4 cups vanilla ice cream

½ cup milk

Pinch table salt

Place two pint glasses in freezer and chill until ready to serve. Let ice cream sit at room temperature to soften slightly, about 15 minutes. Process ice cream, milk, and salt in food processor until smooth, about 1 minute, scraping down sides of bowl as needed. Pour milkshakes into chilled glasses and serve.

Variations

CHOCOLATE-MALT MILKSHAKES

Add ¼ cup malted milk powder and 1 tablespoon unsweetened cocoa powder to processor with other ingredients.

SALTED CARAMEL MILKSHAKES

Increase salt to ¼ teaspoon. Add ¼ cup caramel sauce to processor with other ingredients.

STRAWBERRY MILKSHAKES

Process 1 pound (3½ cups) thawed frozen strawberries in processor until smooth, about 1 minute, scraping down sides of bowl as needed. Reduce ice cream to 2 cups and milk to ¼ cup and add to processor with pureed strawberries and salt and proceed with recipe as directed.

ULTIMATE COOKIES AND IRISH CREAM MILKSHAKES

SERVES 2

Why This Recipe Works It's hard to imagine improving on a milkshake featuring rich, creamy vanilla ice cream and chocolaty cookie crumbles, but we found that a little whiskey turned the cookies-and-cream classic into an indulgent shake worthy of a spot next to one of our ultimate burgers. Instead of starting with cookies-and-cream ice cream, which can have unevenly sized cookie pieces, we made our own cookie crumbs by grinding chocolate wafers in a food processor before adding vanilla ice cream and processing to dreamy, creamy perfection. A pinch of salt intensified the flavor of the vanilla to create a deeply sweet treat. For our adults-only take on this decadent milkshake, we found that Irish whiskey provided the best flavor with its subtle toasted honey notes. Our favorite vanilla ice cream is Ben & Jerry's Vanilla. Tasters' preferences varied as to the amount of liquor they preferred; start with the lesser amount of whiskey and add more to your liking. We prefer to use Irish whiskey here, but American whiskey will work as well. For a nonalcoholic version of this recipe, substitute ½ cup whole milk for the whiskey. This recipe can be easily doubled; simply process the milkshakes in two batches. Garnish with Whipped Cream (recipe follows), chocolate sauce, and extra wafer cookies, if desired.

4 cups vanilla ice cream

10 chocolate wafer cookies, broken into 1-inch pieces

4–6 tablespoons Irish whiskey

Pinch table salt

Place two pint glasses in freezer and chill until ready to serve. Let ice cream sit at room temperature to soften slightly, about 15 minutes. Process cookies in food processor until finely ground, 30 to 60 seconds. Add ice cream, whiskey, and salt and process until smooth, about 1 minute, scraping down sides of bowl as needed. Pour milkshakes into chilled glasses and serve.

WHIPPED CREAM
Makes about ½ cup
This recipe can be easily doubled.

¼ cup heavy cream, chilled

1 teaspoon sugar

¼ teaspoon vanilla extract

Using whisk, whip all ingredients in chilled bowl until soft peaks form, about 2 minutes.

ULTIMATE SALTED CARAMEL APPLE MILKSHAKES

SERVES 2

Why This Recipe Works Ooey, gooey caramel and sweet-tart apple is a favorite autumn pairing, and this over-the-top adult milkshake turns the classic flavor combination into a year-round decadent treat. We knew that the subtle flavor of apple could be easily overpowered by the intense caramel, so we used a generous amount of apple butter, which provided more intense flavor than fresh apples, cider, or dried apples. We found that adding just ¼ teaspoon salt offset the toasty sweetness from the caramel sauce and boosted the apple flavor further. For an adult kick to this deluxe milkshake we opted for brandy, which emphasized the sweet, caramelized fruit flavor profile. A quick whirl in the food processor gave this frosty fall-inspired shake the perfect creamy but sippable texture. Our favorite vanilla ice cream is Ben & Jerry's Vanilla. Tasters' preferences varied as to the amount of liquor they preferred; start with the lesser amount and add more to your liking. For a nonalcoholic version of this recipe, substitute ½ cup whole milk for the brandy. This recipe can be easily doubled; simply process the milkshakes in two batches. Garnish with Whipped Cream (page 207), caramel sauce, apple slices, and graham cracker crumbs, if desired.

4	cups vanilla ice cream
½	cup apple butter
4–6	tablespoons brandy
2	tablespoons caramel sauce
¼	teaspoon table salt

Place two pint glasses in freezer and chill until ready to serve. Let ice cream sit at room temperature to soften slightly, about 15 minutes. Process ice cream, apple butter, brandy, caramel sauce, and salt in food processor until smooth, about 1 minute, scraping down sides of bowl as needed. Pour milkshakes into chilled glasses and serve.

ULTIMATE CHOCOLATE MILKSHAKES

SERVES 2

Why This Recipe Works There are few desserts as nostalgic as a rich and creamy chocolate milkshake, and this grown-up version packs an intense, chocolaty punch. Our tasters were surprised to find that shakes made with just chocolate ice cream had a sour taste. Instead, we settled on a combination of vanilla ice cream and chocolate sorbet, which gave us the chocolate flavor we were after without the sour taste. For an extra burst of deep, rich, chocolate, a little bit of hot fudge sauce went a long way. This twist on the classic chocolate shake is certainly decadent, but for a truly over-the-top drink we turned to amaretto liqueur—the sweet, nutty flavor lent a brownie-like taste that was unbeatably delicious. Our favorite vanilla ice cream is Ben & Jerry's Vanilla. Tasters' preferences varied as to the amount of liqueur they preferred; start with the lesser amount and add more to your liking. For a nonalcoholic version of this recipe, substitute ½ cup whole milk for the amaretto liqueur. This recipe can be easily doubled; simply process the milkshakes in two batches. Garnish with Whipped Cream (page 207), crumbled brownies, and extra fudge sauce, if desired.

2½ cups vanilla ice cream

1½ cups chocolate sorbet

4–6 tablespoons amaretto liqueur

2 tablespoons hot fudge sauce, room temperature

Pinch table salt

Place two pint glasses in freezer and chill until ready to serve. Let ice cream and sorbet sit at room temperature to soften slightly, about 15 minutes. Process ice cream, sorbet, amaretto liqueur, fudge sauce, and salt in food processor until smooth, about 1 minute, scraping down sides of bowl as needed. Pour milkshakes into chilled glasses and serve.

SWEET ICED TEA

SERVES 4 TO 6

Why This Recipe Works When burger night beckons, a chilled pitcher of sweet iced tea is the perfect refreshment to pair with the bold flavors of even the biggest burgers. Our version of iced tea shirks the traditional idea that this drink has to be prepared hot and then cooled down. Instead, we skipped the heat and opted to create a version at room temperature that was still perfectly clear and smooth, without any bitterness. We started by steeping our tea bags in room temperature water, leaving them for a full 45 minutes for a strong-flavored brew without bitter undertones. Without heating the tea, granulated sugar couldn't properly dissolve, leaving us with an unpleasantly grainy texture. Instead of putting the sugar straight in the tea, we sweetened with a simple syrup—equal parts water and sugar heated long enough to dissolve the sugar—that kept our tea both smooth and sweet. For flavor-packed variations, the key was to substitute fruit juice, such as cranberry and pomegranate, for some of the water the tea steeps in. This recipe can be easily doubled.

6 black tea bags

4 cups plus 2 tablespoons water, room temperature, divided

2 tablespoons sugar

1 lemon, halved lengthwise and sliced thin, divided

Ice

1 Tie strings of tea bags together (for easy removal) and place in serving pitcher along with 4 cups water; let steep for 45 minutes.

2 Microwave sugar and remaining 2 tablespoons water in bowl until heated through, about 1 minute. Stir mixture constantly until sugar has dissolved completely. Discard tea bags. Add sugar mixture and half of lemon slices to tea and stir to combine. (Tea can be refrigerated for up to 1 week; lemon flavor will intensify over time.) Serve over ice with remaining lemon slices.

Variations
CRANBERRY-ORANGE ICED TEA
Substitute 3 cups cranberry juice for 3 cups of water in step 1. Substitute ½ orange, halved lengthwise and sliced thin, for lemon.

POMEGRANATE-LIME ICED TEA
Substitute 1 cup pomegranate juice for 1 cup of water in step 1. Substitute lime for lemon.

LEMONADE

SERVES 6 TO 8

Why This Recipe Works Nothing quenches thirst better than a tall, ice-filled glass of tart-sweet lemonade, so make sure you have just the right recipe to whip up a pitcher (or two), when having a crowd over for burgers. For punched up fruity flavor that toned down the sour taste of tart lemons, we muddled the lemon slices with granulated sugar to extract the oils in the peel. Then, we combined the lemons with some water and freshly squeezed lemon juice—no simple syrup needed—and just a bit of whisking dissolved the sugar. Straining the mixture removed the solid bits of lemon for a smooth drink with sweet, lemony flavor. For a simple and fun watermelon lemonade, we found that we just needed to add the watermelon in while we muddled the lemon, and for a more sophisticated take on this childhood classic we created a variation with cucumber and mint that's cool and refreshing. When purchasing lemons, choose large ones that give to gentle pressure; hard lemons have thicker skin and yield less juice. Lemons are commonly waxed to prevent moisture loss, increase shelf life, and protect from bruising during shipping. Scrub them with a vegetable brush under running water to remove wax, or buy organic lemons. Don't worry about the seeds in the extracted juice; the entire juice mixture is strained at the end of the recipe.

1½ cups sugar

13 lemons (2 sliced thin, seeds and ends discarded, 11 juiced to yield 2 cups)

7 cups cold water

Using potato masher, mash sugar and half of lemon slices in large bowl until sugar is completely wet, about 1 minute. Add water and lemon juice and whisk until sugar is completely dissolved, about 1 minute. Strain mixture through fine-mesh strainer set over serving pitcher, pressing on solids to extract as much juice as possible; discard solids. Add remaining lemon slices to lemonade and refrigerate until chilled, about 1 hour. (Lemonade can be refrigerated for up to 1 week.) Stir to recombine before serving over ice.

Variations
WATERMELON LEMONADE
Reduce water to 6 cups. Mash 4 cups coarsely chopped seedless watermelon with lemon slices.

CUCUMBER-MINT LEMONADE
Mash 1 peeled, thinly sliced cucumber and 1 cup fresh mint leaves with lemon slices. Add 1 peeled, thinly sliced cucumber and ½ cup fresh mint leaves to strained lemonade with remaining lemon slices.

7 THE BREAD AISLE

Homemade Hamburger Buns and Rolls

IN THIS CHAPTER

POTATO BUNS

MAKES 8 BUNS

> **Why This Recipe Works** Old-fashioned potato rolls, with their sweet flavor and light, moist crumb, are a classic choice for burgers. But supermarket versions are sometimes so flimsy that they crumble under condiments, and many at-home recipes turn out dense, dry rolls. Creating a solid structure in our rolls started with finding the perfect potato, and high-starch russets worked best; they absorbed the most water for a moister crumb. As we tested different amounts of mashed russet, we discovered that the more potato we used, the less time the dough needed to rise because the potassium in potatoes activates yeast. Potatoes leach almost half their potassium into the water when boiled, so rather than the milk many recipes called for, we simply used some of the cooking water to create our dough; this caused our rise time to drop even lower and produced rolls that were light, moist, and satisfying. Don't salt the water used for boiling the potato.

1 large russet potato (10 ounces), peeled and cut into 1-inch pieces

2 tablespoons unsalted butter, cut into 4 pieces

2¼ cups (12⅓ ounces) bread flour

2 teaspoons instant or rapid-rise yeast

1 teaspoon plus pinch table salt, divided

2 large eggs, room temperature, divided

1 tablespoon sugar

1 tablespoon sesame seeds (optional)

1 Place potatoes in medium saucepan and cover with 1 inch cold water. Bring to simmer over medium-high heat and cook until potatoes are just tender (paring knife can be slipped in and out of potato with little resistance), 8 to 10 minutes.

2 Transfer 5 tablespoons (2½ ounces) potato cooking water to 4-cup liquid measuring cup and let cool completely; drain potatoes. Return potatoes to now-empty saucepan and place over low heat. Cook, shaking saucepan occasionally, until any surface moisture has evaporated, about 30 seconds. Off heat, process potatoes through ricer or food mill or mash well with potato masher. Measure 1 cup very firmly packed potatoes (8 ounces) and transfer to separate bowl. Stir in butter until melted and let mixture cool

completely before using. Discard remaining mashed potatoes or save for another use.

3 Whisk flour, yeast, and 1 teaspoon salt together in bowl of stand mixer. Whisk 1 egg and sugar into potato cooking water until sugar has dissolved. Add mashed potato mixture to flour mixture and mix with your hands until combined (some large lumps are okay).

4 Using dough hook on low speed, slowly add cooking water mixture and mix until cohesive dough starts to form and no dry flour remains, about 2 minutes, scraping down bowl as needed. Increase speed to medium-low and knead until dough is smooth and elastic and clears sides of bowl, about 8 minutes.

5 Transfer dough to lightly floured counter and knead by hand to form smooth, round ball, about 30 seconds. Place dough seam side down in lightly greased large bowl or container, cover tightly with plastic wrap, and let rise until doubled in size, 30 minutes to 1 hour.

6 Press down on dough to deflate. Transfer dough to lightly floured counter; stretch and roll into even 12-inch log. Cut log into 8 equal pieces (about 3½ ounces each) and cover loosely with greased plastic. Working with 1 piece of dough at a time (keep remaining pieces covered), pat into 4-inch disk. Working around circumference of dough, fold edges of dough toward center until ball forms. Flip dough ball seam side down and, using your cupped hand, drag in small circles until dough feels taut and round and all seams are secured on underside of ball. Cover loosely with greased plastic and let rest for 15 minutes.

7 Line 2 rimmed baking sheets with parchment paper. Pat each ball into 3½-inch disk of even thickness and arrange seam side down on prepared sheets, spaced evenly apart. Cover loosely with greased plastic and let rise until nearly doubled in size and dough springs back minimally when poked gently with your knuckle, about 1 hour.

8 Adjust oven racks to upper-middle and lower-middle positions and heat oven to 425 degrees. Lightly beat remaining egg, 1 tablespoon water, and remaining pinch salt together in bowl. Gently brush buns with egg mixture and sprinkle with sesame seeds, if using. Bake until golden brown, 14 to 18 minutes, switching and rotating sheets halfway through baking. Transfer buns to wire rack and let cool completely, about 1 hour, before serving. (Cooled buns can be stored in zipper-lock bag at room temperature for up to 2 days. Wrapped individually in aluminum foil before being placed in bag, buns can be frozen for up to 1 month. To reheat thawed, frozen buns, place them on rimmed baking sheet, still in foil, and bake in 350-degree oven for 10 minutes.)

Variation
POTATO SLIDER BUNS

Cut log into 12 equal pieces (about 2 ounces each) in step 6, then shape into smooth, taut balls as directed. Line single rimmed baking sheet with parchment paper in step 7 and press each ball into 3-inch disk; arrange all balls on prepared sheet. Bake buns on upper-middle rack until deep golden brown, 12 to 14 minutes, rotating sheet halfway through baking. Makes 12 buns.

SHAPING HAMBURGER BUNS

1 Stretch and roll dough into even 12-inch log. Cut log into 8 equal pieces.

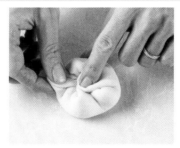

2 Pat 1 piece of dough into 4-inch disk. Working around circumference of dough, fold edges of dough toward center until ball forms.

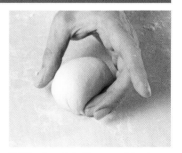

3 Flip dough ball seam side down and, using your cupped hand, drag in small circles until dough feels taut and round and all seams are secured on underside of ball.

Potato Buns

Ciabatta Rolls

CIABATTA ROLLS

MAKES 8 ROLLS

Why This Recipe Works The sturdy but airy interior, full flavor, and crisp, delicate crust of a ciabatta roll make it an unbeatable base for a rich, lavishly topped burger. As with many rustic breads, ciabatta starts with a sponge—a small amount of flour, water, and yeast that ferments for several hours before being added to the dough and that contributes complex flavor and robust texture to the bread. Ciabatta dough is extremely sticky, so we started by kneading the dough with the stand mixer's paddle attachment before switching to the dough hook, and then used a series of folds to reinforce the dough's structure. Rolling the dough into balls was difficult given its tackiness; this step also overworked the dough and inhibited the development of an open, airy crumb. Instead of fussing to create a perfectly round shape, we simply patted and cut the dough into small squares and then gently folded the corners under to form rustic, loose rounds. Whenever possible, use a bowl scraper (or large rubber spatula) and well-floured hands to move and shape this sticky dough. We do not recommend mixing this dough by hand.

SPONGE

- 1 cup (5 ounces) all-purpose flour
- ½ cup (4 ounces) water, room temperature
- ⅛ teaspoon instant or rapid-rise yeast

DOUGH

- 2 cups (10 ounces) all-purpose flour
- 1½ teaspoons plus pinch table salt, divided
- ½ teaspoon instant or rapid-rise yeast
- ¾ cup (6 ounces) plus 1 tablespoon water, room temperature, divided
- ¼ cup (2 ounces) whole milk, room temperature
- 1 large egg

1 **For the sponge** Stir all ingredients in 4-cup liquid measuring cup with wooden spoon until well combined. Cover tightly with plastic wrap and let sit at room temperature until sponge has risen and begins to collapse, about 6 hours (sponge can sit at room temperature for up to 24 hours).

2 **For the dough** Whisk flour, 1½ teaspoons salt, and yeast together in bowl of stand mixer. Stir ¾ cup water and milk into sponge with wooden spoon until well combined. Using paddle on low speed, slowly add sponge mixture to flour mixture and mix until cohesive dough starts to form and no dry flour remains, about 2 minutes, scraping down

Increase speed to medium-low and continue to mix until dough becomes uniform mass that collects on paddle and pulls away from sides of bowl, 4 to 6 minutes.

3 Remove paddle and fit stand mixer with dough hook. Knead on medium-low speed until dough is smooth and shiny (dough will be very sticky), about 10 minutes. Transfer dough to lightly greased large bowl or container, cover tightly with plastic, and let rise until doubled in size, 30 minutes to 1 hour.

4 Using greased bowl scraper (or rubber spatula), fold dough over itself by gently lifting and folding edge of dough toward middle. Turn bowl 45 degrees and fold dough again; repeat turning bowl and folding dough 6 more times (total of 8 folds). Cover tightly with plastic and let rise for 30 minutes. Repeat folding, then

cover bowl tightly with plastic and let dough rise until nearly doubled in size, about 30 minutes.

5 Lightly flour 2 parchment paper–lined rimmed baking sheets. Transfer dough to well-floured counter. Dust top of dough with flour, divide into 2 equal pieces, and cover loosely with plastic. Using your well-floured hands, press and stretch one piece of dough into 8 by 8-inch square (keep second piece of dough covered). Using pizza cutter or bench scraper, cut dough square into quarters (forming four 4 by 4-inch squares). Gently brush excess flour from top of each square. Fold four corners of each square into center to form rough 3½-inch round and pinch edges to seal. Repeat with second piece of dough.

6 Arrange rolls seam side down on prepared sheets, spaced evenly apart. Cover

loosely with greased plastic and let rise until puffy and surfaces develop small bubbles, about 45 minutes.

7 Adjust oven racks to upper-middle and lower-middle positions and heat oven to 450 degrees. Lightly beat egg, remaining pinch salt, and remaining 1 tablespoon water together in bowl. Gently brush rolls with egg mixture and bake until golden brown, 13 to 17 minutes, switching and rotating sheets halfway through baking. Transfer rolls to wire rack and let cool completely, about 1 hour, before serving. (Cooled rolls can be stored in zipper-lock bag at room temperature for up to 2 days. Wrapped in aluminum foil before being placed in bag, rolls can be frozen for up to 1 month. To reheat thawed, frozen rolls, place them on rimmed baking sheet, still in foil, and bake in 350-degree oven for 10 minutes.)

SHAPING CIABATTA ROLLS

1 Transfer dough to well-floured counter. Dust top of dough with flour and divide into 2 equal pieces.

2 Using your well-floured hands, press and stretch 1 piece of dough into an 8 by 8-inch square. Cut dough square into quarters (forming four 4 by 4-inch squares).

3 Fold 4 corners of each square into center to form rough 3½-inch round and pinch edges to seal.

PRETZEL BUNS

MAKES 8 BUNS

> **Why This Recipe Works** With their mahogany-brown crusts, tender interiors, and salty bite, these buns are a great home for big, juicy burgers. Without the food-grade lye professional bakers use to create the dark, distinctly flavored crust unique to soft pretzels, we turned to a dip in a solution of baking soda and boiling water to help create the buns' chewy exterior. We use coarse pretzel salt on the exterior of the buns, but kosher salt may be substituted. Do not use pretzel salt in the dough; if using kosher salt in the dough, increase the amount to 4 teaspoons. For more information on shaping hamburger buns, see page 219. If you don't plan on serving these buns immediately, skip sprinkling them with pretzel salt until you are ready to reheat and serve; over time the salt crystals dissolve and can create a soggy exterior.

3¾ cups (20⅔ ounces) bread flour

2 teaspoons plus pinch table salt, divided

2 teaspoons instant or rapid-rise yeast

1½ cups (12 ounces) plus 1 tablespoon water, room temperature, divided

2 tablespoons vegetable oil

2 tablespoons packed dark brown sugar

¼ cup baking soda

1 teaspoon pretzel salt

1 large egg

1 Whisk flour, 2 teaspoons table salt, and yeast together in bowl of stand mixer. Whisk 1½ cups water, oil, and sugar in 4-cup liquid measuring cup until sugar has dissolved.

2 Using dough hook on low speed, slowly add water mixture to flour mixture and mix until cohesive dough starts to form and no dry flour remains, about 2 minutes, scraping down bowl as needed. Increase speed to medium-low and knead until dough is smooth and elastic and clears sides of bowl, about 8 minutes.

3 Transfer dough to lightly floured counter and knead by hand to form smooth, round ball, about 30 seconds. Place dough seam side down in lightly greased large bowl or container, cover tightly with plastic wrap, and let rise until doubled in size, 1 to 1½ hours.

4 Lightly flour 2 rimmed baking sheets. Press down on dough to deflate. Transfer dough to clean counter; stretch and roll into even 12-inch log. Cut log into 8 equal pieces (about 4 ounces each) and cover loosely with greased plastic. Working with 1 piece of dough at a time (keep remaining pieces covered), pat into 4-inch disk. Working around circumference of dough, fold edges of dough toward center until ball forms. Flip dough ball seam side down and, using your cupped hand, drag in small circles until dough feels taut and round and all seams are secured on underside of ball. Cover loosely with greased plastic and let rest for 15 minutes.

5 Arrange balls seam side down on prepared sheets, spaced evenly apart. Cover loosely with greased plastic and let rise until nearly doubled in size and dough springs back

minimally when poked gently with your knuckle, about 30 minutes.

6 Adjust oven racks to upper-middle and lower-middle positions and heat oven to 425 degrees. Dissolve baking soda in 4 cups water in Dutch oven and bring to boil over medium-high heat. Using slotted spatula, transfer 4 buns seam side up to boiling water and cook for 30 seconds, flipping halfway through cooking. Transfer buns seam side down to wire rack and repeat with remaining 4 buns. Let rest for 5 minutes.

7 Line now-empty sheets with parchment paper and lightly spray with vegetable oil spray. Lightly beat egg, remaining pinch table salt, and remaining 1 tablespoon water together in bowl. Transfer buns seam side down to prepared sheets, spaced evenly apart. Gently brush buns with egg mixture. Using sharp paring knife or single-edge razor blade, make two 2-inch long slashes along top of each bun to form cross. Sprinkle each bun with 1/8 teaspoon pretzel salt.

8 Bake buns until mahogany brown, 16 to 20 minutes, switching and rotating sheets halfway through baking. Transfer buns to wire rack and let cool completely, about 1 hour, before serving. (Cooled buns can be stored in zipper-lock bag at room temperature for up to 2 days. Wrapped in aluminum foil before being placed in bag, buns can be frozen for up to 1 month; thaw before reheating. To serve, mist buns lightly with water, sprinkle with pretzel salt, and bake in 300-degree oven for 5 minutes.)

KAISER ROLLS

MAKES 12 ROLLS

Why This Recipe Works Our biggest and boldest burgers are high-stacked, decked-out creations that need a sturdy bun to keep the loaded towers intact. We thought that kaiser rolls, with their crusty exteriors, would be the perfect choice for our heftiest hamburgers. Aiming to re-create the thin, crisp, golden exterior and moist, sturdy crumb of deli-style rolls, we started by using high-protein bread flour, which yielded tender yet supportive rolls. Many traditional recipes call for malt syrup to add sweetness and boost browning, but our tasters preferred the subtle flavor of white sugar. To achieve a deep golden sheen without the malt, we brushed on an egg wash before baking. Some delis imprint their rolls with a special stamp to create the signature rosette design, but we decided to use a traditional shaping method that was easy with our supple dough and didn't require us to purchase special equipment. Not only did our finished buns have the gorgeous exterior of traditional rolls, but they were also the perfect base for our skyscraper burgers.

- 5 cups (27½ ounces) bread flour
- 4 teaspoons instant or rapid-rise yeast
- 1 tablespoon plus pinch table salt, divided
- 2 cups (16 ounces) plus 1 tablespoon water, room temperature, divided
- 3 tablespoons vegetable oil
- 2 large eggs, room temperature, divided
- 4 teaspoons sugar
- 1 tablespoon poppy seeds (optional)

1 Whisk flour, yeast, and 1 tablespoon salt together in bowl of stand mixer. Whisk 2 cups water, oil, 1 egg, and sugar in 4-cup liquid measuring cup until sugar has dissolved.

2 Using dough hook on low speed, slowly add water mixture to flour mixture and mix until cohesive dough starts to form and no dry flour remains, about 2 minutes, scraping down bowl as needed. Increase speed to medium-low and knead until dough is smooth and elastic and clears sides of bowl but sticks to bottom, about 8 minutes.

3 Transfer dough to lightly floured counter and knead by hand to form smooth, round ball, about 30 seconds. Place dough seam side down in lightly greased large bowl or container, cover tightly with plastic wrap, and let rise until doubled in size, 1 to 1½ hours.

4 Line 2 rimmed baking sheets with parchment paper. Press down on dough to deflate. Transfer dough to clean counter. Press and stretch dough into 12 by 6-inch rectangle, with long side parallel to counter edge. Using pizza cutter or chef's knife, cut dough vertically into 12 (6 by 1-inch) strips and cover loosely with greased plastic.

5 Working with 1 piece of dough at a time (keep remaining pieces covered), stretch and roll into 14-inch rope. Shape rope into U with 2-inch-wide bottom curve and ends facing away from you. Tie ends into single overhand knot, with 1½-inch open loop at bottom. Wrap 1 tail over loop and press through opening from top. Wrap other tail under loop and pinch ends together to seal.

6 Arrange rolls pinched side down on prepared sheets, spaced evenly apart. Cover loosely with greased plastic and let rise until nearly doubled in size and dough springs back minimally when poked gently with your knuckle, 30 minutes to 1 hour.

7 Adjust oven racks to upper-middle and lower-middle positions and heat oven to 350 degrees. Lightly beat remaining egg, remaining 1 tablespoon water, and remaining pinch salt together in bowl. Gently brush rolls with egg mixture and sprinkle with poppy seeds, if using. Bake until golden brown, 30 to 34 minutes, switching and rotating sheets halfway through baking. Transfer rolls to wire rack and let cool completely, about 1 hour, before serving. (Cooled rolls can be stored in zipper-lock bag at room temperature for up to 2 days. Wrapped in aluminum foil before being placed in the bag, rolls can be frozen for up to 1 month. To reheat thawed, frozen rolls, wrap them in foil, place them on rimmed baking sheet, and bake them in 350-degree oven for 10 minutes.)

SHAPING KAISER ROLLS

1 Stretch and roll 1 piece of dough into 14-inch rope, then shape rope into U with 2-inch-wide bottom curve and ends facing away from you.

2 Tie ends into single overhand knot, with 1½-inch open loop at bottom.

3 Wrap 1 tail over loop and press through opening from top. Wrap other tail under loop and pinch ends together to seal.

Whole-Wheat Buns

WHOLE-WHEAT BUNS

MAKES 8 BUNS

> **Why This Recipe Works** A great whole-wheat bun has unmistakable nutty flavor and a hearty yet soft crumb. Its flavor pairs well with poultry and seafood burgers, and because whole wheat is more nutritious than refined white flour, a whole-wheat bun makes a great complement to a protein-rich veggie burger. Our tasters unanimously favored a dough that contained 60 percent whole-wheat flour and 40 percent white flour—more whole-wheat flour than in most recipes. But because whole-wheat flour doesn't form gluten as well as white flour, packing that much whole wheat into our buns compromised their texture. Taking a cue from rustic bakery rolls, we used a sponge—a combination of flour, water, and yeast that allows for earlier fermentation—to help create a more open crumb and better chew. Using high-protein bread flour helped build structure, and we also found that presoaking the whole-wheat flour before making the dough was well worth the extra time; this step helped soften the grain's bran, dulling the sharp edges and preventing the bran from puncturing and deflating the dough. It also converted some of the grain's starches into sugars, thereby reducing the bitterness that can be characteristic of whole-wheat bread. Honey gave our buns a hint of earthy sweetness that complemented the nuttiness of the whole wheat, and adding toasted wheat germ to our dough amped up the deliciously wheaty flavor of these subtly sweet buns. For more information on shaping hamburger buns, see page 219.

SOAKER

- 1½ cups (8¼ ounces) whole-wheat flour
- 1 cup (8 ounces) whole milk
- ¼ cup (¾ ounce) toasted wheat germ

SPONGE

- 1 cup (5½ ounces) bread flour
- ½ cup (4 ounces) water, room temperature
- ¼ teaspoon instant or rapid-rise yeast

DOUGH

- 10 tablespoons (3½ ounces) bread flour
- 3 tablespoons unsalted butter, softened
- 2 tablespoons honey
- 1 tablespoon instant or rapid-rise yeast
- 1 tablespoon vegetable oil
- 2 teaspoons plus pinch table salt, divided
- 1 large egg
- 1 tablespoon water

1 For the soaker Stir all ingredients in large bowl with wooden spoon until shaggy mass forms. Transfer dough to lightly floured counter and knead by hand until smooth, about 3 minutes. Return soaker to bowl, cover tightly with plastic wrap, and refrigerate for at least 8 hours or up to 24 hours.

2 For the sponge Stir all ingredients in 4-cup liquid measuring cup with wooden spoon until well combined. Cover tightly with plastic wrap and let sit at room temperature until sponge has risen and begins to collapse, about 6 hours (sponge can sit at room temperature for up to 24 hours).

3 For the dough Tear soaker into 1-inch pieces and place in bowl of stand mixer fitted with dough hook. Add sponge, flour, butter, honey, yeast, oil, and 2 teaspoons salt and mix on low speed until cohesive dough starts to form, about 2 minutes, scraping down bowl as needed. Increase speed to medium-low and knead until dough is smooth and elastic and clears sides of bowl, about 8 minutes.

4 Transfer dough to lightly floured counter and knead by hand to form smooth, round ball, about 30 seconds. Place dough seam side down in lightly greased large bowl or container, cover tightly with plastic wrap, and let rise until doubled in size, 1 to 1½ hours.

5 Lightly flour 2 parchment paper–lined rimmed baking sheets. Press down on dough to deflate. Transfer dough to lightly floured counter; stretch and roll into even 12-inch log. Cut log into 8 equal pieces (about 4 ounces each) and cover loosely with greased plastic. Working with 1 piece of dough at a time (keep remaining pieces covered), pat into 4-inch disk. Working around circumference of dough, fold edges of dough toward center until ball forms. Flip dough ball seam side down and, using your cupped hand, drag in small circles until dough feels taut and round and all seams are secured on underside of ball.

6 Arrange buns seam side down on prepared sheets, spaced evenly apart. Cover loosely with greased plastic and let rise until nearly doubled in size and dough springs back minimally when poked gently with your knuckle, about 1 hour.

7 Adjust oven racks to upper-middle and lower-middle positions and heat oven to 350 degrees. Lightly beat egg, water, and remaining pinch salt together in bowl. Gently brush buns with egg mixture. Bake until golden brown, 18 to 22 minutes, switching and rotating sheets halfway through baking. Transfer buns to wire rack and let cool completely, about 1 hour, before serving. (Cooled buns can be stored in zipper-lock bag at room temperature for up to 2 days. Wrapped in aluminum foil before being placed in bag, buns can be frozen for up to 1 month. To reheat thawed, frozen buns, place them on rimmed baking sheet, still in foil, and bake in 350-degree oven for 10 minutes.)

NO-KNEAD BRIOCHE BUNS

MAKES 8 BUNS

> **Why This Recipe Works** When you're going for the ultimate burger, a buttery brioche bun can't be beat. It's soft, making even the most stacked burger a pleasure to bite into, and its tender crumb easily soaks up those flavorful meat juices. But making brioche can be a time-consuming affair; for a quicker, easier version we added melted butter to our egg mixture, which made contact with the high-protein bread flour and started to form gluten quickly, allowing us to take a no-knead approach. For beautiful buns, we rolled the dough into tight balls and brushed the tops with an egg wash for a golden-brown crust. For more information on shaping hamburger buns, see page 219. High-protein King Arthur Bread Flour works best here, though other bread flours will suffice. You must let the dough rise for at least 16 hours or up to 48 hours.

3 cups (16½ ounces) bread flour

2¼ teaspoons instant or rapid-rise yeast

1½ teaspoons plus ⅛ teaspoon table salt, divided

5 large eggs, room temperature, divided

½ cup (4 ounces) plus 1 tablespoon water, room temperature, divided

⅓ cup (2⅓ ounces) sugar

12 tablespoons unsalted butter, melted and cooled slightly

1 Whisk flour, yeast, and 1½ teaspoons salt together in large bowl. Whisk 4 eggs, ½ cup water, and sugar together in medium bowl until sugar has dissolved. Whisk in melted butter until smooth. Add egg mixture to flour mixture and stir with wooden spoon until uniform mass forms and no dry flour remains, about 1 minute. Cover bowl with plastic wrap and let sit for 10 minutes.

2 Using greased bowl scraper (or rubber spatula), fold dough over itself by gently lifting and folding edge of dough toward middle. Turn bowl 45 degrees and fold dough again; repeat turning bowl and folding dough 6 more times (total of 8 folds). Cover tightly with plastic and let rise for 30 minutes. Repeat folding and rising every 30 minutes, 3 more times. After fourth set of folds, cover bowl tightly with plastic and refrigerate for at least 16 hours or up to 48 hours.

3 Line 2 rimmed baking sheets with parchment paper. Transfer dough to well-floured counter; stretch and roll into even 12-inch log. Cut log into 8 equal pieces (about 4½ ounces each) and cover loosely with greased plastic. Working with 1 piece of dough at a time (keep remaining pieces covered), pat into 4-inch disk. Working around circumference of dough, fold edges of dough toward center until ball forms. Flip dough ball seam side down and, using your cupped hands, drag in small circles until dough feels taut and round and all seams are secured on underside of ball.

4 Arrange buns seam side down on prepared sheets, spaced evenly apart. Cover loosely with plastic and let rise until nearly doubled in size and dough springs back minimally when poked gently with your knuckle, 2½ to 3 hours.

5 Adjust oven racks to upper-middle and lower-middle positions and heat oven to 350 degrees. Lightly beat remaining egg, remaining 1 tablespoon water, and remaining ⅛ teaspoon salt together in bowl. Gently brush buns with egg mixture and bake until golden brown, 16 to 20 minutes, switching and rotating sheets halfway through baking. Transfer buns to wire rack and let cool completely, about 1 hour, before serving. (Cooled buns can be stored in zipper-lock bag at room temperature for up to 2 days. Wrapped in aluminum foil before being placed in bag, buns can be frozen for up to 1 month. To reheat thawed, frozen buns, place them on rimmed baking sheet, still in foil, and bake in 350-degree oven for 10 minutes.)

NUTRITIONAL INFORMATION FOR OUR RECIPES

To calculate the nutritional values of our recipes per serving, we used Edamam. When using this program, we entered all the ingredients, using weights for important ingredients such as most vegetables. We also used our preferred brands in these analyses. When the recipe called for seasoning with an unspecified amount of salt and pepper, we added ½ teaspoon of salt and ¼ teaspoon of pepper to the analysis. We did not include additional salt or pepper for food that's "seasoned to taste." If there is a range in the serving size, we used the highest number of servings to calculate the nutritional values.

	CALORIES	TOTAL FAT (G)	SAT FAT (G)	CHOLESTEROL	SODIUM (G)	CARBS (G)	DIETARY FIBER (G)	SUGAR (G)	PROTEIN (G)
The Perfect Patty									
Classic Beef Burgers	493	28	10	116	496	21	1	3	36
Classic Turkey Burgers	443	23	8	133	527	22	1	3	38
Ultimate Veggie Burgers	298	14	2	3	314	36	4	4	10
Grind-Your-Own Sirloin Burger Blend	599	45	20	207	408	0	0	0	45
Grind-Your-Own Grass-Fed Beef Burger Blend	430	28	12	152	472	0	0	0	43
Grind-Your-Own Ultimate Beef Burger Blend	488	35	14	159	436	0	0	0	44
Grind-Your-Own Turkey Burger Blend	348	21	4	121	556	2	0	1	37
Ketchup	58	0	0	0	168	14	1	12	1
Smoky Chipotle Ketchup	59	0	0	0	183	14	1	12	1
Balsamic-Spice Ketchup	64	0	0	0	171	15	1	14	1
Dijon Mustard	85	3	0	0	163	5	1	1	2
Classic Burger Sauce	114	11	2	6	162	4	0	3	0
Pub Burger Sauce	161	17	2	8	366	2	0	2	0
Barbecue Sauce	112	2	0	0	439	24	1	20	1
Mayonnaise	263	29	2	49	84	0	0	0	1
Lemon-Garlic Mayonnaise	264	29	2	49	88	1	0	0	1
Smoked Paprika Mayonnaise	265	29	2	49	87	1	0	0	1
Herbed Mayonnaise	264	29	2	49	89	1	0	0	1
Spicy Chipotle-Lime Mayonnaise	266	29	2	49	92	1	0	0	1
Quick Pickled Red Onions	88	0	0	0	148	20	1	18	0
Pickle Relish	71	0	0	0	267	16	1	14	1
Spicy Red Pepper Relish	132	0	0	0	309	32	2	28	1
Quick Pickle Chips	32	0	0	0	216	6	0	4	1
Dill Pickle Chips	32	0	0	0	216	6	0	4	1
Caramelized Onion Jam	93	5	1	0	150	11	1	7	1
Tomato Butter	67	0	0	0	78	17	0	16	0
Sautéed Mushroom Topping	104	9	5	23	147	4	1	2	1
Shoestring Onions	285	8	1	0	494	46	4	9	9
Crispy Bacon	181	17	6	29	288	1	0	0	5
Black Pepper Candied Bacon	198	17	6	29	289	5	0	5	5

	CALORIES	TOTAL FAT (G)	SAT FAT (G)	CHOLESTEROL	SODIUM (G)	CARBS (G)	DIETARY FIBER (G)	SUGAR (G)	PROTEIN (G)
We the People									
Griddled Smashed Burgers	613	42	13	99	934	28	2	6	30
Grilled Steak Burgers	508	34	18	93	1099	37	2	13	15
Grilled Well-Done Burgers	690	40	16	165	405	44	2	6	37
Double-Decker Drive-Thru Burgers	812	42	16	162	862	69	3	12	37
Grilled Smokehouse Barbecue Burgers	714	39	14	154	876	40	3	16	48
Grilled Bacon Burgers with Caramelized Onions and Blue Cheese	837	58	23	175	1032	25	1	5	49
Wisconsin Butter Burgers	633	45	25	156	694	26	1	4	32
Grilled New Mexican Green Chile Cheeseburgers	582	32	13	129	719	30	2	6	41
Oklahoma Fried Onion Burgers	409	23	9	85	446	24	2	4	26
Grilled Jucy Lucy Burgers	625	35	15	135	677	32	2	4	44
Pimento Cheeseburgers	732	49	20	167	687	24	2	4	47
Tex-Mex Queso Fundido Burgers	746	47	20	168	849	27	2	6	50
Connecticut Steamed Cheeseburgers	603	37	16	144	661	23	1	3	43
Easy Beef Sliders	812	55	14	106	1029	46	2	12	32
Patty Melts	734	51	26	191	265	18	2	4	49
Crispy California Turkey Burgers	832	58	12	108	830	46	6	11	33
Grilled Turkey Burgers with Spinach and Feta	420	21	9	126	513	23	1	3	35
with Miso and Ginger	577	24	10	167	679	53	3	7	38
with Herbs and Goat Cheese	479	25	12	129	452	24	1	4	39
Turkey-Veggie Burgers with Lemon-Basil Sauce	455	26	6	91	550	25	2	5	30
Spiced Turkey Burgers with Mango Chutney	516	24	8	135	687	35	2	13	39
Brie-Stuffed Turkey Burgers with Red Pepper Relish	563	31	13	161	703	28	1	8	44
Thai-Style Turkey Sliders	513	22	6	88	873	50	3	17	31
Chicken Burgers with Sun-Dried Tomatoes, Goat Cheese, and Balsamic Glaze	575	34	12	128	396	30	2	9	35
Buffalo Chicken Burgers	569	33	14	187	565	30	2	9	38
Beyond the Beef									
Grilled Bison Burgers with Mexican Corn Salad	717	45	16	134	551	38	3	8	41
Bison Burgers with Piquillo Peppers and Crispy Serrano Ham	969	74	20	209	1313	24	2	3	50
Meatloaf Burgers	637	8	2	40	1391	117	8	24	24
Breakfast Pork Burgers	869	56	21	312	888	42	4	9	48
Banh Mi Burgers	996	69	19	166	1240	46	4	8	45
Italian Pork Burgers with Broccoli Rabe	829	61	16	148	814	34	3	8	37
Grilled Teriyaki Pork Burgers	981	48	18	151	1508	96	4	47	38
Grilled Bayou Burgers with Spicy Mayonnaise	886	66	22	149	1450	26	1	4	37
Lamb Burgers with Halloumi and Beet Tzatziki	932	69	29	179	874	33	2	12	44
Grilled Harissa Lamb Burgers	719	53	19	128	378	25	2	4	33
Hoisin-Glazed Lamb Burgers	657	43	18	125	657	31	2	8	33
Crispy Salmon Burgers with Tomato Chutney	405	13	2	78	722	38	3	10	35
Grilled Southwestern Salmon Burgers	730	55	7	117	520	28	5	4	32
South Carolina Shrimp Burgers with Tartar Sauce	751	53	7	234	1599	37	2	5	29
Grilled Tuna Burgers with Wasabi and Pickled Ginger	371	26	4	57	578	4	2	1	30

	CALORIES	TOTAL FAT (G)	SAT FAT (G)	CHOLESTEROL	SODIUM (G)	CARBS (G)	DIETARY FIBER (G)	SUGAR (G)	PROTEIN (G)
Let's Go for Broke									
French Onion Burgers	923	59	28	246	1309	23	1	4	73
Reuben Burgers	967	64	22	218	1835	33	3	10	65
Grilled Wild Mushroom Burgers	745	45	22	188	994	28	3	6	56
Bistro Burgers with Pâté, Figs, and Watercress	705	37	14	318	896	39	3	15	54
Grilled Crispy Onion–Ranch Burgers	754	46	16	165	907	35	2	6	50
Loaded Nacho Burgers	960	59	26	213	1124	45	3	5	64
Burgers au Poivre	704	43	19	194	863	24	1	4	49
Donut Shop Burgers	752	49	19	187	928	26	1	1	51
Mascarpone Burgers with Wilted Radicchio and Pear	701	41	18	183	849	34	3	11	50
Grilled Blue Cheese Burgers with Bacon and Tomato Relish	665	40	16	170	920	25	2	5	52
Bibimbap Burgers	972	48	15	312	1477	73	3	10	61
Surf and Turf Burgers	700	43	14	192	994	24	2	4	55
Turkey Burgers with Cranberry Relish and Smoked Gouda	757	43	18	213	1001	44	3	22	51
Mediterranean Turkey Burgers with Shaved Zucchini Salad and Ricotta	583	31	6	149	1031	29	3	7	49
Grilled Turkey Caesar Burgers	582	41	7	156	958	11	2	2	45
Jerk Spice–Rubbed Turkey Burgers with Fried Green Tomatoes	1078	57	7	188	1198	90	5	15	53
From the Field and Garden									
Ultimate Veggie Burgers with Sweet and Tangy Napa Slaw	474	28	4	7	658	49	7	13	11
Vegan Pinto Bean and Beet Burgers	451	15	1	0	380	65	10	7	15
Southwestern Black Bean Burgers with Chipotle Sauce	637	21	4	62	457	87	16	5	27
Spicy Brown Rice–Edamame Burgers	509	35	5	11	428	43	4	2	8
Quinoa Burgers with Spinach, Sun-dried Tomatoes, and Marinated Feta	580	41	10	111	538	37	4	2	19
Curried Millet Burgers with Peach-Ginger Chutney	443	19	2	44	455	60	9	17	11
Falafel Burgers with Tahini-Yogurt Sauce	584	24	4	3	526	73	11	12	22
Vegan Grilled Barbecued Tempeh Burgers with Spicy Pickled Jícama	579	14	3	0	894	86	3	47	26
Grilled Portobello Burgers with Goat Cheese and Arugula	282	16	3	7	349	26	2	5	8
Spiced Cauliflower Burgers with Yogurt Sauce	375	17	2	42	623	46	6	14	12
You Want Fries with That?									
Easier French Fries	594	43	3	0	17	50	6	2	6
Chive and Black Pepper Dipping Sauce	145	16	3	12	110	1	0	0	0
Belgian-Style Dipping Sauce	136	14	2	7	147	2	0	2	0
Thick-Cut Oven Fries	290	11	1	0	17	45	5	2	5
Sweet Potato Fries	552	36	3	0	414	55	7	9	4
Kettle Chips	317	23	2	0	9	26	3	1	3
Beer-Battered Onion Rings	395	25	2	0	261	35	2	2	3
Classic Potato Salad	327	23	3	11	516	28	4	2	3
Green Goddess Potato Salad	329	23	3	11	517	29	4	2	4
Horseradish Potato Salad	331	23	3	11	539	29	4	3	4
Smoky Grilled Potato Salad	269	15	3	14	286	28	3	3	6

	CALORIES	TOTAL FAT (G)	SAT FAT (G)	CHOLESTEROL	SODIUM (G)	CARBS (G)	DIETARY FIBER (G)	SUGAR (G)	PROTEIN (G)
You Want Fries with That? (cont.)									
Cool and Creamy Macaroni Salad	344	23	3	11	189	29	1	1	5
with Curry, Apple, and Golden Raisins	396	23	3	11	271	43	2	12	6
with Roasted Red Peppers and Capers	355	24	4	11	254	30	2	2	5
Buttermilk Coleslaw	91	5	1	5	356	11	3	6	2
with Scallions and Cilantro	92	5	1	5	368	11	3	6	3
Lemony Buttermilk Coleslaw	91	5	1	5	358	11	3	6	2
Carrot, Radish, and Asian Pear Slaw	308	21	2	0	354	31	6	20	2
Broccoli Salad with Raisins and Walnuts	244	17	2	8	347	22	4	12	5
Fresh Corn and Tomato Salad	165	8	1	0	410	25	3	9	4
with Arugula and Goat Cheese	192	10	2	4	454	25	3	9	6
with White Beans and Basil	201	8	1	0	520	31	4	10	7
Watermelon Salad with Basil and Feta	157	9	3	13	401	17	2	13	4
Vanilla Milkshakes	584	31	19	122	310	65	2	59	11
Chocolate-Malt Milkshakes	619	33	20	126	410	70	3	62	13
Salted Caramel Milkshakes	687	31	19	123	671	92	2	59	12
Strawberry Milkshakes	365	16	10	61	194	50	5	41	7
Ultimate Cookies and Irish Cream Milkshakes	876	38	20	117	632	106	4	78	13
Whipped Cream	112	11	7	41	11	3	0	3	1
Ultimate Salted Caramel Apple Milkshakes	784	29	18	116	584	106	3	81	10
Ultimate Chocolate Milkshakes	710	20	12	73	282	118	3	104	7
Sweet Iced Tea	18	0	0	0	7	5	0	4	0
Cranberry-Orange Iced Tea	73	0	0	0	3	18	0	16	0
Pomegranate-Lime Iced Tea	24	0	0	0	4	6	0	5	0
Lemonade	159	0	0	0	9	42	0	39	0
Watermelon Lemonade	54	0	0	0	3	15	3	8	2
Cucumber-Mint Lemonade	180	0	0	0	4	48	3	40	1
The Bread Aisle									
Potato Buns	236	5	2	48	223	40	2	2	8
Potato Slider Buns	158	3	2	32	149	27	1	1	5
Ciabatta Rolls	207	1	0	21	153	41	2	1	7
Pretzel Buns	317	5	1	20	1897	57	2	3	10
Kaiser Rolls	285	5	1	27	182	49	2	2	9
Whole-Wheat Buns	322	9	4	34	259	52	4	6	10
No-Knead Brioche Buns	438	21	12	146	270	51	2	9	11

CONVERSIONS AND EQUIVALENTS

Some say cooking is a science and an art. We would say that geography has a hand in it, too. Flours and sugars manufactured in the United Kingdom and elsewhere will feel and taste different from those manufactured in the United States. So we cannot promise that the loaf of bread you bake in Canada or England will taste the same as a loaf baked in the States, but we can offer guidelines for converting weights and measures. We also recommend that you rely on your instincts when making our recipes. Refer to the visual cues provided. If the dough hasn't "come together in a ball" as described, you may need to add more flour—even if the recipe doesn't tell you to. You be the judge.

The recipes in this book were developed using standard U.S. measures following U.S. government guidelines. The charts below offer equivalents for U.S. and metric measures. All conversions are approximate and have been rounded up or down to the nearest whole number.

Example
1 teaspoon = 4.9292 milliliters, rounded up to 5 milliliters
1 ounce = 28.3495 grams, rounded down to 28 grams

Volume Conversions

U.S.	METRIC
1 teaspoon	5 milliliters
2 teaspoons	10 milliliters
1 tablespoon	15 milliliters
2 tablespoons	30 milliliters
¼ cup	59 milliliters
⅓ cup	79 milliliters
½ cup	118 milliliters
¾ cup	177 milliliters
1 cup	237 milliliters
1¼ cups	296 milliliters
1½ cups	355 milliliters
2 cups (1 pint)	473 milliliters
2½ cups	591 milliliters
3 cups	710 milliliters
4 cups (1 quart)	0.946 liter
1.06 quarts	1 liter
4 quarts (1 gallon)	3.8 liters

Weight Conversions

OUNCES	GRAMS
½	14
¾	21
1	28
1½	43
2	57
2½	71
3	85
3½	99
4	113
4½	128
5	142
6	170
7	198
8	227
9	255
10	283
12	340
16 (1 pound)	454

Conversions for Common Baking Ingredients

Baking is an exacting science. Because measuring by weight is far more accurate than measuring by volume, and thus more likely to produce reliable results, in our recipes we provide ounce measures in addition to cup measures for many ingredients. Refer to the chart below to convert these measures into grams.

INGREDIENT	OUNCES	GRAMS
flour		
1 cup all-purpose flour*	5	142
1 cup cake flour	4	113
1 cup whole-wheat flour	5½	156
sugar		
1 cup granulated (white) sugar	7	198
1 cup packed brown sugar (light or dark)	7	198
1 cup confectioners' sugar	4	113
cocoa powder		
1 cup cocoa powder	3	85
butter†		
4 tablespoons (½ stick or ¼ cup)	2	57
8 tablespoons (1 stick or ½ cup)	4	113
16 tablespoons (2 sticks or 1 cup)	8	227

* U.S. all-purpose flour, the most frequently used flour in this book, does not contain leaveners, as some European flours do. These leavened flours are called self-rising or self-raising. If you are using self-rising flour, take this into consideration before adding leaveners to a recipe.

† In the United States, butter is sold both salted and unsalted. We generally recommend unsalted butter. If you are using salted butter, take this into consideration before adding salt to a recipe.

Oven Temperatures

FAHRENHEIT	CELSIUS	GAS MARK
225	105	¼
250	120	½
275	135	1
300	150	2
325	165	3
350	180	4
375	190	5
400	200	6
425	220	7
450	230	8
475	245	9

Converting Temperatures from an Instant-Read Thermometer

We include doneness temperatures in many of the recipes in this book. We recommend an instant-read thermometer for the job. Refer to the table above to convert Fahrenheit degrees to Celsius. Or, for temperatures not represented in the chart, use this simple formula:

Subtract 32 degrees from the Fahrenheit reading, then divide the result by 1.8 to find the Celsius reading.

Example:
"Roast chicken until thighs register 175 degrees."
To convert:
$$175°F - 32 = 143°$$
$$143° \div 1.8 = 79.44°C, \text{ rounded down to } 79°C$$

INDEX

Note: Page references in *italics* indicate photographs.

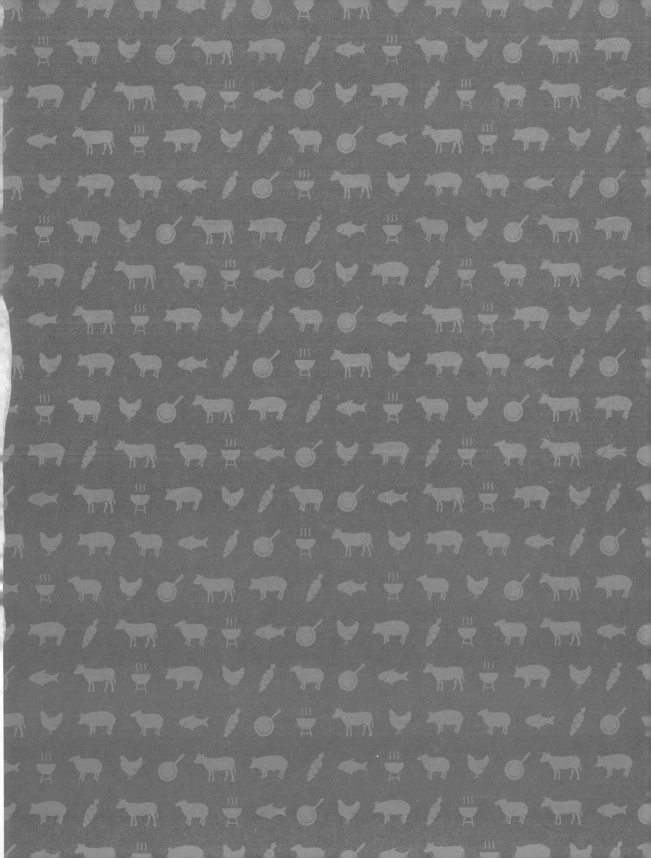

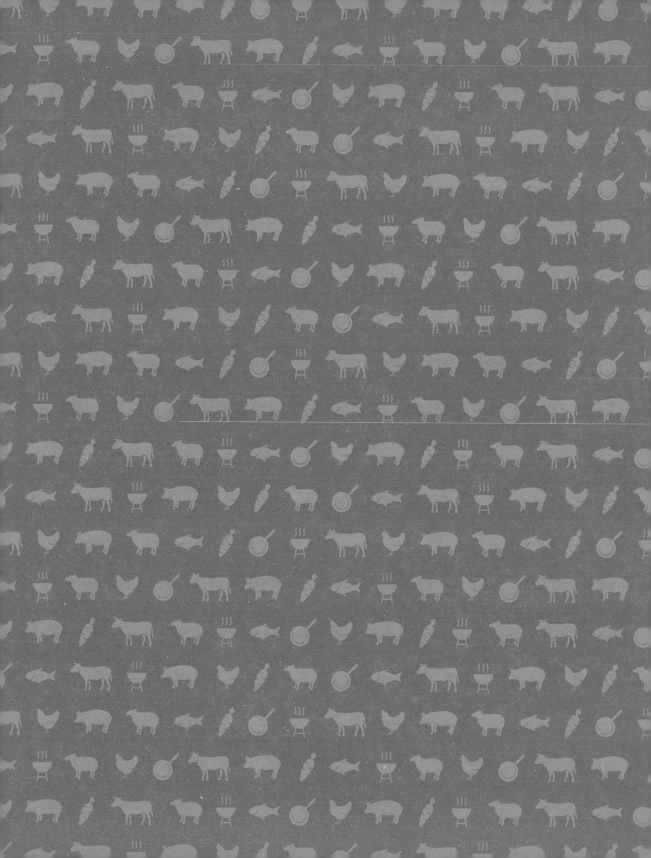